Lineage of Loss

Max Katz

LINEAGE OF LOSS

Counternarratives
of North Indian Music

Wesleyan University Press   Middletown, Connecticut

Wesleyan University Press
Middletown CT 06459
www.wesleyan.edu/wespress
© 2017 Max Katz
All rights reserved
Manufactured in the United States of America
Designed by Mindy Basinger Hill
Typeset in Minion Pro by Tseng Information Systems, Inc.

Sections of Chapter 4 have been excerpted by permission
of the Society for Ethnomusicology from my 2012 article "Institutional
Communalism in North Indian Classical Music,"
Ethnomusicology 56(2): 279–98.

Library of Congress Cataloging-in-Publication Data
Names: Katz, Max, 1976– author.
Title: Lineage of loss: counternarratives of North Indian music /
Max Katz.
Description: Middletown, Connecticut: Wesleyan University Press,
[2017] | Series: Music/culture | Includes bibliographical references
and index. | Identifiers: LCCN 2017019097 (print) | LCCN 2017031327
(ebook) | ISBN 9780819577603 (ebook) | ISBN 9780819577580
(cloth: alk. paper) | ISBN 9780819577597 (pbk.: alk. paper)
Subjects: LCSH: Hindustani music—Social aspects—India—
History. | Musicians—India, North—Lineage—History. |
Hindustani music—India—Lucknow—History and criticism.
Classification: LCC ML3917.14 (ebook) | LCC ML3917.14 K37 2017 (print) |
DDC 780.954/5—dc23
LC record available at https://lccn.loc.gov/2017019097

5   4   3   2   1

CONTENTS

A NOTE ON TRANSLITERATION

This book employs words from Hindi and Urdu, and to a lesser extent Sanskrit, Persian, and Arabic. In my approach to their transliteration, I have endeavored to strike a balance between the two potential extremes of pedantry and ambiguity. On one hand, it is important to me to present readers with enough information about a given word that they may understand its pronunciation and also its likely spelling should they choose to pursue reference materials. On the other hand, I would not like to overburden readers with excessive diacritical markings from multiple contrasting systems suited to the specific linguistic origins of various terms.

Thus, I have chosen to use only a select number of diacritical markings and to employ them as consistently as possible. To indicate long vowel sounds I have used the macron, as in *ashrāf* and *gīt*. For retroflex consonants I have used the underdot, as in *ṭhumrī* and *mukhṛā*. Nasalization is indicated with an "n" with an overdot, as in *Bhairavīṅ* and *saṅgīt*. For fricative sounds I have used a single underline, as in g̲hazal and k̲hyāl. For accuracy of Sanskrit treatise titles, I have additionally marked the palatal "s" with an accent, as in *Nāradīyaśikṣā* and *Nāṭyaśāstra*; I have used the same for patently Sanskrit words such as *śruti*.

I have in most cases avoided the apostrophe or single open quotation mark often used to indicate Urdu's 'ain because the letter does not carry the unique guttural sound in Urdu that it does in Persian and Arabic. Instead, in Urdu, the 'ain is most often pronounced as "ā" or "a." It may also be silent or carry other vowel sounds, such as "e," as in *sher*. For aspirated consonants I have used the single "h," as in *chuṭo* and *Jhinjhoṭī*. This means, however, that the unaspirated "ch" is rendered with only a "c," as in *cācā* and *cikārī*.

Some Hindi/Urdu words have become part of the English lexicon, for example chai, jungle, and verandah. I believe the word *sitar* is one of these, so

I have not rendered it as *sitār* but instead left it in its familiar form. Likewise, for most names of individuals I have not included diacritical specifications. By contrast, some terms that occur throughout the text are rendered exclusively with diacritics (such as *gharānā* and *rāga*) but are italicized only on first appearance. My intention is to retain the emphasis on correct pronunciation without continually marking such words as "foreign" through the use of italics. Some words that appear infrequently in the book are italicized throughout, such as *ālāp*, *mukhṛā*, and *gat*, which are Hindustani musicological terms: the consistent italicization of such terms marks them as part of a specific technical discourse that I enter in only a few sections of the book. Likewise, rāga names remain italicized. For pluralization of transliterated words, I have used the "-s" as in ṭhumrī-s and gharānā-s. In quotations from previous authors, I have reproduced their own spelling, including their use or non-use of diacritics and italics.

ACKNOWLEDGMENTS

The book you hold in your hands is the result of fifteen years of training and research in ethnomusicology and Indian music, an undertaking inconceivable in the absence of countless teachers, guides, colleagues, interlocutors, and loved ones. Their generosity of spirit undergirds every page of this book. With inevitable and regretted omissions, I will attempt to express my gratitude here.

First and foremost I thank my principal scholarly preceptor, Professor Scott Marcus; his commitment to and faith in my work never waivered. I remain forever grateful to Professor Marcus, along with Professors Timothy Cooley, Dolores Hsu, George Lipsitz, and Bishnupriya Ghosh, the members of my doctoral committee at the University of California–Santa Barbara. I have been especially fortunate to receive feedback, support, and instruction from the broad and international community of senior scholars of Indian music. In particular, I have benefited from the guidance and encouragement of Regula Qureshi, Daniel Neuman, Bonnie Wade, Peter Manuel, James Kippen, Richard Widdess, Helen Myers, Stephen Slawek, Lakshmi Subramanian, Allyn Miner, Françoise "Nalini" Delvoye, and Brian Silver. I am further blessed to count among my friends, colleagues, and co-conspirators the brilliant Indian music scholars Katherine Schofield, Margaret Walker, Dard Neuman, Jayson Beaster-Jones, Shalini Ayyagari, Aditi Deo, Rumya Putcha, Anna Schultz, Bradley Shope, Anna Morcom, Kaley Mason, Stefan Fiol, Peter Kvetko, Niko Higgins, Meilu Ho, Sarah Morelli, Davesh Soneji, Amanda Weidman, Zoe Sherinian, Matthew Rahaim, and Justin Scarimbolo. The last two—Matty and Justin—remain for me not only models of intellectual, musical, and personal integrity, but two of my closest and most cherished friends and confidants. Beyond the realm of Indian music, I have enjoyed the friendship of a number of fellow travelers along the path of ethnomusicology. In particular I thank Denise Gill, Kara Attrep, Lillie Gordon, Sonja

Downing, Karen Liu, Ralph Lowi, Kathy Meizel, Eric Ederer, Gibb Schreffler, Revell Carr, Phil Murphy, Laith Ulaby, and Michael Iyanaga.

Over the years many friends and colleagues have given me the gift of close and careful critique of my work, including detailed commentary and numerous discussions that helped shape the present book. In particular, I owe heaping debts of gratitude to Justin Scarimbolo, Matthew Rahaim, Jonathan Glasser, Rob Wallace, Anne Rasmussen, Katherine Schofield, and Allyn Miner. I am likewise grateful to the anonymous reviewers who provided extensive responses to my book manuscript through both the Wesleyan University Press review process and my own tenure review. I am further grateful to the staff at Wesleyan University Press, including Parker Smathers, Suzanna Tamminen, Marla Zubel, and Jaclyn Wilson, and to Susan Abel of University Press of New England and Sara Evangelos. I thank the series editors of the Music/Culture Series of Wesleyan University Press: Deborah Wong, Sherrie Tucker, and especially Jeremy Wallach, who took a keen interest in my project and encouraged me to submit a proposal to the press.

At the College of William and Mary, I have benefited from the care and compassion of my immediate departmental colleagues Kitty Preston, James Armstrong, Jamie Bartlett, Tom Payne, Sophia Serghi, Brian Hulse, Gayle Murchison, David Grandis, Dave Dominique, Richard Marcus, Chris DeLaurenti, and Kathleen DeLaurenti. I have also drawn intellectual and moral sustenance from my colleagues across campus, including Jonathan Glasser, Kathrin Levitan, Francis Tanglao-Aguas, Mark McLaughlin, Patton Burchett, Michael Cronin, Stephen Sheehi, Hiroshi Kitamura, Rani Mullen, Gul Ozyegin, Sibel Zandi-Sayek, Chitralekha Zutshi, Kevin Vose, Arthur Knight, Charles McGovern, and Trent Vinson. I particularly thank my immediate partner in ethnomusicology, Anne Rasmussen: as a colleague, mentor, and friend, she has opened more doors for me than I can recount or repay.

Handling Hindi, Urdu, and Persian texts in insightful and nuanced ways has been a major challenge of writing this book. I would like to thank a number of individuals who assisted me along the way: Ghazala Rafiq, Allyn Miner, James Kippen, Saher Rizvi, Mumtaz Qazilbash, and most importantly Farrokh Namazi. An expert in literary Urdu and Persian, Farrokh spent untold hours poring over the texts of Kaukab Khan, Karamatullah Khan, Sakhawat Husain Khan, and others. Many of the translations in this book owe their genesis to Farrokh.

My research in India has depended on the kindness, generosity, and patience of many. I thank Saleem and Sufia Kidwai for their hospitality and warmth. For their selfless assistance, I thank the staff at the Lucknow branch of the Sangeet Natak Akademi, and the staff of Lucknow's All India Radio station (Akashvani), especially the assistant station director Prithvi Raj Chauhan. At the Bhatkhande Music Institute, I thank sitar instructors Abhinav Sinha, Deepak Chatterjee, and Meeta Saxena; I would also like to thank vice-chancellors Vidyadhar Vyas and Narendra Nath Dhar for the assistance they provided me. I thank the staff of the Uttar Pradesh State Archives. In Delhi, I am grateful to the staff of the National Archive; the Nehru Memorial Museum and Library; Akashvani; and the Sangeet Natak Akademi. In 2016 Lucknow lost a pillar of its intellectual community, the beloved Ram Advani. I remain grateful for the time I spent basking in his warmth and wisdom.

I am indebted to a number of musicians and music lovers in India who helped with my research, but who remain unnamed in the book. In particular I would like to recognize, in Lucknow, vocalist Abdul Majit Khan, shehnai player Ghulam Mohammad Khan, sitarist Kamal David, vocalist Kamla Shrivasto, vocalist Gulshan Bharti, Qazisahab Tahir Nazmi, vocalist and violinist Dauji Goswami, vocalist and sitarist Shahanaz Husain, sitarist Sibte Hasan, sitarists Akhtar and Riyasat Husain Khan, sitar makers Mohammad Sultan and Dilawar Husain, pakhāwaj player Ramakant Pathak, and tablā player Ilmas Khan. In Delhi I would like to thank vocalist Ajit Singh Paintal, sitarist Fateh Ali, scholar and critic S. Kalidas, sarod player Biswajit Roy Chowdhury, scholar and sitarist Sharmista Sen, sitar maker Harichand Kartar, and scholars Vibodh Parthasarathi and Irfan Zuberi. In Bombay I thank the late Ustad Mohammad Sayeed Khan, and Karen "Cubby" Sherman for her warmth, humor, and hospitality.

My research has depended on the support of several institutions, including Fulbright-Hays, the American Musicological Society, the College of William and Mary, and the Reves Center for International Studies. I also thank for its generous support the American Institute of Indian Studies; in particular I thank the director general, Ms. Purnima Mehta, and the associate director general of the Institute's Archives and Research Center for Ethnomusicology, Dr. Shubha Chaudhuri.

Large parts of this book emerged directly from extended interviews and discussions with a small number of musicians and music lovers. In particular, I am deeply grateful to the late Idris Khan, Gulfam Ahmad Khan, Shahid Khan, Aqeel Khan, and finally Irfan Khan, whose insight, knowledge, and generosity were essential to this research.

Ultimately I owe my life in music and scholarship to my parents, Michael and

Betsy Katz, whose love and support made everything possible. I am also grateful to my sister, Anna, for her humor and brilliance. At long last, what can I say of my radiant wife, Eva, and our luminous daughter, Ella? They light my life like the sun and the moon.

This book is dedicated to Ustad Irfan Muhammad Khan, the last of the Mohicans.

Lineage of Loss

Introduction

I arrived in Lucknow in 2007 in search of a culture long declared dead and gone. Like generations of scholars and laypeople before me, I lost myself within the tales of royal decadence leaping from the pages of Abdul Halim Sharar's classic history, *Lucknow: The Last Phase of an Oriental Culture* (2001 [1975]). Populated by poets, dancers, musicians, calligraphers, and pigeon fanciers, Sharar's Lucknow glows as the high-water mark of Islamicate culture in a syncretic and cooperative society shaped by Shia Islam and organized by the principles of courtesy, artistry, and pleasure. And yet, even in the early twentieth century, Sharar (1860–1926) offers only a retrospective nostalgia for a Lucknowi Golden Age he never knew. Subsequent writers on Lucknow dwell in a similar predicament, "becoming maudlin and wistful, longing for the refinement and elegance of a past era" (Kippen 2005 [1988]: xi). As Sharar's translator laments in a preface titled "The Construction and Destruction of Lucknow," the "cultural phoenix" that rose in the once-great city has ultimately "burned again, as it appears, for good" (Hussain 2001: n.p.). What, then, could I expect to find? The final collapse of the grand culture of Lucknow was, according to the literature, a fait accompli: the city described in 1858 by a famed British war correspondent as "more brilliant" and "more vast" than Paris (Russell 1957 [1860]: 57–58, quoted in Kippen 2005 [1988]: 1) was now "rapidly becoming notorious as one of the most hopelessly backward and violent" in all of India (Dalrymple 2004 [1998]: 28).

Yet I possessed an advantage in my search for Lucknow's living past: my subject was music. Guarded and preserved for centuries within long lines of hereditary musicians, India's celebrated "classical" traditions by their very nature breathe life to the past in the present. Thus, despite reports of the city's contemporary cultural obsolescence, I reasoned that if I could locate a living descendant of old Lucknow's master musicians—a carrier of his ancestors' traditions—I could touch the city's musical past even today.

Lucknow marks the approximate center of the vast region of the Indo-Gangetic Plain that spreads from Pakistan to Bangladesh. In the eighteenth and nineteenth centuries, the city was a pivotal site of royal patronage for North India's most elite musicians. Delhi, the capital of the Mughal Empire, was the unrivaled cultural center of North India from the sixteenth to the eighteenth centuries, yet as the empire foundered, Delhi's loss was Lucknow's gain. From the time of its establishment as the capital of the state of Awadh in 1775, Lucknow became a magnet for musicians fleeing the embattled imperial capital.[1] By the mid-nineteenth century, and especially during the reign of its last king, Nawāb Wajid Ali Shah (r. 1847–1856), Lucknow not only was North India's preeminent musical and cultural center, but was the subcontinent's "largest and most prosperous" city outside the new British colonial centers of Calcutta, Bombay, and Madras (Oldenburg 2001 [1984]: 3–4).

Throughout this period, various forms of *rāga*-based art music flourished in the royal courts and salons of Lucknow, where hereditary artists both conserved and transformed the repertoires of the erstwhile Mughal courts. Still North India's most elite and revered musical heritage, today these arts are known collectively as Hindustani music, or Hindustani "classical" music.[2] The specific forms that make up this repertoire span a broad range of vocal genres, from "light" styles, such as the poetic-song genres *ṭhumrī* and *ghazal*, to "heavier" styles, such as *khyāl* and *dhrupad*. Also contained in the category of Hindustani music are instrumental repertoires, including those of the sitar, sarod, and *tablā*, as well as *kathak* dance.

Lucknow's master musicians fled the city when the kingdom was annexed by the British East India Company in February of 1856; the city subsequently collapsed into bloodshed in 1857 and '58 as the Company battled its rebellious subjects in a yearlong military struggle identified in nationalist histories as the first "War of Independence" (Savarkar 1947 [1909]). Demolished and rebuilt as a colonial city, Lucknow emerged in the early twentieth century as a center of both the nationalist movement and the related music reform movement, a project that rebranded long-standing traditions of music and dance as national cultural traditions for India's newly rising bourgeoisie. Independence and partition in 1947 saw a mass exodus of Lucknow's elite Muslim families to Pakistan. By the end of the twentieth century, Lucknow had fully receded into the shadows, while the major commercial centers of Bombay, Delhi, and Calcutta continued to ascend as North India's dominant sites of artistic production, even as Hindustani music rose to global prominence and renown.

Thus, despite the fall of Lucknow, the musical traditions nourished there have ultimately prevailed. Why, then, remain focused on the now-barren site of yesterday's germination if the garden—uprooted, replanted, and newly cultivated—flourishes elsewhere today? Was my very focus on Lucknow an act of nostalgia borrowed from the pages of Abdul Halim Sharar? Or was it possible that Lucknow's tale of local decline could tell us something important about a musical tradition in global ascent? As a student of the sitar, I was particularly entranced by Lucknow's instrumental legacy: it is common knowledge among musicians that the most exciting, fast-paced instrumental repertoire— promulgated globally by superstar sitar and sarod players today—was born in the city's nineteenth-century royal court. Accordingly, I began a search for the living legacy of the instrumental masters of old Lucknow.

Before long, my quest led to the door of Idris Khan (1955–2013), shown in Figure 1. Sitting on his bed in the very room occupied eighty years earlier by his famed grandfather, and strumming his own father's weathered but resonant sitar, Idris regaled me with stories of his glorious family lineage. I heard of his great-great-grandfather's invention of the modern sarod, his great-grandfather's debut in Paris, and his grandfather's performances before Hitler, Stalin, Mussolini, and Jawaharlal Nehru. Idris reveled in the renown and accomplishment of successive generations of his ancestors, from distant Paṭhān forefathers who led Afghan armies into battle with the power of their horseback *rabāb* to his own father and uncle, who trained legions of middle-class students while maintaining the purity of their inherited repertoire at home and on the stage. As I would soon learn, Idris possessed a direct hereditary connection to Abdul Halim Sharar's Lucknow. In the short sections on music in his book, Sharar quotes extensively an expert named Asadullah "Kaukab" Khan. A towering instrumentalist of his day, Kaukab (ca. 1850–1915) propagated the traditions of his father in a continuous hereditary instrumental line embodied in 2007 only by Idris Khan and a small number of his remaining relatives. Sitting with Idris, absorbed in his tales of the larger-than-life figures who had shaped the sitar and sarod traditions of Lucknow, I felt that I had finally found the conduit to the past I was searching for.

And yet, while Idris's "house" of music (his *gharānā*, or family tradition) stood proudly in his tales of court grandeur, his actual ancestral home was crumbling around him. Idris himself was gaunt and impoverished. He had lan-

FIGURE 1 Idris Khan, Lucknow, March 7, 2008. Still from video by author.

guished in unemployment for the three preceding years, and remained entirely unknown in the contemporary world of Hindustani music. Beyond his own inability to perpetuate the musical inheritance of his lineage, Idris acknowledged that no children of the next generation were being groomed within his family tradition. Not only was Idris struggling for survival, but the living legacy of his musical inheritance was itself moribund. Only four or five living descendants still carried the inherited repertoire of their family line; among them, only two continued to perform and teach.

Despite their marginality today, these men descend from a musical lineage of rare distinction in the annals of modern Hindustani music history. Idris Khan's great-great-grandfather was Niamatullah Khan (d. 1903), a court musician of the last nawāb of Lucknow. Niamatullah Khan's renown is well documented, especially in the written works of his two sons, Karamatullah Khan (1848–1933) and Kaukab Khan (ca. 1850–1915), themselves among the most famous instrumentalists of their day. Idris Khan's grandfather, Sakhawat Husain Khan (1875–1955), ranked among the top three sarod players of his own day—comparable in his generation only to the sarod immortals Allauddin Khan and Hafiz Ali Khan—and traveled the world displaying his artistry. Idris Khan's father and uncle, the sitarist Ilyas Khan (1924–1989) and the sarod player Umar Khan (1916–1982), respectively, shone among their peers in the second half of the twentieth century.[3] In each generation, written documents reveal the family's ongoing musical and intellectual contributions to the contemporary Hindustani tradition. Moreover, the family perpetuated an oral history that still lives today. Drawing on archival documents, manuscripts, published writings, and oral interviews, this book is my attempt to document the modern history of Hindustani music from the point of view of a once-grand musical dynasty, a lineage known today as the Lucknow gharānā.

This book is far from the first to identify Idris Khan's lineage as one of the most significant in modern Hindustani music history (see Bagchee 1998; Chatterjee 1996; Chaubey 1958; Das Munim 1924; Khan 2000; Khan 1959; Manuel 1989a; McNeil 2007a; Misra 1985, 1991; Naqvi 2010; Schofield forthcoming; Sharar 2001 [1975]; Williams 2014).[4] During their own lifetimes, Idris Khan's father and uncle were deemed authoritative sources by numerous scholars in pursuit of the oral history and embodied repertoire of North Indian music (for example, Kippen 2005 [1988]; Miner 1997 [1993]; Sen 1992; Solis 1970). The chief of the gharānā today, Idris's cousin Irfan Khan (b. 1954), has himself been embraced by several scholars as a living source of such knowledge today (Barlow 2007; McNeil 2004; Tamori 2008; Trasoff 1999). Yet, while the history of the Lucknow gharānā peppers the works of notable scholars reaching back to the early twentieth century, the voices of the lineage serve largely as footnotes, playing supporting roles in someone else's story. In part, this is because authors such as Barlow (2007), Kippen (2005 [1988]), McNeil (2004), Miner (1997 [1993]), Sen (1992), Solis (1970), Tamori (2008), and Trasoff (1999) are all themselves practitioners who, while drawing extensively on the oral knowledge of the Lucknow gharānā, owe their allegiances to other—even rival—lineages. The present work, by contrast, keeps the Lucknow gharānā at the center of its focus throughout.

Since 2007 I have been dwelling within the world made by the Lucknow gharānā: in its embodied repertoire, in its documentary history, and in its living historical consciousness. In this book I experiment with a phenomenological perspective on the experience of the lineage, positing the gharānā as a coherent transgenerational subject that arises, lives, and declines. In this way, I "read back" the lineage identity, locating within it nineteenth- and early twentieth-century figures who could not have foreseen their own position within a connected genealogical chain stretching to the present day. Such an approach allows me to unfold in this book a set of interlinked historical counternarratives that weave self-understandings advanced by lineage musicians past and present together with archival and theoretical materials external to the lineage traditions. In the process I play with the line between disinterested and partisan representation, employing overlapping frames of reference that juxtapose the insights of the genealogical ethos with critical historiography and questions of broader scholarly inquiry.

Of what use is such an exercise? Why flout the accepted scholarly procedures that grant agency only to discrete individuals and that evaluate oral historical claims only against an impartial written record? Despite the obvious openings for scholarly criticisms of my own lack of objectivity, I maintain that my engagement with the world of the Lucknow gharānā offers a glimpse through the looking glass that turns upside down much of the commonplace knowledge of modern North Indian music history. As incredible as the view from the Lucknow gharānā sometimes may appear, it throws into relief the accepted history, much of which itself rests on a foundation of oral narrative enshrined in texts that obscure their own contingency.

A destablizing dose of counterhistory is vital today because the world of North Indian music now includes a body of official historical knowledge compiled through some four decades of intensive study by Western scholars. In particular, the literature produced in the field of ethnomusicology since the 1970s has contributed to a dense discursive web that shapes the way insiders and outsiders alike conceptualize the culture and history of Indian music. For example, the ethnomusicologist James Kippen acknowledges that when he first set out to conduct research in India in 1981, his agenda, orientation, and expectations were already shaped by the pioneering work of Daniel Neuman, who began his own research in the late 1960s (Kippen 2008: 125–26). Since that time a generation of scholars has produced a canon of definitive works on the dominant genres of Hindustani music (Du Perron 2007; Magriel and Du Perron 2013; Manuel 1989a; Sanyal and Widdess 2004; Wade 1997 [1984]), its instruments (Kippen 2005 [1988]; Miner 1997 [1993]; Qureshi 2007; Bor 1986/1987; Slawek 2000 [1987]; McNeil 2004), its melodic and rhythmic theory (Clayton 2000; Jairazbhoy 1995 [1971]; Levy 1982; Powers 1970; Rowell 1998 [1992]; Widdess 1995), and its social history (Erdman 1985; Daniel Neuman 1990 [1980]; Purohit 1988; Van der Meer 1980; Wade 1998).[5] In general, this literature tells the story of resilient musical traditions that maintained their essential integrity while adapting to changing social, economic, and political conditions.

While emphasizing the continuity of musical traditions, much of this literature nevertheless illuminates "radical changes" (Silver and Burghardt 1976:

28) in the social structure of Hindustani music in the twentieth century. Such changes include a geographical shift from regional courts to large urban centers as the preeminent sites of patronage, the rise of new public audiences, and the birth of new institutions of music education and dissemination. Both cause and consequence of these phenomena, perhaps the most dramatic and vexing social change within modern Indian music history concerns the ascendance of new populations of performers. As stated forthrightly by Harold Powers, and recognized by numerous scholars, "by the end of the 17th century virtually all Hindustani musicians were Muslim" (1980: 23; see also Manuel 1989a: 4 and 2007 [1996]: 122; Wade 1997 [1984]: 2; Slawek 2007: 507). Yet, as Powers continues, "the shift of patronage of Hindustani music to the growing urban and predominately Hindu middle class" brought "an ever-growing flood of Hindu professional musicians" (1980: 26). Until the late twentieth and early twenty-first centuries, most scholars held that the shift from Muslim to Hindu predominance within Hindustani music was a salutary, natural, and unavoidable result of the rise of nationalism and the democratization of performing arts traditions that had long been monopolized by hereditary (and often Muslim) professional artists.

More recently, a new trajectory in the literature focuses a critical lens on nationalism, colonialism, and the contradictions of modernity as they shaped the arts known today as "classical" music and dance in both North and South India (see Allen 1997; Bakhle 2005; Capwell 1991; Farrell 1997; Kobayashi 2003; Maciszewski 2006, 2007; Morcom 2013; Peterson and Soneji 2008; Qureshi 1991; Rosse 1995; Soneji 2012; Subramanian 2006, 2008; Walker 2014; Weidman 2007 [2006]). These works reveal the late nineteenth and early twentieth centuries as a caldron of reinvention in which elite forms of Indian music and dance were recast as national traditions available to the burgeoning middle class. Unlike many previous scholars, the authors of this "critical turn" (Peterson and Soneji 2008: 3) highlight the loss of prestige suffered by hereditary musicians as their traditions were appropriated and rebranded by a reform movement led by English-educated, urban, upper-caste elites. Paving the way into this discourse, Regula Qureshi contends that "music, newly re-Hinduized, symbolized self-assertion vis-à-vis the British as well as the Muslims" (1991: 160). The remaining Muslim hereditary professional musicians in India today are thus merely "left over"; they have little chance of survival in the absence of the Muslim patrons they and their ancestors once served (ibid.: 162). According to Qureshi, the situation is so stark that "within a generation most of these musicians, along with their oral musical heritage, can be fully expected to fade away" (ibid.). Reflecting and encapsulating the concerns of the new trajectory, Weidman emphasizes in her book "the exclusions that the consolidation of classical music had brought about" (2007 [2006]: 22). Peterson and Soneji summarize the proposition perhaps most starkly when they write that "the Hinduization of musical traditions in particular served to marginalize and exclude the hereditary—and principally Muslim—performers of north Indian music and dance [. . .] and to claim Hindustani music as the classical music of the nation as a whole" (2008: 7–8).

Yet despite such axiomatic statements, few scholars have pursued ethnographic studies of Muslim loss in the modern history of Hindustani music. The most rigorous investigations of demographic change instead concern gender, revealing the radical disenfranchisement of formerly privileged communities of professional courtesans and the transformation of many to common sex workers (Maciszewski 2006; Morcom 2013). Morcom in particular argues that the process by which the Hindustani performing arts were ennobled and nationalized in the late nineteenth and early twentieth centuries was predicated on the exclusion of female artists whose traditions were branded as illicit. Pushed to the periphery, these traditions echo today in the underworld of Bombay "dance bars" (Morcom 2013: 73), a far cry indeed from the nineteenth-century *koṭhā*-s (salons) where North India's courtesans were known to wield cultural, economic, and even political power. Morcom is exemplary of the new generation of scholars who have thrown into question the narrative of Indian music's successful adaptation to the conditions of modernity and its essential continuity across the radical disjunctures that created the Indian nation-state.

By contrast, the small number of works that directly pursue the history and ethnography of male Muslim hereditary Hindustani musicians depict a vibrant and adaptable tradition that meets the challenges of nationalist modernity, prevailing through its inherent artistic and cultural integrity. For example, the historian Janaki Bakhle, though criticized for overemphasizing "Muslim loss and Hindu gain" (Slawek 2007: 507), actually presents a qualified "story of triumph and success" that highlights the continued cultural centrality of Muslim master musicians—*ustād*-s—at the heart of a "national art that was never completely disciplined by the juggernaut of colonial or nationalist modernity" (Bakhle 2005: 253, 14; see also Clayton 2007). Dard Neuman arrives at a similar conclusion, holding that "the case of Hindustani music represents one of the few instances where the modernizing project to discipline and appropriate 'old-world' traditions stumbled against an alternative history in which the traditional practitioners were more successful in modulating into and through history" (2004: 435). An allied interpretation is offered by Daniel Neuman, who maintains that because Muslim musicians had no need for texts, institutions, or musical literacy, they simply "ignored" the machinations of the nationalist reformers (2014: 297). As he writes, Muslim hereditary musicians "survived and have in many cases thrived, precisely because they operated in a quite separate historical stream" (ibid.). At the extreme, some scholars have flatly denied that there ever was a concerted conspiracy to undermine the authority of Muslim musicians, arguing instead that Hindus and Muslims worked together to shape musical modernity in harmony and mutual respect (see Pradhan 2014: 3–4; Kobayashi 2003).

The most convincing account of the modern ascent of hereditary ustād-s comes from Dard Neuman, who unfolds a fascinating story of triumph over adversity in which degraded musicians not only raised their status but soared to national celebrity in the twentieth century. Significantly, Dard Neuman reorients the analysis of sociomusical conflict away from religion (Hindu versus Muslim) and instead illuminates a clash of classes within the tradition of Muslim hereditary specialists. This story concerns a fundamental hierarchy of prestige discussed in detail by Daniel Neuman: the Hindustani music tradition requires both soloists (artists who possess rarified, hereditary musical knowledge) and accompanists (artisans who provide rhythmic or melodic support to the soloist) (1990 [1980]: 136, passim). The senior Neuman theorizes that this division of musical labor ultimately led to the birth of an occupational caste that produced highly trained but socially stigmatized musicians to perform as accompanists, players of the tablā (drums) and the *sāraṅgī* (fiddle). By the early twentieth century, this sociomusical hierarchy was so entrenched that members of subordinated accompanist communities—known as *ḍhāḍhī*-s or *mīrāsī*-s— were assigned inferior social status irrespective of their musical attainment. For instance, in Alladiya Khan's memoirs, dictated in the 1940s but largely addressing the decades surrounding the turn of the twentieth century, the famed vocalist notes that "singers from Dhadi and Mirasi communities and women singers were not considered as belonging to a tradition, even though they had also learnt from the traditional singers" (Khan 2000: 71). Thus, despite the artistic renown of a given musician, membership in a community of accompanists negated one's eligibility to claim membership in a "tradition," that is, a named and recognized lineage or gharānā.

And yet Dard Neuman reveals that these degraded classes of musicians eventually "took the musical world by storm, defining dominant trends in the twentieth century" (2004: 238). As both Daniel Neuman and Dard Neuman affirm, the present-day scene for Hindustani music has resulted from the rise of superstar musicians from the ranks of the accompanist classes, their adoption of new roles as vocalists and solo instrumentalists, and their triumph over the older, elite lineages of hereditary musicians. Dard Neuman characterizes this story as a transition from orthodox to heterodox hegemony: as he argues, musicians of humble origins eagerly enriched their repertoires and thus came to dominate and invigorate the Hindustani tradition in the twentieth century while elite lineages of orthodox musicians "died a slow death" (2004: 307; see also Daniel Neuman 1978: 186). This large-scale sociomusical coup exposes a fundamental flaw in the ideological insistence on a social gulf between the realms of the soloist and the accompanist: in fact, the performance tradition depends on intimate proximity. Sāraṅgī players in particular were able to imbibe the repertoire of orthodox singers through extended musical contact while remaining largely in the shadows and rarely receiving formal training (Dard Neuman 2004: 301–7). Through this "ghost" mode, individual musicians of the accompanist class rose to constitute a new dominance as soloists, crafting an innovative repertoire of their own by combining materials from a great variety of sources (ibid.). By contrast, the orthodox classes refused to adapt and evolve, thus securing their own extinction.

As outlined by the foregoing discussion, the contemporary scholarship contains an apparent conflict between one trajectory that highlights the Hindu nationalist appropriation of India's "classical" traditions and another that emphasizes the triumph of Muslim hereditary musicians who overcame adversity to command the national stage. Taken together, however, the key works that address twentieth-century sociomusical change in Hindustani music complement rather than contradict one another: the Hindu middle class rose in the twentieth century to dominate the tradition in raw numbers of teachers, students, and performers, while simultaneously a new class of Muslim hereditary artists capable of meeting the demands of the new audience ascended the ranks of celebrity and renown.

There are good reasons to champion both the shared cultural pride and the triumph of innovative musical underclasses that birthed the Hindustani tradition as we know it. In this book, however, I channel the voices and visions of an elite hereditary tradition that finds little to celebrate in the culture of North

Indian music today. As *ashrāf*—high-status—Muslims from Afghanistan, and as players of the newly invented sarod, the ancestors of the Lucknow gharānā defined the new orthodoxy of Hindustani instrumental traditions in the late nineteenth and early twentieth centuries, succeeding the elite lineages that prevailed in the Mughal courts from the sixteenth to the nineteenth centuries. The oral histories and manuscripts of the Lucknow gharānā present a window into an alternate universe where we may attend to voices of dissent that reject the triumphant narrative of Hindustani music's successful transition to modernity in the twentieth century. Instead, these voices echo themes of displacement, loss of prestige, and erasure from the collective memory, in effect narrating their own "slow death" (Dard Neuman 2004: 307). As Daniel Neuman has recently noted, the memories and traditions of Paṭhān sarod lineages such as the family discussed in this book "constitute another separate musical historical reality, another important stream in Indian music history" (2014: 292–93) that has largely remained outside the dominant historical narratives of the tradition.[6] And yet, for the moment, this stream of music and memory flows on.

A Chain of Hearts

The continuity of musical repertoire and collective memory cultivated by lineages of hereditary musicians is premised on an intensive, family-based, one-on-one method of instruction. This method is described as *sīna-ba-sīna*—"chest-to-chest," or "father-to-son" (Platts 2004 [1884]: 714), or even as "heart-to-heart" (see also Qureshi 2009: 167). Ostensibly the purpose of this method was to transmit musical materials, yet the process itself produced a *silsila*: a linked lineage, a continuous chain of memory through which the voices of the ancestors are carried into the present (Ho 2006).

While hereditary musical materials have, over the course of the twentieth and twenty-first centuries, become widely available and are now practiced in homes and schools across the country with little connection to the families that once cultivated them, melody and rhythm were not the only practices transmitted through the hereditary chain of hearts. Lineages such as the Lucknow gharānā channel the generation-to-generation transmission of dispositions, postures, self-understandings, and historical consciousness: an embodied epistemology of music and meaning.

In his book *Musicking Bodies* (2012), Matthew Rahaim argues for increased attention to physical disciplines in musical pedagogy and practice. Revealing the limitations of a two-dimensional conception of melody as a sequence of discrete notes, Rahaim suggests a parallel understanding in which melody constitutes three-dimensional bodily pathways through a virtual musical space. Focusing on the gestures and movements that accompany the performance and transmission of melodic trajectories, Rahaim builds on the Sanskrit term *paramparā* (succession), coining the term *paramparic body* to address "embodied musical dispositions that are passed down through generations of teachers and students" (2012: 108). Here I extend Rahaim's metaphor of melody-as-pathway to the understanding of hereditary musicians themselves: they exist as individual agents (that is, as sequences of discrete notes) but also as participants in a lineage that can be conceived as a pathway through time and space (that is, as Rahaim's notion of three-dimensional shapes and rāga-spaces). As a stream of memory, the lineage forms a flow that connects the present to the past, and—ideally—also allows residents of the present to project their identity into the future through the belief in the ongoing viability of the lineage.

The paramparic body thus constitutes a spatiotemporal node of music and memory. Dard Neuman complicates the role of memory in the craft of the hereditary Hindustani musician through a reinterpretation of the meaning of practice. As he argues, musicians endure grueling regimes of repetitive drilling not to memorize materials by rote, but rather to transform their "hands or throat" into agents of their own (2012: 446). In the moment of performance, Neuman argues, Hindustani musicians rely on the preparation of muscles and bones to autonomously explore the gamut of musical possibilities, the body remaining "several steps ahead of the comprehending mind" (2004: 164). I would add, however, that while the musician's methods may not rely on conscious memory, the social apparatus that makes such practice rituals possible (the extended family of hereditary musicians) constitutes a vital and self-conscious conduit for extramusical memories, family stories, and self-understandings.

The Instrumentalist Paradigm

As renowned and authentic as their musical traditions may have been, why should we trust the visions and versions of history offered by the living representatives of the Lucknow gharānā today? This small handful of remaining musicians—spread across North India in the cities of Delhi, Lucknow, Calcutta, and Gauhati—are virtually unknown in the contemporary culture of Hindustani music, and thus might appear motivated to advance a sense of history that devalues the contributions of the dominant musical figures today and tarnishes the legacies of competing hereditary lines. In this regard, a wary analyst would naturally interpret the oral histories of the Lucknow gharānā within an "instrumentalist paradigm" that assumes oral historical narratives are primarily crafted with present concerns in mind, and should thus be read as retrospective stories that tell us more about who is telling them than about the documentable historical past (Glasser 2015).

The instrumentalist paradigm is well established in the anthropological literature, most famously articulated by Evans-Pritchard in his influential text *The Nuer* (1940). As he wrote, the history available in the oral traditions of tribal groups is best understood as "a projection into the past of the actual relations between groups of persons [in the present]. It is less a means of co-ordinating events than of co-ordinating relationships, and is therefore mainly a looking backwards, since relationships must be explained in terms of the past" (1940: 108, quoted in Shryock 1997: 21, brackets added). Even ethnomusicologists who ostensibly embrace the primacy of the musician's perspective agree that oral historical narratives should be approached with scrupulous skepticism. For example, Richard Widdess contends that "oral history is largely unverifiable, and must be viewed as statements as much about the present as about the past" (2010: 119). Likewise, James Kippen avers that "genealogical and historical data should not be taken literally as true accounts of the descent and history of musical families [. . . .] Instead, we should treat such data as symbolic of *contemporary ideas* concerning both the past and present states of being a musician in India, and also as 'texts' available for manipulation in specific situations" (2005 [1988]: 84–85, emphasis added).

Beyond identifying the tendency of contemporary musicians to misrepresent the past, some writers have extended their critique to include scholars themselves, especially those who base their research on the dubious oral accounts of musicians. Bakhle, for instance, frames her 2005 book as a corrective to flawed works by ethnomusicologists who, she argues, too often forge intimate bonds with their informants, suspend their critical faculty, and thus accept erroneous, exaggerated, or invented memories as historical fact. Dard Neuman suggests a similar critique when he identifies "a politics of ethnographic affiliation" that leads scholars to become uncritical partisans of their research informants (2004: 234). Such politics are especially problematic when, as ethnomusicologist Stephen Slawek suggests, the primary sociomusical unit of Hindustani music today—gharānā—serves not only to preserve and perpetuate musical knowledge, but also to consolidate social identity and prestige in the manner of a tribe or political party. As Slawek writes of his famed sitar teacher, "[Ravi] Shankar conceptualizes gharānā as a mechanism through which one's musical status can be preserved. The stronger the alliance, the higher and more stable the status. Weaken the alliance and you create conditions that will allow the propaganda of rival groups to be taken for historical fact" (1991: 174, brackets added).

As all of these scholars suggest, writing music history on the basis of oral testimony from living informants is tricky business. Especially when working within a tradition that prizes descent from glorious ancestors, we have every reason to remain skeptical of origin stories that privilege the lineage of the storyteller and denigrate the ancestors of competing lines. And yet aggrandizing tales are the currency of history among hereditary musicians. Following anthropologist Andrew Shryock, I argue that the lineage-based historical consciousness constitutes a valid historical epistemology at the heart of many traditions premised on genealogical descent. In his book *Nationalism and the Genealogical Imagination: Oral History and Textual Authority in Tribal Jordan* (1997), Shryock identifies this epistemology as the "genealogical imagination," a way of knowing the past in which "reliable forms of human knowledge [. . .] are reproduced genealogically, whether in biological pedigrees or intellectual chains of transmission" (1997: 6).

Taking the genealogical imagination seriously is important because for too long anthropologists and ethnomusicologists have propounded an uncritical conception of history. Shryock observes that since the 1970s, anthropologists have increasingly embraced "history in the analysis of social change" (1997: 25), but have rarely engaged critically what they mean by "history." Shryock identifies three unspoken assumptions he believes underlie dominant conceptions of legitimate history: (1) it should be premised on textual documents; (2) it should embrace a uniform chronology; and (3) it should take the final form of a linear narrative (ibid.: 28). Shryock contends that this conception of history—the "commonsense epistemology of the modern intellectual classes"— serves to subordinate "other histories to hegemonically Western ones" (ibid.). In Shryock's colorful language, Western modes of historiography thus "envelop foreign conceptions of history as readily as colonial powers once amassed foreign soil" (ibid.: 26).

Shryock is not the first to argue for the value of oral historical traditions, yet celebrations of orality often contain caveats. Alessandro Portelli, for instance, insists, "Oral sources are credible but with a *different* credibility." He continues, suggesting that "'wrong' statements are still psychologically 'true,' and [...] this truth may be equally as important as factually reliable accounts" (1991: 51). Of course I agree in principle with Portelli's prescription for "factual verification" (ibid.), yet history rarely comes to us as a list of verifiable events and dates; instead, as indicated by Shryock's third criterion, it most often takes the form of a narrative. The critique of narrative in history writing is of vital importance to the argument of this book, and thus I will address it here in some detail.

Narrative and Counternarrative

In this book I proceed from the philosophical perspective that history is always contested and that acts of historical interpretation are necessarily fraught with political and ethical peril. The scholar's choices of what to study, which sources to access, and how to forge disparate traces of the past into a coherent narrative are themselves acts of power with ideological causes and consequences. As I hope to convince you, the story of the Lucknow gharānā reveals that the contest over how to interpret music history is not simply a matter of whose sources are more accurate or reliable. Instead, it is a matter of the historian's own political and ethical decisions and dispositions. As George Lipsitz contends, historians always confront "multiple, conflicting, and contradictory realities and truths" (2007: 105) that require them to make perilous and politically charged choices to highlight "some parts of the past over others" (1995: 704).

Fredric Jameson, in his book *Postmodernism, Or, the Cultural Logic of Late Capitalism* (1991), addresses this very dimension of historical scholarship when he argues, "The decision as to whether one faces a break or a continuity—whether the present is to be seen as a historical originality or as the simple prolongation of more of the same under different sheep's clothing—is not an empirically justifiable or philosophically arguable one, since it is itself the inaugural narrative act that grounds the perception and interpretation of the events to be narrated" (1991: xii–xiii). Here Jameson contends that because our grasp of the past is itself shaped by quasi-literary narratives, we cannot expect to base our narrative choices on the facts of history alone. If we cannot select our narratives solely on the basis of past events, then what can serve as the basis for such decisions? How do we select which parts of the past to emphasize in order to compose a coherent historical narrative, and how do we justify the accuracy of our conclusions?

The historian Hayden White supplies a radical answer to these questions: "it is not a matter of choosing between objectivity and distortion, but rather between different strategies for constituting 'reality' in thought so as to deal with it in different ways, each of which has its own ethical implications" (1978: 22). White thus argues that various narrative interpretations of the same historical phenomena demand evaluation not merely on the grounds of objective veracity, but as regards their "ethical implications." White's formulation resonates with Jameson's own statement that the "problem of postmodernism" is both "an aesthetic and a political one" (1991: 55). As Jameson continues, "The various positions that can logically be taken on [the problem of postmodernism], whatever terms they are couched in, can always be shown to articulate visions of history in which the evaluation of the social moment in which we live today is the object of an essentially political affirmation or repudiation" (ibid.). That is, once again, theoretical positions and narrative choices constitute political decisions made by scholars on the ground and in the present.

My political and ethical choices have led me to lionize the voices of a hereditary lineage that has collapsed into near nonexistence today. The voices themselves offer stories that contrast and conflict with dominant narratives in Indian music history; I have chosen to select, amplify, thematize, and frame those stories as a set of interlocking counternarratives. I do not maintain that the resulting history constitutes a correct version meant to supersede existing narratives. Following Derrida, I offer the "counter" as a "with-against" that "not only means to oppose or contradict, but also, inseparably, to engage, meet, make contact" (Wortham 2006: 20). I thus embrace the contradiction of constructing narratives in the service of narrative critique, and hope that this work finds a place both parallel and perpendicular to the canon of scholarship on Indian music history.

Overview

The story at the heart of this book takes place in the short century between 1856 and 1947, the pivotal period of Indian music's transformation from elite court art to national cultural tradition. The iconic historical moment that marks the commencement of this transformation occurs in Lucknow when the final king is overthrown, ousted, and exiled by the British East India Company. As I discuss in Chapter 1, this very moment is memorialized in a well-known ṭhumrī (light classical song) titled "Bābul Morā" that celebrates the Lucknow that was, while simultaneously mourning its ignominious loss. Moreover, as I learn in a music lesson with Irfan Khan, the ṭhumrī itself continues to inform the inherited repertoire of the Lucknow gharānā today. I argue in this chapter that a close reading of the central musical phrase of the ṭhumrī "Bābul Morā" illuminates both the history of Lucknow and the intertwined but distinct history of the Lucknow gharānā. The fall of the city precipitates a musical diaspora that finds the Lucknow gharānā putting down roots in Calcutta, Kathmandu, and Allahabad. By the second decade of the twentieth century, the central representative of the gharānā—Sakhawat Husain Khan—takes his lineage traditions around the globe, finally returning to a much-diminished Lucknow to play his part in establishing India's preeminent institution of music education. Using the ṭhumrī as a framing device, Chapter 1 presents the early history of the Lucknow gharānā as a Pyrrhic victory in which the rising tide of sociopolitical change propels the gharānā to renown, while simultaneously preparing the conditions for its collapse.

Chapter 2 investigates the musical dimensions of the gharānā's Pyrrhic victory: the lived contradictions of musical modernity are revealed through a common thread in the writings of several generations of the lineage that rejects ṭhumrī—the very musical form most closely associated with the changing musical world of the mid-nineteenth century—as a detriment to the hoary traditions of Hindustani music. Yet ṭhumrī was itself a key element in the musical transformations that accompanied the rise of the Lucknow gharānā. Chapter 2 traces the thread, as successive members of the musical lineage dive ambivalently into a new cultural world, simultaneously embodying in their own inherited repertoire and rejecting in their own recorded statements the most modern of musical forms.

Chapter 3 embraces the gharānā's genealogical imagination, exploring the oral history as relayed to me by Irfan Khan and Gulfam Ahmad Khan. Many of the stories of this chapter concern the struggle to retain ideological centrality through the repetition of historical narratives that deny the claims to greatness of rival lineages. And yet the primary shared characteristic of the rival lines is that they are dominant today, and thus have been able to craft their own histories, which are now embedded in the collective memory of Hindustani musical culture.

At the same time that its members were challenged by the rise of competing lineages, the Lucknow gharānā faced the appropriation of the Hindustani tradition by the forces of religious nationalism. Denigrated as illiterate, ignorant, and intransigent, Muslim hereditary musicians were targeted by the Hindu leaders of the late nineteenth- and early twentieth-century reform movement as the primary obstacles to music's modernity. Chapter 4 explores the relationship between the college[7] established by leading reformist V. N. Bhatkhande, and Muslim hereditary artists such as Sakhawat Husain Khan, arguing that the institution propagated a Hindu-centric ideology inimical to Muslim musical authority. Drawing on archival state documents as well as on the public writings and unpublished private memoirs of Sakhawat Husain Khan, this chapter presents a historical counternarrative marked by irony. Even as the new institutions of music defined, in principle, an all-inclusive national cultural tradition, their very structure alienated and disenfranchised the hereditary musicians who had laid the local and pre-national foundations for that tradition.

And yet the Lucknow gharānā proposed an alternative. Chapter 5 introduces two towering figures of the lineage: literate, educated, hereditary Muslim musicians who actively engaged the reform movement through both participation and resistance, wrote their own versions of music history, envisioned a robust and national future for Hindustani music, and insisted on the rightful place of Muslim artistry and Islamicate epistemology at its center. In particular, this chapter addresses the active agency of Muslim musicians in resistance to the Hinduization of their traditions through close readings of long out-of-print and unpublished Urdu texts by the brothers Karamatullah and Kaukab Khan. Focused on the writings of these two stalwarts of the Lucknow gharānā, Chapter 5 unfolds a historical counternarrative in which Muslim musicians recognized and resisted the threat posed to their prestige by the burgeoning reform movement in the early twentieth century.

We begin in the middle: the year is 1925, the place is Lucknow, and onstage the renowned vocalist Faiyaz Khan presents a prescient critique of the modern history of Indian music in five short words.

ONE

"Oh Father, My Home Is Being Left Behind"

From 1916 to 1925, the celebrated music scholar Vishnu Narayan Bhatkhande (1860–1936) convened a series of All-India Music Conferences bringing together for the first time the most prestigious musicians of the day with the community of music scholars and the general public. Among the most significant of these was the Fourth All-India Music Conference, held in Lucknow in January of 1925. The events of the conference took place within a large *paṇḍāl* (temporary pavilion designed for a religious or otherwise festive gathering) erected within the grounds of the Qaiserbagh Baradari, the performance hall at the heart of Wajid Ali Shah's erstwhile palace complex (Report 1925: 40). Here at the symbolic center of old Lucknow, the celebrated singer Faiyaz Khan intoned the ṭhumrī "Bābul Morā Naihara Chūṭo Jāya," a song widely known as the final statement of loss by the deposed king upon his ouster from Lucknow nearly seventy years earlier in 1856 (ibid.: 104). Indeed, the words of the ṭhumrī reference, even memorialize, the traumatic separation of the king from his kingdom, and thus evoke the massive political and cultural calamity that befell the city—and likewise the entire country—in the wake of the ouster. In this regard, "Bābul Morā" has become an icon of loss that enshrines the defeat of the king of Lucknow as a pivotal moment in Indian history.

The song's recurring refrain literally references the pain of separation felt by a young bride as she is carried away from her childhood home to the household of her husband's family. In this regard the song draws on the tradition of the wedding lament, a performance practice found in patriarchal societies throughout the world that acknowledges and soothes the trauma suffered by young women as they are torn from their family home on their wedding day (see Sugarman 1989: 193). The ubiquity of the wedding lament as a standard song genre throughout the Mediterranean and Muslim world indexes a widely shared understanding of marriage as a moment of both great joy and grievous loss. In *Sunlight on a Broken Column* (1992 [1961]), a novel set in mid-twentieth-century Lucknow, the author Attia Hosain likewise mines the emotional complexity of South Asian marriage as a window into broader social change. In the novel, the young female protagonist, Laila, defies centuries of tradition by rejecting an arranged marriage, marrying instead for love, and thereby embracing the very modernity that will ultimately disenfranchise her entire clan. While the story revolves around Laila's own ambivalent freedom struggle, it simultaneously depicts the last days of British rule in India, highlighting the dependence of the Indian feudal aristocracy on the economic and political structures of colonialism. Because of this dependency, the birth of independent India as a democratic republic in 1947 toppled not only the British Empire, but also those families—like Laila's—whose refined culture and generous patronage of the arts were premised on a long-standing system of feudal exploitation supported by the colonial state. Laila's family is torn apart both by the forfeiture of their fortune and by emigration to Pakistan, India's conjoined twin, separated at birth through a bloody and brutal partition whose pain is still felt today.

In South Asia, as in much of the world, marriage is virtually unavoidable. It constitutes one of life's most significant rites of passage, opening a new future even as it marks a wrenching rupture with the past. Likewise, the defeat of colonialism, the death of feudalism, the rise of democracy, and the birth of the nation brought not only liberation but tragic loss. This twofold structure characterizes dominant interpretations of modernity, an internally conflicted historical moment that pits enhanced lifestyles against diminished lifeways. For example, in his classic study *All That Is Solid Melts into Air* (1988 [1982]), the Marxist scholar Marshall Berman acknowledges that the experience of modernity entails a painful rupture with the past, yet encourages us to become "immune to nostalgic yearnings for the world we have lost," and to instead embrace our unstable existence in a shifting and disorienting cultural landscape (ibid.: 60). Similarly, the scholar of rhetoric Dilip Parameshwar Gaonkar maintains that the experience of loss is not a side effect of modernity, but instead a central aspect of it: modernity constitutes a "double consciousness" and a "poisoned gift" (1999: 3).

In his book *A Singular Modernity*, Fredric Jameson argues that the term *modernity* is overused and imprecise: it may refer to any historical period that entailed a self-conscious distance from its own immediate past. For instance, Jameson offers a preliminary "inventory of possibilities" that includes fourteen significant moments of historical rupture over a period of nearly five centuries, each a potentially persuasive "narrative option" in the origin story of modernity (2002: 31–32). The discussion of modernity in the non-Western world is further complicated by the dominant understanding of modernity as a European invention that originated in the cosmopolitan center and spread only later to the colonial periphery (Anderson 1991 [1983]; Chatterjee 1993 [1986], 1993). Dipesh Chakrabarty (2008 [2000], 2002) and others have maintained that modernity developed in Europe and the colonies conterminously, but strenuous debate continues over the relationship between colonialism and modernity in India. Sanjay Subrahmanyam (1998), for instance, argues for India's precolonial modernity beginning as early as the fifteenth century.

In the context of scholarship on Indian music, however, the term *modernity* is fairly well defined. It refers to thoroughgoing changes consciously implemented by nationalist reformers in the late nineteenth and early twentieth centuries, and also to the adaptive strategies of hereditary musicians during the same period. In this chapter and the next I argue for a distinctive intermediate period connecting the musical traditions of the Mughal courts (sixteenth to nineteenth centuries) to the rebranded and redefined practices nationalized in the late nineteenth and early twentieth centuries as North Indian "classical" music, showing that a new world of music was being born in the mid-nineteenth century and was rapidly disseminated as a result of the war of 1857–58.

An iconic memorial of the events that led to the war, the thumrī "Bābul Morā" suggests a counterinterpretation of musical modernity in India. The song draws on the metaphor of marriage to evoke a widely shared sense of loss, but Hindustani music has not generally been associated with lamentation, loss, or grief. Quite the opposite, Hindustani music is broadly understood as a powerful and continuous tradition that defied colonialism and modernity, asserting its rightful place as the highest art tradition of the Indian people in this or any era. While postcolonial India celebrates its modernity—highlighting especially its status as a nuclear power, its contributions to information technology, its international corporate connectivity, and its achievements in space exploration—it also clings to significant threads of continuity with the past, championing "classical" music as a definitive conduit to antiquity through claims of a two-thousand-year-old tradition. In fact, the most striking and consistent element of continuity within Indian music history is the discursive emphasis on continuity itself (Scarimbolo 2014: 160), but there is nevertheless a strong sense among musicians and music lovers that the performance traditions of today allow modern subjects to touch the ancient world. The assertion of that continuity in the nationalist and postcolonial age, however, entailed social and cultural changes that marginalized many. In this chapter I explore the experience of the Lucknow gharānā as it transitioned into and through modernity, focusing in particular on the ṭhumrī "Bābul Morā" as both an element of the gharānā's repertoire and a potent metaphor illuminating the relationship between the gharānā and modernity at large. While Lucknow remains at the center of this story, I first discovered these interrelationships far from the city as I traveled in pursuit of the living k̲h̲alīfa (chief) of the Lucknow gharānā today.

Meeting the K̲h̲alīfa

In early 2009 I boarded a flight from Delhi to Jorhat, a small city in the state of Assam, far in the northeast of India, close to the borders with Bangladesh, Burma, Bhutan, and China. From Jorhat I traveled another two hours by car to the remote town of Numaligarh, nestled in a vast expanse of tea plantations, not far from the Kaziranga wildlife park, a UNESCO World Heritage Site home to large numbers of the Indian one-horned rhinoceros. Here I finally met Irfan Khan, the senior performing artist and presiding k̲h̲alīfa of the Lucknow gharānā. Irfan Khan served as head of the department of music of the Delhi Public School (the conventional British term—Americans would call it an elite *private* school) serving the township of Numaligarh, a heavily guarded residential compound housing a colony of oil refinery workers and their families. Because the northeast region of India has long been home to separatist militants, oil refineries such as Numaligarh are targets for terrorist attacks, thus necessitating the concentric rings of roadblocks and armed guards I crossed when entering the township. Passing the security corridor, I found a lush and manicured landscape maintained by a phalanx of gardeners quietly trimming, weeding, and watering throughout the day. The dormitory accommodations Irfan Khan had arranged for me in the township were spacious and spotless. In the cafeteria, I ate my daily meals with large numbers of refinery professionals and heard the sounds of Assamese language spoken at tables all around me.

In sum, Numaligarh could hardly have presented a greater contrast to my primary field site in Lucknow—a historical center of cultivated Urdu language, a crowded and polluted state capital in the plains of North India, a centuries-old city marked by ornate Indo-Persian architecture. Yet sitting for daily music lessons with Irfan Khan on the floor of my Numaligarh dormitory room, I experienced a connection to the musical traditions of Lucknow I had not found in the city itself. While Idris Khan (introduced in the preceding chapter) offered lively narrative anecdotes concerning his family history, Idris's cousin Irfan Khan was willing and able to perform and teach numerous musical compositions attributed to specific gharānā ancestors, orally annotating these with stories of the lineage that evoked a continuous musical genealogy reaching back to the eighteenth century. And yet the very musical repertoire and inherited historical dispositions that connect Irfan Khan to the glorious past also yoke him to an ongoing experience of loss of pride and prestige. Indeed, since the 1960s, the lineage has steadily declined and has nearly been forgotten today. In this chapter, I argue that the sense of loss experienced by Irfan Khan and his remaining gharānā brothers is sustained through the continuity—not the rupture—of the hereditary tradition and is communicated in and through the embodied repertoire itself.

This chapter explores the relationship between loss and embodiment through an interpretive reading of a small piece of Irfan Khan's inherited repertoire. Unpacking the meanings of one musical phrase entails a journey into the past that illuminates the origins and adventures of the Lucknow gharānā. From Assam of 2009, we are transported back to Lucknow of 1856, and further back to Afghanistan of the eighteenth century before following the Lucknow gharānā's primary mid-twentieth-century artist on his journeys around the globe. Beyond the historical insights it offers, our study of a single musical gesture from Irfan Khan's repertoire ultimately reveals an alternate reading of the present. As a counternarrative thwarting dominant frameworks that celebrate the adaptability of Hindustani music in the modern era, the legacy of Irfan Khan's lineage suggests a critique of modernity as a double-edged sword that brings both progress and pain, predicating the tremendous success of the Hindustani tradition in the twentieth and twenty-first centuries on grievous loss for some. To begin the discovery of the insights available through the embodied traditions of a hereditary lineage, we return to my dormitory room in Numaligarh, where I sit on the floor for a lesson with the _khalīfa_ of the Lucknow gharānā.

A Lesson in Rāga *Bhairavīṅ*

Irfan Khan is playing his hereditary instrument, the sarod, a fretless, plucked lute. Striking his main string with a thick plectrum called *jāwā* in his right hand, he slides up and down the sarod's polished steel fingerboard with the nails of the first two fingers of his left hand. When those nails wear down, he employs on these fingers (as per his family tradition) thimble-like conical caps today made of cellulose, but in the past made of dried, hardened fish scales (Solis 1970: 50). The instrument itself, shown in the hands of Irfan Khan's father, Umar Khan, in Figure 2, is a short-necked lute of carved wood with a sound chamber covered by stretched goatskin. The bridge is supported only by the stretched skin, thus contributing to the sarod's characteristic percussive sound, somewhat akin to that of the Western banjo. Unlike today's banjo, the sarod features a fingerboard devoid of frets, and includes an array of sympathetically vibrating strings tuned to the notes of the scale to be played.

One of the specialties of Hindustani instrumental music is the great variety of techniques available on various instruments to imitate the human voice. While "fixed pitch" instruments like the harmonium are tuned to a limited number of predetermined melodic steps, the singing voice may range freely within the broad spectrum of musical sound, producing a theoretically limitless number of discrete pitches and transitioning seamlessly between them. The technique of connecting musical steps through smooth melodic portamento is central to the aesthetics of Indian music in both north and south. Sarod players achieve this vocal-like technique by pressing the string against the polished steel finger-board, and, while exciting the string with the plectrum in the right hand, main-taining that left-hand pressure and sliding, sometimes in virtuosic recursive patterns, along a given string. By contrast, the sitar, shown in the hands of Irfan Khan's uncle, Ilyas Khan, in Figure 3, features a succession of parallel frets much like the guitar. Unlike the guitar, however, the frets of the sitar are long and curved. As a student of the sitar, I was required to translate the fluid slides of Irfan Khan's sarod onto my instrument by pulling and displacing the main string across the curvature of the frets. Though the two instruments require different techniques, and produce different timbres, it is not uncommon for a sitarist to learn from a sarod player, or vice versa. Beyond the compatibility of various instruments, the unity and coherence of the Hindustani tradition allows instrumental music of all kinds to be taught vocally, the teacher singing phrases for the student to echo on her instrument. Even in the case of a student learning

FIGURE 2 Umar Khan,
Calcutta, 1982. Photo by
Ismail Ali Doodha,
courtesy of Irfan Khan.

FIGURE 3 Ilyas Khan, Lucknow,
1984. Photo by Irfan Khan,
courtesy of Irfan Khan.

vocal music, shapes and gestures—communicated by a great variety of movements of the hands, arms, torso, and head—are at the heart of musical transmission in Hindustani music (Rahaim 2012; Clayton 2000: 4).

Learning to move your body and shape musical phrases as your teacher does is central to the transmission process known as *tālīm*, or formal training. Participating in *tālīm* requires an extraordinary degree of commitment from both parties. Even today, in the era of easy access to Indian music and its methods through public institutions or online lessons, a master musician sitting with a new student would not usually reveal much, and would expect the pupil to grasp even less. One does not have to look far for stories of disciples who patiently waited for years for the lessons to begin, or who were instructed to repeat the most mundane of exercises until they lost interest and gave up (for example, Dard Neuman 2012: 437). Yet I came to Irfan Khan primarily as a researcher and brought years of sitar practice already under my belt. Moreover, as a music school teacher for most of his career, Irfan was accustomed to readily revealing his repertoire, and—far from fearful that someone might steal his music—welcomed anyone interested in participating in his gharānā's traditions. For these reasons, he was ready to perform the specialties of his gharānā, and in the third week of our lessons began teaching a rāga with particular significance for his family, rāga *Bhairavīṅ*. Beyond its special meanings for the Lucknow gharānā, *Bhairavīṅ* is also known and beloved by Hindustani musicians and aficionados throughout the world.

This is one of the most common rāga-s of Hindustani music today, usually spelled *Bhairavī*. Though uncommon in the broader culture, the nasalization of the final long *i* vowel constitutes a variant spelling found in some Urdu texts and used by members of the Lucknow gharānā both in their writings and in their spoken discourse today. The rāga itself is understood to have as its most basic structure a heptatonic (seven-note) scale with lowered 2nd, 3rd, 6th, and 7th degrees. Yet one learns early in the study of Indian music that a rāga is a musical entity of far greater complexity than a mere scale. Rāga-s entail inherent melodic tendencies, movements, phrases, and relative points of emphasis such that many different and otherwise unrelated rāga-s may share a common scale. Some rāga-s additionally incorporate specific phrases that include notes outside the basic scale: *Bhairavīṅ* is most famous among these, theoretically allowing for all five accidentals, and thus the use of all twelve notes of the chromatic scale. However, one would rarely run a step-wise chromatic line all the way through an octave of the scale. Instead, over the course of a performance,

FIGURE 4 *Bhairavīṅ* scale with its most common accidentals.

one may cumulatively include all five accidentals—each in its own idiomatic context—though only four accidentals are commonly employed. (*Bhairavīṅ*'s basic scale, along with its most common accidentals, is illustrated in Figure 4.) Because of its propensity to include notes outside its basic scale, *Bhairavīṅ* is often used for "light" vocal forms such as ṭhumrī and *dādrā*, rather than dhrupad and khyāl. It is also usually reserved for a concluding piece, in part because it is so widely beloved that it would be hard to follow with any other rāga, and also because it may provide a familiar and accessible conclusion to what might have been a demanding main musical event.

An in-depth understanding of Hindustani music requires technical language and specialized skills, but the great majority of those who know and love rāga-based music connect with it not through esoteric theory or disciplined practice, but rather through its emotional appeal. Since the earliest texts in which the term is defined, *rāga* has referred to a combination of modal structure and emotional affect (Widdess 1995: 42). The word *rāga* derives from the Sanskrit *ranj*, meaning "to color"—for centuries rāga-s have been understood to "give color." The best-known contemporary definition of rāga is "that which colors the mind," suggesting that the capacity to evoke emotions, feelings, or colors remains the defining characteristic of rāga music today (Shankar 2007 [1968]: 28). Moreover, rāga-s are associated with seasons, times of the day, and even, in some cases, geographic locations. Such is the case with *Bhairavīṅ*, which is an early-morning rāga, but is also associated with the city of Lucknow. In Abdul Halim Sharar's book *Lucknow: The Last Phase of an Oriental Culture*, the author extensively cites musician and scholar Asadullah "Kaukab" Khan—Irfan Khan's own great-grandfather—who notes, "Today Lucknow's *bhairvin* raginis, sung in the early morning, have become as famous throughout India as Lucknow's melons" (2001 [1975]: 138).[1]

"Oh Father": The *Mukhṛā*

Although the rāga itself is an abstract melodic entity capable of a vast variety of musical manifestations, Irfan Khan focused our lessons on the *ālāp* (slow,

FIGURE 5 *Mukhṛā* as played by Irfan Khan.

nai- har- a   chū-   ṭo   hī   jāya

FIGURE 6 *Mukhṛā* as sung by Girja Devi.

unmetered introduction), employing a small melodic statement known as a *mukhṛā* to punctuate the *ālāp*'s successive developmental sections. The particular *mukhṛā* Irfan Khan taught me is notated in Figure 5, using rough rhythmic approximations as it does not conform to a formal pulse. The notes bearing "x" instead of a regular note head indicate the use of high-pitched drone strings known as *cikārī* (tuned to the tonic and dominant pitches) that participate in the rhythmic but not the melodic contour of the phrase. In our lessons Irfan Khan emphasized that this *mukhṛā* should be used repeatedly throughout the performance of the *Bhairavīṅ ālāp* as a temporal signpost much the way many musicians use a *mohṛā* or stand-alone, cadential phrase.[2]

When I inquired about the origins of this particular *mukhṛā*, Irfan Khan revealed that it constituted a melodic fragment from the well-known ṭhumrī "Bābul Morā" and that musicians of his family have been employing it within performances of *Bhairavīṅ* since the song was first composed in the nineteenth century. Yet the song is hardly limited to Irfan Khan's family repertoire: "Bābul Morā" is perhaps the most famous ṭhumrī in India, widely disseminated by the beloved singer and actor K. L. Saigal in the 1938 film *Street Singer*. "Bābul Morā" has also been performed and recorded by numerous Hindustani vocalists. For purposes of comparison with the *mukhṛā* played by Irfan Khan, Figure 6 presents a transcription of the same *mukhṛā* as sung by famed vocalist Girja Devi from a 1977 recording by All India Radio, released as a commercial cassette in 1995.

Figure 6 shows only Girja Devi's first statement of the *mukhṛā*, which comes at the end of her short introductory *ālāp*. The words of the *mukhṛā* are *naihara chūṭo jāya*, thus constituting the final three words of the ṭhumrī's first line, yet including the word *hī* interposed between *chūṭo* and *jāya*. As Hindi language scholar Lalita Du Perron explains in her book on the lyrics of ṭhumrī songs, performance often includes small changes to fixed texts (2007: 85–90); within performances of "Bābul Morā," it is exceedingly common for singers to include the word *hī* in the manner reflected here. *Hī* is simply an amplifying word, suggesting that the home is "verily" left behind. The final word of the *mukhṛā* in this initial statement coincides with the first beat of the fourteen-beat *tāla* (rhythm cycle) that continues until the end of the nearly quarter-hour recording. Like the transcription of Irfan Khan's performance of the *mukhṛā*, the transcription in Figure 6 does not include a time signature and uses designations of pitch duration somewhat loosely.

The structural similarities between the two renderings of the *mukhṛā* are striking: it appears that Irfan Khan generally applies a plectrum stroke for each syllable of the text and performs a melismatic elaboration with much the same contour and pitch content as that sung by Girja Devi. Moreover, the alternative scale degrees of natural 2 and natural 7 are used in similar ways, with the raised 2nd degree employed throughout the passage until the final cadence, where flat 2 is reintroduced and followed immediately by the raised 7th degree before the resolution on the tonic pitch. It is true that similar melodic shapes are used in other ṭhumrī-s in rāga *Bhairavīṅ* (for instance, "Ras Ke Bhare Tore Naina"), but "Bābul Morā" is by far the most famous of these.

My argument here is not that Irfan Khan's performance was influenced by that of Girja Devi, or vice versa; instead, both performances draw on a widely shared knowledge of this famous ṭhumrī. In the case of Irfan Khan's performance, however, the ṭhumrī has particular resonance for the history of his own lineage and thus carries meanings and associations unique to his tradition. For not only is rāga *Bhairavīṅ* associated with Lucknow, but the specific ṭhumrī "Bābul Morā" (always set in *Bhairavīṅ*) is understood to reference the collapse of the city in the mid-nineteenth century, a pivotal historical moment that shaped the trajectory of Irfan Khan's lineage. Indeed, authorship of the ṭhumrī is most often ascribed to the family's most prestigious patron, the final king of Lucknow himself. To uncover the connections between "Bābul Morā," the genre of ṭhumrī, and both the rise and the fall of the Lucknow gharānā, we must return to the court of Lucknow and review the circumstances that led to its demise early in 1856.

"A Cherry Which Will Drop into Our Mouths"

The decline of the Mughal Empire in the eighteenth century opened the door for new, independent princely states to emerge and prosper. The largest and wealthiest of these was the state of Awadh, ruled by a succession of Shia Muslims of Persian extraction known as nawāb-s. From 1775 until 1856, the nawāb-s of Awadh ruled their kingdom from the capital city of Lucknow, which was the most significant administrative, commercial, and cultural center of India beyond the newly established colonial port cities of Calcutta, Bombay, and Madras. However, the collapse of the unified Mughal Empire also empowered the British East India Company, whose appetite for expansion gradually eroded the area and autonomy of Awadh. The British Resident in Lucknow wielded "indirect" control over matters of finance and government, yet Awadh remained, nominally, an autonomous kingdom.[3]

The final king of Awadh, Nawāb Wajid Ali Shah, ruled from 1847 to 1856. Because of his complex and fraught relationship with British imperial power, Wajid Ali Shah's legacy is contested today, but there is no doubt that in his own time he was an unrivaled patron of music, dance, and poetry who fostered a profusion of artistic output and sealed Lucknow's reputation as a preeminent city of the arts.

Despite his renown as a powerful patron, and as a visionary artist himself, Wajid Ali Shah's political power was underwritten by the British East India Company, whose interests demanded greater control over the political and economic administration of Awadh. Lord Dalhousie, the British governor-general of India from 1848 to 1856, saw Awadh as a territory crucial to the expansion of the British Empire, famously describing it as "a cherry which will drop into our mouths some day" (Dalhousie 1910: 169; Mukherjee 2001 [1984]: 32). In January of 1856, as a finale to his tenure as governor-general, Dalhousie ordered General James Outram, the Lucknow Resident, to present the king of Awadh with an ultimatum: sign a new treaty ceding all administrative responsibilities for the kingdom to the British East India Company or face a military attack.

Captain Fletcher Hayes was among General Outram's small entourage present at the fateful meeting with Nawāb Wajid Ali Shah on the morning of February 4, 1856. As Hayes documents in his eyewitness report, at the conclusion of the meeting Wajid Ali Shah removed his turban, handed it to General Outram, and stated that he was now "in the hands of the British Government" which could, "at its pleasure, consign him to obscurity" ("Oude Blue

Book" 1856: 288–89; Bhatnagar 1968: 149). Though he disbanded his military and offered no immediate resistance, the king was outraged by the insult of his ouster, refused to sign a new treaty, and vowed to seek immediate redress at the highest levels of government, first in the Company's administrative center of Calcutta, and then, if necessary, in London before the queen herself (Bhatnagar 1968: 150). On March 13, 1856, the king departed Lucknow, never to return.

According to legend, it was at this very moment of crisis, as the king fled his kingdom, that he penned the ṭhumrī "Bābul Morā." The lyrics of the most common version of the ṭhumrī are as follows:

Bābul morā naihara chūṭo jāya
Cār kahār mili ḍoliyān uṭhāe
Apanā bigānā chūṭo jāya

Father, my maternal home is being left behind.
Four water-carriers together lift up my palanquin;
what's mine, what's not, it's all being left behind. (Du Perron 2007: 161)

It is especially significant that Wajid Ali Shah should choose to lament his ouster with a ṭhumrī, for not only was he believed by many—though incorrectly—to have invented the genre of ṭhumrī itself (Manuel 1989a: 34; Du Perron 2007: 52), but his very reputation as a lover of music, dance, and poetry provided Lord Dalhousie with his primary justification for the overthrow of the king: the nawāb was neglecting the affairs of the state.

The claim of "misrule" was documented by Dalhousie through reference to the reports of successive British Residents, close witnesses to the Lucknow court. For example, Colonel William Sleeman (Resident from 1849 to 1854) writes in an undated letter to Lord Dalhousie that the "King's ambition seems to be limited to the reputation of being the best drum-beater, dancer, and poet of the day" (quoted in Chatterjee 2004: 4161). In his own statement to the East India Company's court of directors in London, Lord Dalhousie insists that it is the solemn responsibility of the British government to protect the people of Awadh from the depredations of their successive rulers, citing "avarice, as in one; intemperance, as in another; or, as in the present King, effeminate sensuality, indulged among singers, musicians, and eunuchs, the sole companions of his confidence, and the sole agents of his power" ("Oude Blue Book" 1856: 180). Even contemporaneous critics of the British Empire understood that such claims against the nawāb merely justified an a priori policy decision (see Lucas

1857), yet in the popular imagination, the notion remains that Wajid Ali Shah was deposed as a consequence of his "misrule," itself a result of his excessive fascination with dance, poetry, and music.

In this regard, "Bābul Morā" constitutes an art song written in lament of a fate that was itself a consequence of the love of art song. Yet the ṭhumrī carries further historical significance still: as a document of the exile of Wajid Ali Shah from his kingdom, "Bābul Morā" marks a pivotal moment of historical rupture. Although Dalhousie was convinced that the administration of Awadh must be transferred to the Company, he was not in favor of outright annexation. As Dalhousie writes in explanation of his position, "we should lower the dignity and authority of the Sovereigns of Oude no further than is absolutely necessary for the accomplishment of our righteous ends" ("Oude Blue Book" 1856: 184). Of course Dalhousie's concern for the "dignity" of the king was entirely strategic: as noted by Colonel Sleeman, "Were we to take advantage of the occasion to *annex* or *confiscate* Oude, or any part of it, our good name in India would inevitably suffer" (quoted in Chatterjee 2004: 4161). As it turned out, the nawāb thwarted Dalhousie's plan quietly to take over the administration of Awadh when he refused to sign a new treaty, instead fleeing his own kingdom in humiliation, and thereby forcing Dalhousie to annex the territory directly. The result, much more terrible than that feared by Sleeman or Dalhousie, was the righteous indignation of the entire population of Awadh, which joined a broad rebellion against the British colonizers in a yearlong war that permanently tore the fabric of North Indian society.

As numerous historians have argued, the war of 1857–58, though beginning as a mutiny by soldiers of the Bengal Army in the city of Meerut, quickly spread throughout North India as a popular uprising embraced by all levels of society. Fighting was particularly fierce in Awadh, where peasants and landlords were unified by their shared outrage at the ignominious ouster of their king (see Metcalf and Metcalf 2002: 100; Bhattacharya 2010 [2007]: xv; Mukherjee 2001 [1984]: 82–134). Because of the radical social and political rupture of the war, the year of 1857, as noted by historians Barbara Metcalf and Thomas Metcalf, has "conventionally been taken as the dividing point that marks the beginning of modern India" (2002: 91).

Scholars continue to debate the idea that the war constituted the birth of the nationalist movement in India, but there is no doubt that it was an unprecedented anticolonial rebellion and continues to live in the collective memory of

the subcontinent today: as historians Bose and Jalal write, 1857 is a "date to con-
jure with in modern South Asian history" (1998: 88). Although the leaders of
the rebellion did not themselves advocate thoroughgoing changes to the social
order (Bhattacharya 2010 [2007]: xxv-xxvi), they did observe democratic principles of organization, and during their rule produced newspapers that spoke
to a new conception of the public at large, presenting it with "enticing vistas of
what it would gain from an Indian (not necessarily, royal) regime" (Habib 2010
[2007]: 61). Moreover, events that culminated along with the war highlight massive shifts in the politics, economy, culture, and communications of India, including the birth of "the railway, the telegraph, the postal service, and improved
steam transport" (Metcalf and Metcalf 2002: 95).

The shift to modernity in India did not take place in a momentous epiphany,
and scholars still debate the roles of colonialism, capitalism, and precolonial
history in shaping India's modernity. However, if one were to posit that a single
historical tableau might capture the emotional experience of India's entrance to
modernity, the meeting of Wajid Ali Shah with General Outram on February 4,
1856, would not be an entirely outlandish choice. The king's resignation, his pain
and anger, the war that followed, and the resulting transformation of Indian
social life all speak to the radical ruptures characteristic of modernity. In this
regard, the nawāb's lament — "Bābul Morā" — may be understood as an iconic
artistic rendering of the painful process through which modern India was born.

Wajid Ali Shah's famous ṭhumrī has been interpreted on several levels. For
instance, beyond the understanding of the song as a wedding lament, scholars
note that the image from the second line of the ṭhumrī of a bride being carried
away on a palanquin may also be read as a reference to the funeral procession
that carries away the deceased (see Manuel 1989a: 20; Du Perron 2007: 57). In
this way, the ordeal of the young bride and her journey to her new home may
also be interpreted as the exile from the material realm and the transition to the
afterlife. Here I argue for an additional interpretation in which the ṭhumrī can
be read as a trenchant critique of modernity itself, drawing on the metaphor of
marriage to highlight the loss that accompanies epochal shifts such as the rise
of the modern world. Moreover, the critique of modernity couched within the
metaphor of marriage not only illuminates a broad sense of modern alienation,
but also highlights a significant dimension of modern music history at the heart
of the experience of the Lucknow gharānā.

The Rise and Fall of a Gharānā

The Lucknow gharānā finds its earliest known progenitors in eighteenth-century Afghanistan. Following their migration to India, the gharānā's rabāb-playing forbears ultimately arrived at the lavish court of Lucknow—capital of the kingdom of Awadh—where they encountered orthodox court musicians and participated in the proliferation of new musical forms and compositions for which the Lucknow court remains famous today. Yet as we have seen, this effervescent musical hotbed collapsed early in 1856 when the king of Awadh was deposed, his kingdom annexed by the land-hungry East India Company. After two years of imprisonment in Calcutta during and after the uprising of 1857–58, the erstwhile king of Awadh settled in the nearby township of Matiyaburj (Bhatnagar 1968: 154; Llewellyn-Jones 2014: 6; Sharar 2001 [1975]: 65–70). Wajid Ali Shah remained in Matiyaburj for thirty years (more than three times longer than his rule as the king of Awadh), draining his family fortune and his British pension in an effort to recreate the culture and atmosphere of Lucknow until his death in 1887 (Sharar 2001 [1975]: 65–70). Among the nawāb's retinue of performing artists to shift from Lucknow to Matiyaburj were the elite descendants of the highest-ranking musicians of the Mughal courts. One of the most renowned among these was Basat Khan, who adorned Wajid Ali Shah's new court-in-exile, along with his disciple Niamatullah Khan, Irfan Khan's great-great-grandfather. Niamatullah Khan's only known portrait is shown in Figure 7.[4]

Niamatullah Khan (d. 1903) completed his discipleship with Basat Khan in Wajid Ali Shah's court-in-exile. Niamatullah Khan's own son writes that Niamatullah Khan departed the court in 1865 (Asadullah "Kaukab" Khan 1915: n.p.), but a newspaper account from 1872 includes Niamatullah Khan among the musicians performing at a private soiree held by Amir Ali, "the manager at Matiyaburj" (Williams 2014: 176). Sometime in the vicinity of these dates, Basat Khan retired to Bihar and Niamatullah Khan settled in Kathmandu, Nepal, where he enjoyed thirty years of patronage in the court of Mahārājā Jang Bahadur.[5] In 1903 Niamatullah Khan visited Delhi to attend the coronation of King Edward VII and Queen Alexandra as emperor and empress of India; he passed away during or shortly after the festivities. In his time, Niamatullah Khan reigned as one of the most highly regarded instrumentalists in India. He is credited with the transformation of the rabāb (early sarod) into the prototype of the modern sarod through the incorporation of a metal fingerboard and metal strings, a modification that quickly proliferated in the hands of legions of players of the

FIGURE 7 Niamatullah Khan.
Courtesy of Irfan Khan.

new instrument. Allyn Miner, preeminent historian of instrumental music in eighteenth- and nineteenth-century North India, has described Niamatullah Khan as the earliest sarod player to settle in Bengal, and thus as the progenitor of the sarod tradition in that region (1997 [1993]: 153). Indian music scholar Jon Barlow argues that by virtue of his close association with the elite instrumentalists of Wajid Ali Shah's court, as well as his own achievements, Niamatullah Khan became "an honorary Seniya," a reference to the highest-ranking Mughal court musicians and their descendants (2007: 109). Barlow further notes that the renowned dhrupad singer Allabande Khan (1853–1927) attested to the Birendra Kishore Roy Chowdhury that Niamatullah was "the fastest of all the Sarod players" (ibid.).

The lives, careers, and writings of Niamatullah Khan's two sons, Karamatullah Khan (1848–1933) and Asadullah "Kaukab" Khan (ca. 1850–1915), are the subject of extensive discussion in Chapter 5. For now, suffice it to say that the brothers were leading sarod players of the early twentieth century who established music schools, performed in Europe, trained large numbers of disciples, served powerful patrons, and authored significant Urdu-language theoretical treatises on music. Together they trained Sakhawat Husain Khan (1875–1955), who rose to the top of the realm of Hindustani instrumental performance in the first half of the twentieth century, and whose career spans a pivotal moment of sociomusical change including the end of British colonialism and the birth of the nation in 1947.

Sakhawat Husain Khan's paternal grandfather was Enayat Ali Khan (1790–1883), sarod player of Shahjahanpur, one of the Paṭhān enclaves east of Delhi established in the eighteenth century. Like his cousin Niamatullah Khan, Enayat Ali Khan relocated in the mid-nineteenth century to Bengal, where he was retained under the patronage of Mahārājā Narayan Ray, ruler of the Bhawal state in present-day Bangladesh. Several authors agree that Enayat Ali Khan was one of the earliest Hindustani musicians to travel abroad, performing in London in 1877 for "the fortieth anniversary of the reign of the English monarch Victoria" (McNeil 2004: 120; see also Barlow 2007: 99, 110; Misra 1991: 88; Sharma 1993: 197).[6] Enayat Ali Khan's son, Shafayat Khan (1838–1915), was likewise a renowned sarod player, and married a daughter of Niamatullah Khan, thus becoming brother-in-law to Karamatullah and Kaukab Khan. Sakhawat Husain Khan was the son of Shafayat Khan, thus the nephew of both Karamatullah and Kaukab Khan. Through this family connection, Sakhawat Husain Khan imbibed the musical heritage of the Lucknow gharānā, first from Karamatullah Khan and then from Kaukab Khan. Permissible in Islam and characteristic of the gharānā system, Sakhawat Husain married his first cousin, the daughter of his uncle and ustād, Kaukab Khan. When his first wife passed away, Sakhawat Husain Khan married his own aunt, the widow of Karamatullah Khan.

In some accounts, the marriage of Sakhawat Husain Khan to the daughter of Kaukab Khan is depicted as the decisive moment of merger of two gharānā-s — the Lucknow or Bulandshahr gharānā of Niamatullah Khan and the Shahjahanpur gharānā of Enayat Ali Khan (McNeil 2004: 146; Tamori 2008: 192). It is true that over time the two lines joined, but this merger was not dependent on Sakhawat Husain Khan's marriage. Enayat Ali Khan and Niamatullah Khan already belonged to the same Bangash clan of Paṭhān rabābiyā-s; there was no question of Sakhawat Husain Khan being considered an "outsider" by Karamatullah and Kaukab Khan. Indeed, as statements by his sons attest, Sakhawat Husain Khan was welcomed into the musical fold of the Lucknow gharānā *before* his marriage to Kaukab Khan's daughter. As Sakhawat Husain Khan's younger son, Ilyas Khan, writes, "my father learned from the famous sarod players of Allahabad and Calcutta, Ustad Karamatullah Khan and his younger brother Asadullah Khan, and even became his son-in-law" (1986: 48). Sakhawat Husain Khan's own journal contains an entry in Devanāgarī script authored by his student, Devrani Chatterjee. As an introduction to the life and works of her ustād, Chatterjee writes,

> The Ustād's initial training was from his father. Later he learned from Karama-tullah Khan who was the uncle of Ustād, and who was regarded as the most learned sarod player of his time. Ustād became the disciple of Karamatullah Khansaheb with lots of pomp and splendor [a reference to a lavish *shāgirdī*, or discipleship ceremony] and learned a lot of things from him. Later when he married the daughter of Karamatullah Khansaheb's younger brother, Profes-sor Asadullah Khan Kaukab, he also learned from him for quite a long time. (Khan n.d.: n.p.)

Drawing on an interview with Sakhawat Husain Khan's elder son, Ted Solis writes, "Asadullah Khan [. . .] approached Safayat Khan, father of the groom, asking that he be allowed to impart his seniya knowledge of *ālāp* to Sakhawat Khan, so that the latter's bāj [style] would be complete, enabling him to properly provide for Asadullah's daughter" (1970: 41). These accounts suggest that the marriage of Sakhawat Husain Khan to the daughter of Kaukab Khan was surely significant, but took place subsequent to the young sarodist's embrace by the leading lights of the Lucknow gharānā.

Despite the scholarly disagreement just noted, none doubt that in the early decades of the twentieth century, Sakhawat Husain Khan emerged as the prin-cipal representative of the combined lineages of Niamatullah Khan and Enayat Ali Khan. Born in 1875 in Shahjahanpur, Sakhawat Husain Khan came of age under court patronage and played a role in establishing the new system of insti-tutionalized and nationalized music education. In this regard, his career spans a critical juncture and is thus worth studying in some depth. Fortunately, his service at Bhatkhande's music college from 1927 to 1955 (discussed in detail in Chapter 4) afforded him the opportunity to publish some of his writings; be-yond these, Sakhawat Husain's handwritten journal was made available to me by Irfan Khan (in whose possession the journal remains) and has now been thoroughly examined and translated for the first time, offering tremendous new insights into Sakhawat Husain Khan's biography, career, and opinions.[7]

In his memoirs, Sakhawat Husain Khan highlights the powerful patrons who honored him, often with "gold medals," throughout his career. Though he began his career as a court musician in a number of princely states, especially Kasimpur in Bengal and Gidhaur in Bihar (Ilyas Khan 1986: 48), Sakhawat Husain's memoirs focus largely on his relationships with powerful political figures and on his foreign travel. For instance, describing his earliest experience with royalty, Sakhawat Husain Khan notes that he performed for the Prince of Wales during the latter's visit to Calcutta in 1912 (Khan n.d.: n.p.), receiving from him a certificate and a medal. Likewise, Sakhawat Husain Khan mentions that he performed for Lord Hardinge (governor-general of India from 1910 to 1916), who gave him "a gold watch with his [Hardinge's] picture in it" (ibid.).

Among the celebrated achievements of his career, Sakhawat Husain Khan is most often remembered for his global travels for several years in the mid-1930s as a musician in the company of Madame Menaka's dance troupe. Famed kathak dancer Damayanti Joshi (1928–2004) acknowledges that her formative years as a young dancer were shaped within Madame Menaka's dance troupe, a professional ensemble that enjoyed widespread renown in the 1930s, touring extensively in India, Southeast Asia, and Europe (Joshi 1989: 7). Though she has been largely forgotten in contemporary historical narratives of Indian dance, Madame Menaka (1899–1947), a Bengali Brahman, was a pivotal figure in the transformation of the derided tradition of "nautch" (dance performed by professional courtesans) into kathak as a respectable middle-class pursuit (Chakravorty 2006: 117–18). Indeed, the anti-nautch movement that sought to cleanse the new national culture had already cast a shadow of disrepute on the traditional culture bearers of North Indian dance. As Margaret Walker shows, the 1930s saw the birth of kathak as a classical dance in part as a result of its appropriation by "high-caste, educated women" (2014: 118) such as Menaka, who made it available to the world through an exoticized display of so-called ballets that conformed to established aesthetics of "Oriental Dance" (ibid.: 120).

Though she eschewed the tainted figure of the courtesan (instead populating her dance troupe with girls from respected middle-class families), Menaka had no qualms about hiring eminent hereditary Muslim musicians to serve in her orchestra. According to Joshi, Menaka avoided the traditional sārangī/tablā ensemble, and instead commissioned original "rāga-based" compositions for an "orchestral" group including "sarod, shehnai, tabla, pakhawaj, ghanta, nal, the xylophone and clappers" (1989: 18). Joshi cites Ambika Charan Mazumdar as the troupe's longest-serving music director, noting that he was "an early graduate of Marris College, Lucknow" (ibid.); in discussing the musicians of the orchestra, Joshi begins with Sakhawat Husain Khan, "a noted sarod player" who was "a teacher at Marris College before joining the troupe" (ibid.: 19).

According to the oral history of the Lucknow gharānā, Sakhawat Husain Khan was not merely a musician in the orchestra, but the troupe's primary music director. There is no disagreement, however, that Sakhawat Husain Khan traveled extensively with Madame Menaka, beginning in 1935 with a tour of India (including performances in Ahmedabad, Surat, Baroda, Lucknow, Calcutta, and Chittagon), Burma, Singapore, Malaysia, and Sri Lanka (Joshi 1989: 24–25). From 1936 to 1938, Sakhawat Husain Khan accompanied Menaka's troupe on a tour of Europe that entailed some 750 performances. Beginning in January of 1936 in Switzerland, the troupe proceeded to Luxembourg, Germany, Belgium, the Netherlands, Denmark, Norway, Sweden, Finland, Poland, Czechoslovakia, Hungary, the Balkans, Lithuania, Latvia, Estonia, England, France, and Austria (ibid.: 25–26).[8]

The most prestigious of these hundreds of performances took place at the International Dance Olympiad as part of the Olympics of 1936, held in Berlin under the auspices of the Nazi government and attended by Adolph Hitler (Joshi 1989: 26). Viewers of the Olympics in the present era may forget that from 1912 to 1948, international Olympic Games included competitions in the arts as well as athletics. Joshi writes that the "Menaka Indian Ballet received the first prize [. . .] Ramnarayan and Gauri Shankar receiving Honour Prizes additionally" (ibid.), thus proclaiming, "With three prizes out of 13 at the Olympiad, the Indian troupe triumphed over all its rivals to a preeminent position in the world of dance" (ibid.: 27).

In Europe, Sakhawat Husain Khan enjoyed the patronage of towering heads of state, including the king of Kabul (whom he met once in India and once in Italy), Mussolini (whom he met in his "palace" while ruler of Italy), and Adolf Hitler. The last offered not only a "medal from the Olympic club," but also "a certificate written by the hand of Hitler the Great himself," which was personally presented when Sakhawat Husain Khan was invited "for tea in his [Hitler's] house" (Khan n.d.: n.p.). Sakhawat Husain Khan further includes Joseph Stalin among his patrons in Europe, noting that the Soviet leader gave him "a very expensive watch, which unfortunately was stolen by someone in Switzerland" (ibid.). Finally, Sakhawat Husain Khan documents a performance in Holland for Kaiser Wilhelm II (ibid.).

Beyond such political figures, Sakhawat Husain Khan was able to reach a broader global audience with his sarod playing through solo items within Menaka's show. For instance, in a review of a performance in Munich, critic K. Ude writes, "The prelude to the performance was an 'unending melody' on the Sarod—a melodious string instrument played by Ustad Sakhawat Hussain Khan. The Sarod created a magical spell and took the audience to the exotic East" (May 12, 1937, translated by Rashmi Misra, quoted in Joshi 1989: 48). Moreover, while in Germany, Menaka's troupe appeared in a feature film titled *Der Tiger von Eschnapur* by Berlin's Tobis Studio (Joshi 1989: 28). The film includes two major dance pieces, both accompanied by the troupe's orchestra, and both including clear and sustained shots of Sakhawat Husain Khan playing his sarod.

While proud of his individual achievements and international travels, Sakhawat Husain Khan emphasizes his investment in the past and future of his musical lineage, as well as his responsibility in propagating the musical heritage of the nation. As he writes, "I am trying to keep my ancestors' names alive, which I did by spending seven years performing in India's biggest music conferences, receiving many medals and awards" (Khan n.d.: n.p.). Sakhawat Husain Khan acknowledges his great gift from God and the blessings of his elders, asserting that he continues to accrue renown because the musicians of "my lineage have been the custodians of the sarod, rabāb, and sursiṅgār from Mughal times, whose branches have spread all over the land of India" (ibid.). Taking credit on behalf of his gharānā, Sakhawat Husain Khan notes that "all those playing sarod today are the special blossoms from the garden of my family" (ibid.).

Among Sakhawat Husain Khan's own sons and nephews were a number of outstanding performing artists; none of these, however, was able to attain renown comparable to that of Sakhawat Husain himself. Sakhawat Husain Khan's first son, Umar Khan, was born in 1916 in Dhaka (today the capital city of Bangladesh) while Sakhawat Husain was serving the nawāb of Dhaka as a court musician. Not long after Umar Khan's birth, Sakhawat Husain Khan moved his family back to Lucknow, where Umar Khan spent his youth, traveling frequently as he grew to adolescence to look after family-owned property in nearby Bagrasi (in the district of Bulandshahr) and Shahjahanpur. Umar Khan briefly held a position as court musician in Panna State (today in the state of Madhya Pradesh), and also taught briefly at the Bhatkhande College while his father was away in Europe. During World War II, Umar Khan served as a staff artist at the All India Radio station in Bombay, where he spent time learning vocal music from the famous rivals Rajab Ali Khan and Alladiya Khan. After a few years in Bombay, Umar Khan returned to Lucknow, where he remained until the mid-1950s.

Around 1950 Waliullah Khan, son of Kaukab Khan, had fallen ill. Feeling he could no longer carry on as the court musician to Musharraf Hussain (the nawāb of Jalpaiguri), and as the ustād of the begam sahiba (the nawāb's daughter), Waliullah Khan (1892–1951) nominated his nephew, Umar Khan, as his own replacement. The residence of the nawāb was in Calcutta, and thus, accepting the nawāb's invitation, Umar Khan settled in that city in the mid-1950s. At the same time, Umar Khan also began offering lessons in his new Calcutta home, largely teaching sitar and sarod to middle-class Bengali girls. In the evenings he enjoyed social visits from dhrupad singer Rahim Fahimuddin Dagar and khyāl singer Munawar Khan, who were nearly daily guests at Umar Khan's house.

The patronage of the nawāb was a mixed blessing for Umar Khan: although supplying steady employment, the nawāb and the begam did not allow Umar Khan to perform extensively outside their own palace. Irfan Khan suggests that this condition eventually crushed his father's spirit, and denied him the chance to become a very big name in post-independence India. On February 22, 1982, while performing in Dhaka—the city of his birth—Umar Khan suffered a stroke and passed away. His body was returned to Calcutta, where his funeral was attended by such musicians as Munawar Khan, Rahim Fahimuddin Dagar, Mushtaq Ali Khan, Karan Saheb, Malvika Kanan, Sunil Bose, the Kishlu Brothers, Latafat Khan, Nisar Husain Khan, and many more.

Ishtiaq Khan, son of Karamatullah Khan, was born in 1920 in Bagrasi. His initial training was imparted by Karamatullah Khan, who passed away in 1933 when Ishtiaq Khan was still a young man. Upon the death of his father, Ishtiaq Khan lived with Sakhawat Husain Khan, who married Karamatullah Khan's widow. Yet Ishtiaq Khan stayed in Lucknow only briefly, moving back to Bagrasi, where he was trained by the sitar and *surbahār* (bass sitar) player Shafiqullah Khan, who had himself learned from Karamatullah Khan. Shafiqullah Khan's brother, Rafiqullah (also trained by Karamatullah Khan) became Ishtiaq Khan's father-in-law. Shafiqullah and Rafiqullah were close kinsmen to Karamatullah Khan: their father, Kifayet Khan, was the son of Niamatullah Khan's first cousin. As his first job away from home, Ishtiaq Khan worked briefly as a staff artist at All India Radio in Bombay, but disliked the distance from his young wife. Umar Khan thus requested a position for Ishtiaq Khan as a staff artist at All India Radio, Delhi, so that the lovelorn sarodist could be reunited with his wife. Ishtiaq Khan obtained that position and remained in service at the Delhi radio station until he passed away in 1967. He imparted training to his son Mukhtiyar, but passed away before he could begin training his younger son, Gulfam, in earnest.

Ilyas Khan, the second son of Sakhawat Husain Khan, was born in 1924 in Shahjahanpur. He grew up in Lucknow, where he was trained by his father and also by the sitarist Yusuf Ali Khan, a close friend of Sakhawat Husain Khan (see Katz 2014). Because Ilyas Khan suffered from poor eyesight, he was not able to continue his schooling past class (grade) 6. He worked briefly in the Bombay film industry, but in 1955—the year of Sakhawat Husain Khan's death—he took up a post at the Bhatkhande College, carrying on the tradition started by his own father. Ilyas Khan concertized extensively, especially in Delhi and Kashmir, but remained committed to his teaching position at the college throughout his life. A compact disc of his performance at a historic concert in Delhi in 1956 has recently been released by Sangeet Natak Akademi; otherwise, though he recorded extensively for All India Radio, there are no commercial recordings of Ilyas Khan. Beyond his legions of students at the college, Ilyas Khan trained his own son, Idris, as well as his two nephews, Shahid and Irfan, at home. Ilyas Khan passed away in Lucknow in 1989.

Akhtar Khan, born in Shahjahanpur in 1936, was not himself a blood descendant of the line. Yet he received training in sitar from Musharraf Khan, who was Sakhawat Husain Khan's paternal uncle (his father's sister's husband). Akhtar Khan's brother, Afaq Hussain Khan, likewise learned sitar, and held a position in All India Radio, Bombay. Akhtar also moved to Bombay, where he began learning from Zia Mohiuddin Dagar, the renowned bīn player and descendant of the Dagar line of dhrupad singers. In the 1950s Akhtar Khan settled in Kanpur (near Lucknow) and began a discipleship under the sitarist Yusuf Ali Khan. Sometime after the passing of Sakhawat Husain Khan in 1955, Sakhawat Husain Khan's sister arranged the marriage of Akhtar Khan to one of Sakhawat Husain Khan's daughters; in this way Akhtar Khan married into the Lucknow gharānā. In 1966 he accepted a position as staff artist at All India Radio, Gauhati, and permanently resettled his family in Assam, where he passed away in 1989.

————

In this chapter I have introduced the thumrī "Bābul Morā" as a window into the history of the Lucknow gharānā, while also arguing that the thumrī may be read more broadly as a critique of musical modernity, and of modernity writ large. Marriage serves as a powerful vehicle for such a critique. The ultimate purpose of marriage is to create a genealogical continuity—to produce the succeeding generation. And yet "Bābul Morā" reminds us that the very production of continuity depends on a violent severance: as the reed is cut from the reed bed to produce a flute, so the girl is torn from her natal home to become a bride. As introduced here, and discussed further in the following chapters, the thumrī "Bābul Morā" proved prophetic for the Lucknow gharānā. It seems that the very processes that created the conditions for the gharānā's rise also undermined its ability to survive. The collapse of nawābī Lucknow inaugurated a new era of nationalist resistance that would ultimately lead to the downfall of feudalism and colonialism; yet the collapse also saw the loss of one of India's great cities of art.

Yet again, it was the city's fall that propelled the gharānā to renown in the Lucknowi diaspora. Throughout the late nineteenth century and the first half of the twentieth, the Lucknow gharānā produced successive generations of top-ranking artists. Yet the contemporary generation—including the sons of Umar Khan, Ilyas Khan, Ishtiaq Khan, and Akhtar Khan—experienced the collapse and eclipse of their own lineage despite its tenuous viability even today. The trajectories of rise and fall of the city and the gharānā are thus related but chronologically offset. Ultimately, the changes that undermined royal patronage in Lucknow culminated in a broad shift to nationalist modernity that saw the Lucknow gharānā displaced and overtaken by rival lineages and new constituencies, as discussed in subsequent chapters of this book. While disinterested scholarship may approach this shift from the point of view of large-scale social change, the Lucknow gharānā offers its own explanation. How does a self-consciously modern family of musicians that enjoyed great renown and influence in the early 1900s understand its own marginality to the culture of Hindustani music by the century's end? The next chapter explores this question through a focus on the challenge of thumrī.

TWO

The Challenge of Ṭhumrī

In March of 2009, I made a trip to Delhi to meet Gulfam Ahmad Khan, sarod player of the Lucknow gharānā. Leaving the heart of New Delhi, I crossed the Yamuna River, eventually finding Gulfam's neighborhood, where I was aided by a succession of generous neighbors who guided me through the narrow walkways to Gulfam's front door. Inside his home, Gulfam welcomed me into his music room, where he sat on a carpet with an array of stringed instruments he was eager to show me. As I set up my video camera, Gulfam began an organological history lesson, tracing the musical evolution of his lineage through the meeting and metamorphosis of musical instruments.

He began with a demonstration of the "Seniya" rabāb, an archaic instrument I had seen only in line drawings and reproductions of centuries-old artworks. As shown in Figure 8, Gulfam assumed a posture similar to yoga's *vīrāsana*, or "hero" pose, sitting on his heels with his knees together and the instrument held vertically in front of him. With closed eyes he began a slow and stately *ālāp* in the rāga *Shuddha Kalyān*. Evoking the dhrupad style with which the instrument is historically associated, he played a succession of integral phrases using spare ornamentation, progressing systematically from the lower end to the higher end of the scale.

Following his short performance on the Seniya rabāb, Gulfam explained that this was the instrument played by Hindustani music's sixteenth-century patriarch, Tansen (d. 1589).[1] Chief musician to the Mughal court of Emperor Akbar (the greatest of the "Great Mughals"), Tansen has since become a mythic figure to whom supernatural musical powers are ascribed. Even in his own time Tansen was showered with hyperbolic praise: Akbar's official court chronicler, Abul

Fazl, famously wrote that Tansen's "equal has not appeared in a thousand years" (quoted in Delvoye 1997: 195). As Gulfam explained, Tansen transmitted his mastery of the Seniya rabāb to his own son, Bilas Khan, who in turn propagated a nearly four-century-long hereditary tradition that culminated in the hands of the brothers Basat Khan, Pyar Khan, and Jaffar Khan, celebrated court musicians of Wajid Ali Shah in mid-nineteenth-century Lucknow. The Seniya rabāb virtually vanished from the scene by the late nineteenth century, along with the cloistered families that cultivated it. However, while Basat Khan and his brothers refused to impart the knowledge of their own hereditary instrument to nonhereditary disciples, they offered training to such students in related yet distinct instruments such as the sitar and sarod. According to Gulfam, the most significant figure among these nonfamily students was Basat Khan's primary disciple, Niamatullah Khan, Gulfam's own great-grandfather and patriarch of the Lucknow gharānā.

Introducing now the meeting of Niamatullah Khan with Basat Khan, Gulfam laid aside the Seniya rabāb and took up the much smaller Afghani or Kabuli rabāb, shown in Figure 9. As Gulfam adopted the more familiar cross-legged posture, his demeanor shifted from meditative to athletic and he treated me to a volley of rapid-fire, virtuosic runs across the gamut of rāga *Bhairaviṅ*. Like the Seniya rabāb, the Afghani rabāb features gut strings, but its shorter scale length allowed Gulfam to let loose the strength of his picking hand, and thus to highlight exciting rhythms rather than purity of rāga grammar. Gulfam himself has performed extensively in Kabul and the surrounding areas in recent years, perpetuating the musical connections between India and Afghanistan through his virtuoso performances of Hindustani rāga music on the Afghani instrument. Indeed, Hindustani musicians were consistently retained in the royal court of Kabul beginning in the 1860s, and Hindustani music was likely present in Afghanistan under the Mughal Empire as early as the sixteenth century (Baily 1988: 24–25).

As detailed by Irfan Khan's father, early forms of the Afghani rabāb were introduced to India with the armies of Emperor Babur in the early sixteenth century (Umar Khan 1976). Yet Afghani rabāb players—including military musicians, horse traders, and mercenaries—began arriving in India in large numbers only in the eighteenth century. Gulfam's ancestors were among these migrants, eventually obtaining court patronage in centers such as Lucknow, where they came into contact with Seniya rabāb players such as Basat Khan. By the time Niamatullah Khan began learning from Basat Khan in the mid-nineteenth

FIGURE 8 Gulfam Ahmad Khan, Delhi, March 17, 2009. Still from video by author.

FIGURE 9 Gulfam Ahmad Khan, Delhi, March 17, 2009. Still from video by author.

century, the Afghani rabāb had already been in India for perhaps two centuries, and had already begun to change: though retaining its gut strings, wooden fingerboard, and tied gut frets, its size had expanded, and presumably the style of music played by its Paṭhān specialists had begun to reflect the demands of the new patrons in India.

Gulfam completed the organological history lesson by taking up the present-day sarod, illustrating the final outcome of the meeting between the Seniya rabāb and the Afghani rabāb through a presentation of a *gat* (short composition) in rāga *Jhinjhoṭī*. As documented in Karamatullah Khan's 1908 book, within a decade of the demise of Lucknow in 1856, Niamatullah Khan together with his teacher Basat Khan made changes to the Paṭhān's instrument that constituted the invention of the modern sarod: the gut strings were replaced by steel, the frets were removed, and the wooden fingerboard was covered with a metal plate. Though further refinements were made, most famously and influentially by sarodist Allauddin Khan and his brother Ayet Ali Khan in the early twentieth century (Trasoff 1999: 307), evidence supports the assertion that the path to the contemporary sarod was paved through the meeting of Basat Khan and Niamatullah Khan described to me by Niamatullah Khan's own great-grandson, Gulfam Ahmad Khan.

Yet Gulfam's three-part demonstration does not merely represent a historical succession of instrumental technique and evolution of design. The presentation also sketches a narrative of authority, authenticity, and legitimacy that highlights the injustice faced by his lineage in the present day. Gulfam addressed this dimension of his demonstration explicitly when he described the historical origins of the Seniya rabāb, noting that the instrument is traced directly to the great musical patriarch Tansen. He further noted, however, that the Seniya rabāb is not the only instrument associated with Tansen's family line: much more widely known, and even still played by a small number of specialists, the bīn or rudra veena reigns in the collective Hindustani musical imagination as the most prestigious of the archaic instruments associated with the court of Emperor Akbar. Gulfam explained, however, that there was a clear and important difference between the rabāb and the bīn: they were the hereditary specializations of two distinct and unequal branches of Tansen's descendants. According to Gulfam, the line descending from Tansen's son, Bilas Khan, specialized in the rabāb, while the line descending from Tansen's daughter, Saraswati, specialized in the bīn. Not surprisingly, Gulfam insisted that the musical knowledge of the son's line is far superior to that of the daughter's.

The assertion of superiority of the son's line rests on the patriarchal structure of inheritance practiced globally, but especially in India: as discussed in Chapter 1, when a daughter marries, she is believed to become part of her husband's family, leaving her natal home behind. The privileging of the son over the daughter is especially pronounced within hereditary musical families, where daughters are not expected to participate in hereditary musical traditions. As many scholars have argued, musicians tend to reserve their most revered repertoire and techniques for their direct male descendants.[2] In this regard, Gulfam's tripartite organological performance stakes a bold claim for the primacy of the Lucknow gharānā: essentially, Gulfam argues that the pure transmission of musical knowledge traveled from Tansen through his son's line to Basat Khan, and then from Basat Khan to his disciple Niamatullah Khan, where it is maintained through the lineage of the Lucknow gharānā to the present day. The further implication of this argument is that other musical families claiming direct discipular descent from Tansen have received inferior knowledge and training, as such families generally claim their connection through the line of Tansen's daughter. This chapter explores the ramifications of Gulfam's narrative, focusing in particular on the musical consequences of the meeting between the Seniya Basat Khan and the Paṭhān Niamatullah Khan.

Out of Afghanistan

The Afghani or Kabuli rabāb (Figure 9) is a short-necked lute with two tied gut frets that is played in "Baluchistan, Tajikistan, Pakistan, and Kashmir" (Baily 1988: 26), yet is associated most immediately with Afghanistan, where it is widely embraced as the national instrument (Sakata 1983: 197; Baily 1976: 56 n. 4; Slobin 1976: 57). Carved sculptures in Afghanistan from the second century of the Common Era depict instruments resembling the present-day Afghani rabāb (Sarmast 2009: 21). The instrument is found again illustrated in a fourteenth-century treatise (ibid.: 138), and later still in sixteenth-century Mughal paintings (ibid.: 139). It is impossible to say that all of these representations refer to the same basic instrument, but their similarities suggest a long continuity of forms related to the rabāb in Afghanistan. What is known is that as early as the sixteenth century, a certain kind of rabāb was known as "surod," and this is undoubtedly the instrument that was transformed in India into the Hindustani sarod (ibid.: 135; see also Trasoff 1999: 210–11; McNeil 2004: 22–23).[3] The ethnic group associated with the rabāb, and with the surod in particular, is known in Afghanistan as Pashtūn. The Pashtūn-s, dominant in eastern Afghanistan, came to be known as Paṭhān-s in India (Gommans 1995: 9).

Writing in the early twentieth century, Gulfam Ahmad Khan's grandfather, Karamatullah Khan, notes that the "sarod has been used in Afghanistan for a thousand years because its sound brings forth the enthusiasm and tumult needed for courage and valor. This is why the rabāb is the musical instrument for war" (1908: 160). The association between the Afghani rabāb and the military is frequently repeated. Indeed, the Afghani rabāb was played on horseback, and was used to lead armies of warriors as they marched into battle or to conquer new territories. Adrian McNeil insightfully observes that the instrument itself resembles a club-like weapon (2004: 25). The connections between the rabāb/sarod and military might were expressed viscerally by Irfan Khan's grandfather, Sakhawat Husain Khan, the primary disciple of Karamatullah Khan:

> The people of Afghanistan play the instrument while singing warlike songs in battle which transport the Afghan into a state whereby killing and dying becomes a game, and dancing with sword in hand, he confronts the enemy with all his might. When the rousing sound of the sarod reaches his ears, he attacks his enemy with the vigor of youth and either becomes a martyr himself or kills the enemy and then rests. In the Afghan military band, the sarod is played with the *ḍhol* [drum] in front of it, which by its beat and rise and fall rouses the lovers of martyrdom towards it. (Khan n.d.: n.p.)[4]

As this discussion reveals, for a significant period of time in India, the terms *sarod* and *rabāb* were somewhat interchangeable. For instance, Karamatullah Khan writes that "the sarod has gained tradition and is being played in India since about two hundred and fifty years, and has undergone numerous improvements, developments and changes before taking its present form" (1908: 160). The understanding from Karamatullah Khan seems to be that the term *sarod* refers to both the ancient Afghani rabāb ("used in Afghanistan for a thousand years") and the contemporary Indian instrument, with the caveat that it has seen numerous changes in its design.

As suggested by Karamatullah Khan, the instrument was brought to India and introduced into the Mughal courts as early as the sixteenth century, along with successive waves of immigration from the west. As the Mughal Empire declined in the eighteenth century, new waves of Paṭhān-s settled in Afghan-dominated areas of North India. Among these immigrants were the ancestors of the Lucknow gharānā. Based on interviews with Ilyas Khan in the 1980s,

McNeil reports that Najaf Ali Khan (1705–1760)—"a mercenary and a musician"—was the first of the family's rabāb-playing ancestors to migrate to India, sometime in the early eighteenth century (2004: 51). These musicians all descended from the Bangash clan, and settled in Paṭhān-dominated areas east of Delhi. Among these, the districts of Shahjahanpur and Bulandshahr were renowned as concentrated centers of rabāb/sarod players.[5]

In the late eighteenth century, the expanding colonial project of the British weakened Paṭhān power, and many musicians consequently left these areas for greater opportunities in the newly established princely states of North India, most especially Awadh, with its capital first at Faizabad, and then at Lucknow. It was in Lucknow that Irfan Khan's Paṭhān ancestors forged the discipular connections that would propel the lineage to fame and fortune in the late nineteenth and early twentieth centuries.

The Shift to Lucknow

Within the oral history of the Lucknow gharānā, the shift to Lucknow in the late eighteenth century marks a critical turning point, bringing the ethnic Paṭhān-s—players of the Afghani rabāb and its Indian transformations—into contact with the most esteemed Hindustani musicians of the era, court musicians of Lucknow, and players of the Seniya rabāb. Significant similarities between the instruments allowed the Afghani rabāb players to begin to learn orthodox, rāga-based music from the renowned players of the Seniya rabāb. The meeting between these two streams of musicians is encapsulated in the relationship between Niamatullah Khan (d. 1903), Paṭhān of Bulandshahr, and Basat Khan (d. ca. 1887), elite court musician of Wajid Ali Shah and a descendant of the most prized musicians of the Mughal courts. This relationship is critical because it forges a direct connection between the Lucknow gharānā and the musical traditions of the Mughal court, most famously represented by Tansen, the famed court musician of Emperor Akbar (r. 1556–1605).

Since the late nineteenth century, musicians have claimed authority in Hindustani music's instrumental traditions through tracing a connection to the family of Tansen. As Daniel Neuman points out, because virtually all instrumentalists in the present day will claim stylistic descent from Tansen, the genealogical argument amounts to a struggle over who is "more Seniya" (1990 [1980]: 108). Claims of descent from Tansen, however, rest on shaky ground. In fact, the most prestigious instrumentalists of the eighteenth and nineteenth

centuries did not assert descent from Tansen at all. Instead, such musicians—
known as *kalāwant*-s—descended from one of several lines that comprised the
Delhi kalāwant *birāderī* (brotherhood) (Schofield forthcoming). Through a
study of twenty Persian-language sources from 1593 to 1857, Katherine Schofield
has been able to reconstruct "the complete lineage of the chief kalawants to
the Mughal emperors all the way down from Akbar (r. 1556–1605) to the last
Mughal emperor Bahadur Shah Zafar (r. 1837–1858)" (ibid.). Her research
confirms that Tansen was a dominant figure within the Delhi kalāwant birāderī whose direct heirs prevailed as chief musicians to the Mughal emperors
throughout the seventeenth century. In the eighteenth century, however, a new
dominant figure rose. Known widely as "Sadarang," he was chief musician to
the Mughal ruler Muhammad Shah (r. 1719–1748). Basat Khan and his brothers,
Pyar Khan and Jaffar Khan, were most likely direct blood descendants of Firoz
Khan "Adarang," the nephew and principal disciple of Sadarang (ibid.). Indeed,
throughout the eighteenth and nineteenth centuries, it was the musical dynasty
of Sadarang within the broader kalāwant birāderī that prevailed in the Mughal
courts and then in their successor courts, such as Lucknow. As Schofield notes,
the genealogy is difficult to trace beyond the upheaval of 1857–58, but it is clear
that the lineage of Sadarang through his primary disciple Adarang continued
to thrive in Lucknow under the patronage of Wajid Ali Shah. Within the entire
network of the kalāwant birāderī with its origins in the Mughal court of Delhi,
Basat Khan appears to have been the final figure to propagate his inheritance;
according to Schofield's research, there is only one living line of discipleship that
can trace its lineage back to the Mughal kalāwant-s, and that line rests on the
discipleship between Basat Khan and Niamatullah Khan.

The relationship between Basat Khan and Niamatullah is documented in Karamatullah Khan's published book, in Abdul Halim Sharar's book, and in Kaukab Khan's unpublished manuscript. Yet all three of these sources ultimately
depend on the written claims of Niamatullah Khan's sons as to the relationship between their father and Basat Khan. One more piece of available evidence
should thus be considered: the unpublished manuscript by Basat Khan, which
remains in the possession of Irfan Khan today. According to the oral history,
Basat Khan bequeathed it to his disciple (Niamatullah Khan), who passed it to
one of his sons (either Karamatullah Khan or Kaukab Khan), who passed it
to their nephew and primary disciple (Sakhawat Husain Khan), who passed it
to his son (Umar Khan), who passed it to his son (Irfan Khan). Unfortunately,
the text itself, written in Persian language, tells us little about Basat Khan and

nothing about his disciples. According to Schofield, the manuscript is not an original work, but is apparently a compendium consisting of copies of three earlier treatises on music: an incomplete version of the *Shams al-Aṣwāt* by Ras Baras Khan (1698), the *Saṅgīt Sarāvatī* by Rashik Kalyan, and a hasty copy of the *Uṣūl al-Naghmāt-i Āṣafī* by Ghulam Raza Sabir Ali (1793) (Schofield, personal communication, September 7, 2013).

It remains unclear whether the text contains new additions or annotations by Basat Khan, but the calligrapher's seal provides some important contextual information. The seal appears at two points in the manuscript, along with nearly identical statements of the scribe's name, lineage, and address, as well as the name and address of Basat Khan. The two dates are a month and a half apart — July 12, 1856, and August 28, 1856 — suggesting that the manuscript was completed in sections over a period of time. Most significant, however, is the general time frame: by this time Wajid Ali Shah had already abdicated and fled Lucknow, and it seems that Basat Khan had already left Lucknow as well. The address given is Muradpur mohalla (neighborhood), in the Sahibganj qasba (town), of the Bihar zila (region), of the Bengal Presidency. From several other documents, we know that Basat Khan's son, Mohammad Ali, was a court musician of Gidhaur, an important center also in Bihar. From this information we gain some insight into Basat Khan's itinerary, for he clearly spent some time in Bihar before attending Wajid Ali Shah's court in exile in Bengal. After his time in Bengal, the oral history relates that Basat Khan returned to Bihar for the remainder of his life.

Disciples beyond Borders

Among the central mythic structures of Hindustani music is the idea that significant relationships between teachers and students not only form a connected chain, or *silsila*, but also cross significant social, cultural, and musical boundaries. The oldest such relationship still celebrated in the oral history of Hindustani music is that between Nizamuddin Auliya (ca. 1244–1325) and his disciple Amir Khusrau (1254–1325). Nizamuddin is remembered as a Sufi saint who propagated the Chishti order of Islamic mysticism in and around Delhi; the Chishti order stands out for its embrace of music and dance as pathways to achieve ecstatic union with God. While Nizamuddin remained aloof from the court, his disciple Amir Khusrau served a succession of rulers of the Delhi Sultanate as court poet and musician. Amir Khusrau is remembered today as a pivotal figure in the establishment of a hybrid Indo-Islamic culture, most especially through his investments in language and music. In this regard, his patronage by the sultans of Delhi provided a conduit between Nizamuddin's world of religious mysticism — reaching back in principle to Prophet Muhammad himself — and the contemporary musical culture of the Delhi court (Brown [Schofield] 2010: 161).

Another, even more central relationship in the lore of Hindustani music is that between Tansen (d. 1589) and Swami Haridas. Research by Nalini Delvoye reveals that the discipleship of Tansen to Haridas was likely a latter-day fabrication; as she notes, it was not until the eighteenth century that "the famous saint-musician Svāmī Haridās of Vrindaban" is first mentioned as the guru of Tansen (1997: 206; see also 2001: 238).[6] Nevertheless, the relationship remains prominent in the collective imagination of Hindustani musicians and music lovers; it is widely accepted that Swami Haridas (a religious ascetic like Nizamuddin before him) imparted his musical knowledge to Tansen, who (like Amir Khusrau before him) was a celebrated court musician. Both of these boundary-crossing discipleships index significant social shifts. In the case of Nizamuddin and Amir Khusrau, the relationship marks the proliferation of Sufi mysticism in North India in the thirteenth and fourteenth centuries, especially highlighting the role of music in connecting esoteric religious practice to a wider consuming public. The relationship between Haridas and Tansen evokes a similar duality, signifying today both the tension between Hindustani music as a spiritual practice versus a secular profession, and also the broad shift in association from Hindu sacrality to Muslim entertainment (Daniel Neuman 1990 [1980]).

In this same vein, the relationship between Basat Khan (primary representative of the Delhi kalāwant-s) and Niamatullah Khan (Afghani rabāb player of the Bangash clan) encapsulates a further shift that took place in the mid-nineteenth century: the direct bloodlines of the kalāwant birāderī began to disappear, and new lines of hereditary musicians began to adopt the mantle of the Mughal musical traditions. Two significant factors shaped the nature of this transmission: the orthodoxy of the kalāwant-s required that they withhold the knowledge of their own hereditary instruments, and the changing atmosphere of the world around them required that they teach a new kind of repertoire demanded by their nineteenth-century patrons. Both of these changes came together in the court of Wajid Ali Shah, first in Lucknow and then later in exile in Bengal. Moreover, both of these factors are highlighted in the relationship between Basat Khan and Niamatullah Khan.

One of the telling signs of the transition from kalāwant supremacy to the rise of new lines of professional musicians is instrumentation. As documented by numerous scholars, the kalāwant musicians of the nineteenth century were vocalists as well as players of two major instruments: the bīn (also known as the rudra veena) and the rabāb (also known as the Seniya rabāb). One apparently universal stricture observed by the kalāwant-s (glossed today as "Seniyas") was their refusal to teach their own hereditary instruments to their nonfamily disciples. Ted Solis, in his 1970 thesis, cites an interview with musician and scholar Birendra Kishore Roy Chowdhury, who stated that "seniya instrumentalists played only the bīn, rabāb, and sursiṅgār in public, while teaching the surbahar, sitar, and other instruments to their disciples" (Solis 1970: 34). In the middle of the nineteenth century, the most significant "other" instrument was the sarod. As Solis suggests, "The sarod may have been invented by seniyas to circumvent the teaching of rabab, although its technique was approximated" (ibid.: 35). As already introduced, the construction of the prototypical modern sarod (an enlarged Afghani rabāb with metal strings and a metal fingerboard) was a primary result of the meeting between Niamatullah Khan and Basat Khan. The Lucknow gharānā was thus at the center of the epochal shift from kalāwant authority to the rise of new, unrelated lines and is also credited with implementing the changes that would give birth to the contemporary sarod; moreover, the gharānā was pivotal to the propagation of a new musical repertoire that would come to redefine Hindustani instrumental music in the twentieth century.

A New Style Born

By the sixteenth century, rāga practice had bifurcated geographically with the development of distinct forms, instruments, and techniques in the north versus those of the south. In the north, where rāga music cultivated in the royal courts came to be known as Hindustani music, the dominant form was a genre known as dhrupad, distinguished by its "vocal style and technique, metrical structure, rhythmic style, instruments, poetry, performance structure, historical tradition and social and religious identity" (Sanyal and Widdess 2004: 42). The ethnomusicologist Richard Widdess demonstrates that dhrupad today is as much an ideology as a musical style (2010: 118–19), but also provides strong evidence for continuities of practice that suggest a relatively coherent musical aesthetic emerging in the fifteenth-century Gwalior court of Man Singh Tomar, and then becoming the dominant form in the Mughal courts in the sixteenth and seventeenth centuries. In the Mughal courts, dhrupad was performed by various classes of musicians, yet it was centrally the prerogative of the kalāwant-s, the "high-ranking vocal soloists employed at the court" (ibid.: 127). Paintings from Akbar's court reveal that the primary instruments used within dhrupad performance were the bīn, the rabāb, and the double-headed *pakhāwaj* drum.

Dhrupad held sway in the Mughal courts only until the mid-eighteenth century, when the new vocal genre of khyāl—pioneered by a Delhi-based, hereditary lineage of Sufi musicians known as the *qawwāl-bacce*—rose to prominence (Brown [Schofield] 2010: 161, passim). By the end of the eighteenth century, new instruments such as the sitar and tablā began to replace the now old-fashioned bīn, rabāb, and pakhāwaj. Simultaneously, a new vocal form known as thumrī was born in Delhi, and subsequently flowered in Wajid Ali Shah's mid-nineteenth-century Lucknow court. The new style flourished as an alternative to more austere and serious vocal forms and suited the flamboyance and superficiality of the Lucknow aristocracy. Today thumrī has become a ubiquitous "light" genre most often heard at the end of a recital by a khyāl singer. This new status as a "dessert" piece (Manuel 1986: 482) is the result of ongoing changes in the style and performance of thumrī over the past two centuries. As Peter Manuel notes, the thumrī-s prevalent in the court of Wajid Ali Shah were known as *bandish* thumrī-s, a term that highlights the fixity and centrality of the composition as opposed to the florid improvisations of thumrī performance today (1989a: 62, passim). Though associated most commonly with evocative poetry, *bandish* thumrī-s were essentially fixed melodies that could support dozens of different texts over time.

In the same time and place—mid-nineteenth century Lucknow—a new instrumental style was born, associated with the sitarist Ghulam Raza Khan, beloved court musician and intimate companion of his patron, Wajid Ali Shah. Ghulam Raza was a colorful character who wielded great influence in the first two years of Wajid Ali Shah's rule, rising to prominence not only as a musician but as a court officer. Ultimately betraying his patron through an affair with one of the nawāb's most cherished wives, Ghulam Raza was banished from the kingdom in 1849 (along with several other musicians). The astonishing tales of Ghulam Raza are documented in Allyn Miner's work (1997 [1993]; 2014), but for the moment his most significant characteristic was his social and musical distance from the kalāwant-s of the court. According to Imam, who personally witnessed Ghulam Raza's performance in the court, "Ustads are averse to this style, and the connoisseurs are ashamed of it" (Imam 1959 [ca. 1857]: 23).

As described by Imam, Ghulam Raza's new sitar style was based on the ṭhumrī vocal form. We do not know exactly what this means, except that Ghulam Raza probably composed his *gat*-s (instrumental compositions) in rāga-s associated with ṭhumrī, highlighted exciting rhythms and accelerated tempos, and may have also employed the melodies of *bandish* ṭhumrī-s popular at the time. Beyond Imam's description, Miner offers another insight into the connections between Wajid Ali Shah, ṭhumrī, and Ghulam Raza's new style. According to Wajid Ali Shah's own memoirs, the king fell in love with ṭhumrī in "about 1843" through the presence in the court of two ṭhumrī singers, the sisters Amman and Amaman. As the king writes, "From that time I acquired the piercing love for well-composed ṭhumrī-s" (quoted and translated in Miner 2014: 4). The sitarist Ghulam Raza Khan was invited to the court on the recommendation of Amman and Amaman, his sisters (Miner 2014).

At the same time that Ghulam Raza's new style was catching on, the elite kalāwant-s of Wajid Ali Shah's court were also creating a new repertoire characterized by fast-speed compositions for sitar, and later, sarod. The compositions of Basat Khan, Pyar Khan, and Jaffar Khan are now treasured examples of Seniya style, yet it is clear that the kalāwant composers (associated with the oldest and most austere forms of the day) were responding to the changing demands of their patrons, and also to the requirement of a new basis for pedagogy that would not threaten their patrimony, and would suit the new instruments of the day. This new repertoire of the Seniyas came to be known as the *Purab bāj*, or Eastern style, to distinguish it from the older style associated with Delhi (to the west). This style must have been distinct from that of Ghulam Raza and yet, most confusingly, both of these new styles were rapidly conflated under the name *Razākẖānī bāj*. Moreover, this new style (which perhaps bore traces of both the Seniya material and the original compositions of Ghulam Raza) quickly became a standard part of the repertoire for all sitar players, including those in Delhi and elsewhere.

Sadiq Ali Khan's 1869 text *Sarmāya-i 'Ishrat* is the earliest known practical musical performance manual in Urdu. It shows that by the last quarter of the nineteenth century, the *Razākẖānī bāj* (here associated with Ghulam Raza's son, Ali Raza) had become ubiquitous: "Note that there are two types of sitar bāj: one is the purab bāj connected with Ali Raza Khan, and the defining thing about it is

that the gats are played in *drut lay* [fast tempo] and their *bol*-s [rhythmic struc-
tures] are *āṛe tiche* [complex and crooked]" (Khan 1875 [1869]: 203).[7] Despite
what might have been an antipathy between Ghulam Raza and the kalāwant-s
of Wajid Ali Shah's court, within a few decades of its invention, the *gat* form
characteristic of the *Razākhānī bāj* (as opposed to a specific composition by
Ghulam Raza) was adopted as a vital component of the teaching repertoire of
the kalāwant musicians of Wajid Ali Shah's court themselves. For instance, Karamatullah Khan includes in his text a transcription of a *gat* in rāga *Kāfi*, writing, "This Ghulam Raza Khani gat was the composition of the late Miyāṅ Pyar
Khansahab rabāb player, who was the elder brother of late Ustad Basat Ali Khan
and a descendant of the late Tansen" (1908: 219). Thus, within the very teaching
line of Basat Khan, the *Razākhānī* (or here, *Ghulām Razākhānī*) *gat* was embraced as a vehicle for elite composition.

The Lucknow Gharānā and the Changing Musical World

The birth of the *Purab* or *Razākhānī bāj* as a distinct style associated today
with the Lucknow gharānā presents a succinct encapsulation of the contradictions characteristic of this vital moment of musical and social change, a result
of the collision of conflicting classes of musicians, along with the demands of
new strata of patrons. While the kalāwant-s were the bearers of a centuries-old
musical tradition, and practitioners of elite instruments, the world they faced
demanded innovation. Tradition prohibited their own adoption of new instruments for new styles of performance; instead, they taught these to their nonfamily students. As the primary existing lineage to inherit the new repertoire,
the Lucknow gharānā provides a direct historical conduit to the court of Wajid
Ali Shah and to the contradictory musical changes happening there. In this regard, the "tradition" of the Lucknow gharānā is itself a direct and primary product of Hindustani music's mid-nineteenth-century modernity.

We thus face a conundrum: in the present day, the Lucknow gharānā celebrates its connection to the kalāwant-s (Seniyas) of Wajid Ali Shah's court as
the primary source of the line's repertoire, an old collection of compositions
understood as orthodox, authentic, and pure. But the presence of ṭhumrī as an
important ingredient in the construction of this repertoire threatens to undermine such claims to orthodoxy. For instance, the composition referenced earlier
by Karamatullah Khan—which he attributes directly to Pyar Khan—has since
become perhaps the "single most famous *gat* in *sitār* playing"; Miner notes that

it is found "in virtually every collection of sitar music, oral and written" (1997 [1993]: 216). Yet this very composition, ostensibly an example of the Seniya purity preserved in the repertoire of the Lucknow court's most orthodox musicians, is clearly based directly on one of the most popular *bandish* ṭhumrī-s of the nineteenth century. As Peter Manuel writes, this very melody "serves as the basis of dozens of *bandish* ṭhumrīs which differ from one another only in text, or minor melodic details. Lallan Piya set at least fourteen texts to variants of this tune" (1989a: 99).

Thus, even though the kalāwant-s must have looked askance at Ghulam Raza (claiming both musical and social superiority over him), there was at the same time a fluid and shared repertoire in the court that crossed the boundary between "popular" and "serious" music. Niamatullah Khan's sons were propelled to the heights of renown in part by this very repertoire and were ready to use it to meet the new demands of the twentieth century: the brothers wrote books, established educational institutions, traveled widely, mastered many instruments, made commercial recordings, and participated in the nationalist movement. Thus the Lucknow gharānā emerged into the limelight in the early twentieth century with a new instrument, a new repertoire, and a new outlook on the nature of patronage while simultaneously claiming a privileged continuity with the hoariest of Hindustani traditions.

The paradox of both embracing and rejecting musical modernity comes clearly to the fore in the writings of Niamatullah Khan's own son, Kaukab Khan, who documents his discomfort with the changing musical world of the early twentieth century. Kaukab assigns significant blame to professional performing artists in sullying the art and science of music, explaining that "professionals played a big hand in its neglect and contempt" and thus "[t]hose rules and regulations that had been encoded from former times became nonexistent" (1915: 114). Yet performers are not the primary target of Kaukab Khan's ire. Noting that when "*dhrupad* is sung, the listeners become restless" (ibid.), Kaukab suggests that perhaps knowledgeable artists remain, but that patrons are lacking. Indeed, in Kaukab's writings, the primary agent of musical degeneration is not the professional musician but the patron, whose declining sophistication erodes the musical environment, creating a demand for frivolous, unsystematic, and unworthy musical forms. In Kaukab's eyes, primary among these inimical musical fads is ṭhumrī itself.[8]

"Vices of the King"

Though Kaukab's book was never completed and never published, his critique of ṭhumrī has been publicly available for a hundred years in the published works of Abdul Halim Sharar. Originating in an Urdu letter written to Sharar in the early twentieth century, then printed as a quotation in Sharar's own publications, Kaukab's statements on ṭhumrī were finally translated into English in the sections on music within Sharar's book, *Lucknow: The Last Phase of an Oriental Culture* (2001 [1975]: 135). Originally published as a series of articles between 1914 and 1919, Sharar's text constitutes nostalgic depictions of pre-Mutiny Lucknow "distilled from memory in exile," as the author was born only after the fall of the city, and came of age in Wajid Ali Shah's court in Matiyaburj, Bengal (Perkins 2011: 304). Recent scholarship argues for a reappraisal of Sharar's accuracy in representing both nawābī Lucknow and the court in exile (Perkins 2011; Naim 2012), yet the compilation and translation by E. S. Harcourt and Fakhir Hussain has, since its publication over forty years ago, become the seminal source on the courtly culture of the legendary city. The two chapters on music—"The Origins and Growth of North Indian Music" and "The Development of Light Classical and Instrumental Music"—are based largely on extended quotations from Kaukab Khan's personal letters to Sharar (2001 [1975]: 132–41).

C. Ryan Perkins, in his dissertation on Sharar and the role of print culture in late colonial India, argues that Sharar anxiously sought to document living memories of pre-Mutiny Lucknow while those who saw it were still alive (2011: 339). In this regard, Perkins notes that Sharar turned over his authorial voice to Kaukab Khan in the chapters on music, choosing to "reproduce word for word" (Sharar 2001 [1975]: 135) the statements of an expert in the field regarding "music of the period before Sharar's time" (Perkins 2011: 340). However, while both Sharar and Perkins seem to have assumed that Kaukab was one of the rapidly disappearing "eyewitnesses to that past world" (ibid.), in fact Kaukab—like Sharar himself—never knew the glory of pre-Mutiny Lucknow. Coming of age in Matiyaburj and Kathmandu (successive sites of his father's employment as a court musician), Kaukab draws on secondhand knowledge in his depictions of the musical world of Wajid Ali Shah's Lucknow, evoking in large measure the official colonial judgment of the king as an irresponsible degenerate concerned only with his own entertainment.[9]

Specifically, Kaukab condemns the court of Wajid Ali Shah as inhospitable to the most prestigious forms of Hindustani music, lamenting that "Ghazals and thumris were the vogue" while the orthodox forms of "*dhurpad* and *hori*" withered on the vine (Sharar 2001 [1975]: 138).[10] Indeed, Kaukab argues that Lucknow's fame as a musical center in the nineteenth century was premised on the rise of new forms of music that were distinctly light, unsophisticated, popular, and entertaining—genres such as g͟hazal and t̤humrī—and that these were destructive to the orthodox core of Hindustani music—genres such as dhrupad and horī. As reflected in Kaukab's passages reproduced in Sharar's work, Kaukab Khan believed strongly that lighter forms of music enjoyed by uninitiated patrons were responsible for the downfall of orthodox Hindustani music. Kaukab even specifies particular rāga-s—*Khamāj, Jhinjhoṭī, Bhairavīṅ, Sindhurā, Tilak Kāmod,* and *Pīlū*—describing them as "small and tasty rāginī-s selected for the talent of comic entertainers," and further noting that "these were the very rāga-s that the nawāb himself preferred" (Sharar 2006: 184).

Likewise, in his own unpublished manuscript, Kaukab lays blame at the feet of Wajid Ali Shah, framing his patronage as a detriment to the art in its simple fascination with "the minor points of music" (1915: 130). As evidence, Kaukab Khan asks, if Wajid Ali Shah were such a great patron of music, why then was no "reliable or worthy book ever written during his reign" (ibid.)? Here Kaukab specifies three Persian texts at the heart of his own writings, lamenting that "not even a translation of such books as [*Uṣūl al-*]*Naghmāt-i Āṣafī* [1793], *Tuḥfat al-Hind* [ca. 1675], or *Shams al-Aṣwāt* [1698]" were produced under Wajid Ali Shah (ibid.). Invoking a pen name he ascribes to Wajid Ali Shah, Kaukab states that whatever proper musical practice remained up until the mid-nineteenth century was "ruined by Kadar Piya's t̤humrī-s" (ibid.).[11] Kaukab summarizes his critique of the relationship between Wajid Ali Shah's improper patronage and its musical consequences with the Persian epithet, *'aibe ke sultān bepasandad hunar ast*—"vices of the king become art" (ibid.).

It is true that t̤humrī flourished in Wajid Ali Shah's court, but Kaukab Khan is far off the mark when he claims that the king was ignorant of dhrupad and unsupportive of new scholarship. In fact, recent research by music historian Richard Williams shows that Wajid Ali Shah himself composed, collected, and published volumes of dhrupad-s and other genres, and authored a number of treatises on music, including one in Persian—*Saut al-Mubārak* (1852–1853)— and at least four in Urdu (Williams 2014: 140). These sources reveal that Wajid Ali was personally familiar with numerous Indo-Persian music treatises, including the *Uṣūl al-Naghmāt-i Āṣafī*, which Kaukab specifically notes was neglected in the nawāb's court. As Williams observes, the *Uṣūl al-Naghmāt-i Āṣafī* was "named for its patron and Wajid 'Ali's predecessor Nawāb Asafuddaulah (r. 1775–1797), so it would have been surprising if Wajid 'Ali had ignored it entirely" (2014: 140).

Kaukab was surely aware of Wajid Ali Shah's contributions as erudite author and refined patron and composer, as the nawāb's works were published from his own press in Matiyaburj and were known among the court musicians (Williams 2014: 141). Ignoring these, Kaukab appears to adopt the colonial perception of the king as a debauched and dissolute ruler. I argue, however, that the exaggerated portrayal of Wajid Ali Shah as a musical lightweight serves a specific rhetorical purpose within Kaukab Khan's larger argument: ultimately, Kaukab is motivated not to vilify Wajid Ali Shah, but to distinguish his own orthodox lineage from the low-status musical activity of the court, thus protecting the prestige of his family for posterity. Yet the question remains: How do we understand the categorical rejection of ṭhumrī by Kaukab Khan when we know that ṭhumrī played a central role in the repertoire of his own lineage? How does Kaukab simultaneously align himself with the orthodoxy of kalāwant musicians such as Pyar Khan (see Sharar 2001 [1975]: 138) while simultaneously denigrating the very ṭhumrī-based repertoire Pyar Khan himself helped create?

Despite Kaukab Khan's claims of orthodoxy, the Lucknow gharānā was certainly associated with ṭhumrī in the broader culture of Hindustani music. For instance, Prabhakar Chinchore, one of V. N. Bhatkhande's disciples, offers a brief anecdote from Bhatkhande's travel diaries concerning a meeting in Calcutta in December of 1907 between Bhatkhande and a small number of ṭhumrī experts. Among these experts, Bhatkhande specifically names Kaukab Khan (Chinchore 1988: 22). Bhatkhande's journals are not publicly accessible, and thus we know little else about the meeting, but at the very least, this episode reflects the widely recognized connection between the Lucknow gharānā and the genre of ṭhumrī in the early twentieth century.

In the succeeding generation, the Lucknow gharānā was represented most centrally by Sakhawat Husain Khan (1875–1955), the primary disciple of both Karamatullah Khan and Kaukab Khan. In his writings, Sakhawat Husain specifically addresses the erosion and degradation of the orthodox instrumental style of his family, expressing great anxiety over pernicious trends in Hindustani music that mix vocal techniques into instrumental music. As he writes,

Instrumental music has a style of its own and with the blessings of God I am steadfast in the teaching of my ancestors and have not made any changes whatsoever because I don't think I am more capable than them. Which form and which thing have they not done before? Nowadays a lot of *gāyakī* [vocal style] is becoming fashionable. Here you find *tān-s* [melodic runs] of *gāyakī*, and there you find thumrī style. And sometimes excessive importance is given to the rhythms of tablā and dance. And the argument is that it is for the sake of the development of music. Neither is there any beauty of *gat-toḍā* [instrumental compositions and variations] nor any mood for rhythmic technique (*lay kā mizāj*). I am surprised when people request me to play these things. What should be my reply and how should I explain? (Khan n.d.: n.p.)

Here Sakhawat Husain Khan, the primary exponent of the gharānā from the 1920s to the 1950s—shown with his son, Umar Khan, in Figure 10—decries *gāyakī* in instrumental music as well as the influence of thumrī, but does not acknowledge the extent to which thumrī vocal music served as a pillar of the repertoire of his ancestors. As in the writings of Kaukab Khan, we see the discursive rejection of thumrī and the simultaneous celebration of an orthodox instrumental style that was premised in part on thumrī itself.

Yet Sakhawat Husain's statements regarding *gāyakī*, written most likely in the early 1950s, were perceptive. As Peter Manuel has discussed, *gāyakī* or *gāyakī-aṅg* refers to an imitation of the singing voice on instruments such as the sarod and sitar, is associated with such towering figures of twentieth-century music as Vilayat Khan and Hafiz Ali Khan, and is often premised on the thumrī style of vocal music (1989a: 170–73). There is no doubt that an embrace of vocal-like embellishments and even the playing of vocal compositions—the primary hallmark of *gāyakī-aṅg*—became a dominant force in Hindustani instrumental music in the second half of the twentieth century. Ted Solis provides a powerful illustration of the ubiquity of *gāyakī* style in his thesis from 1970 on traditional sarod repertoire.

Solis states that his research methodology required that he find and analyze recordings only of the pure sarod style as played and taught by Amir Khan (like the members of the Lucknow gharānā, a direct descendant of Paṭhān rabāb players from Afghanistan). These include recordings by Amir Khan himself and by his famous student Radhika Mohan Maitra (1917–1981). Yet Solis notes that in looking for recordings of Radhika Mohan Maitra that most reflected Amir Khan's style, he could find only one recording "relatively free of vocal influences" (1970: 45). Solis's sarod teacher and research guide was Radhika Mohan Maitra's most renowned disciple, Buddhadev Das Gupta, often considered the

FIGURE 10 Sakhawat Husain and Umar Khan, Bombay, ca. 1930. Courtesy of Irfan Khan.

most traditional sarod player of the high-ranking artists today. Das Gupta, however, "disqualified himself from inclusion due, he said, to the excessive influence of sitāriyā Vilayat Khan and vocalist Bare Ghulam Ali Khan upon his playing" (ibid.). Thus, Buddhadev Das Gupta, as Solis's guide in the quest to understand and document the traditional sarod style of Amir Khan, acknowledges his own departure from that tradition through his choice to pursue *gāyakī* style instead. In this regard, we can see that Sakhawat Husain's statements document pervasive changes in the world of instrumental music at midcentury.

In the generation succeeding Sakhawat Husain Khan, both of his sons likewise reject and decry the unorthodox incorporation of ṭhumrī and vocal styles into instrumental playing. In an interview conducted by ethnomusicologist James Kippen in 1981, Sakhawat Husain Khan's eldest son, Umar Khan (shown in Figures 2 and 10), notes that he has received the message that the consuming public is not interested in his family's musical traditions. As he declares, "I stopped my radio programs, I stopped my conference programs, because people don't like my playing. They want me to play *bhāṭiālī* [a type of Bengali folk song]. They are shouting, 'Play *bhāṭiālī!* Play this ṭhumrī!' I am not going to play all those things on the stage. I'm not going to play" (interview by James Kippen, August 11, 1981). In this interview, Umar Khan, father of Irfan Khan, notes that for thirty years he has been living in Calcutta, the center of instrumental Hindustani music throughout the twentieth century, yet laments that the city's ostensibly sophisticated audiences demand such things as *bhāṭiālī* and, of course, ṭhumrī. The implication is that vocal influence and ṭhumrī style in instrumental music had by 1981 become so ubiquitous that Umar Khan felt alienated from Calcutta's music lovers and unwelcome on the concert stage.

In an interview for All India Radio in Lucknow, Umar Khan's younger brother, sitarist Ilyas Khan (shown in Figure 3), acknowledges nineteenth-century ṭhumrī as the basis of his instrumental repertoire, yet strongly distinguishes between the ṭhumrī of that era—which he argues was cultivated, classical, and canonical—and the ṭhumrī of the late twentieth century. As he states, "I know 200–300 *Purab bāj gat*-s [. . . .] They were created on the basis of ṭhumrī, but which ṭhumrī? These are *bandish* ṭhumrī-s in *tīntāl* and *āḍāchau-tāl* [rhythm cycles associated with the classical repertoire]. They were in such rāga-s as *Darbārī, Māligaurā, Pūrvī*, not like today when ṭhumrī-s are only in *Khamāj, Pīlū*, and *mishra* [mixed] rāga-s" (interview by Shrimati Shaheen Sultana, ca. 1979). Ilyas Khan stresses the point that *Purab bāj gat*-s may have been created on the basis of ṭhumrī-s, but these were not the newfangled *bol banāo* ṭhumrī-s (which proliferated in the late nineteenth and early twentieth centuries, especially in Banaras); instead, they were *bandish* ṭhumrī-s, which employed sophisticated rāga-s in serious tāla-s. Further supporting his argument for the ennobling of the old ṭhumrī-s, Ilyas Khan ascribes the invention of the *Razākẖānī gat* not to the low-status sitarist Ghulam Raza, but instead to an earlier Ghulam Raza, author of the eighteenth-century text *Uṣūl al-Naghmāt-i Āṣafī* (ibid.). Here Ilyas Khan presents an anachronism, but one that surely contributes to the retrospective classicization of the ṭhumrī-based repertoire of the Lucknow gharānā.

Ilyas Khan's defense further highlights the challenge of ṭhumrī for the lineage: the Lucknow gharānā owes its entrance into the fold of Hindustani classical music to the teachings of Basat Khan, believed to be a descendant of Tansen. The instruction and repertoire imbibed by Niamatullah Khan and passed down through his family line is thus celebrated as orthodox, pure, and untainted by the excessive fascination with vocal music of the present day. The purity of this repertoire is especially emphasized in the statements of Umar Khan—the grandson of Kaukab Khan—who refuses to perform or record for the radio because of the pervasive popularity of light and vocal-inflected instrumental forms in his day. Yet we also know that the repertoire deemed elite, orthodox, and pure by the Lucknow gharānā achieved maturity in the court of Wajid Ali Shah, and reflects the popularity of ṭhumrī in mid-nineteenth-century Lucknow. Nevertheless, each generation clung tightly to the distinction between *gat*-s that may have been premised on ṭhumrī-s (celebrated explicitly by Ilyas Khan), as compared to the direct imitation of vocal music that came to dominate instrumental performance practice in the second half of the twentieth century. As Lucknow-based journalist S. K. Chaubey wrote of his contemporary, Sakhawat Husain Khan, "He was renowned for playing his *gats*, but he would never play ṭhumrī *bols* [plectrum strokes in imitation of a vocal composition] just to please his audience. He would play wonderful gats in Pīlū-Janglā, but never Pīlū in ṭhumrī style. Being a traditionalist, he never violated the dignity of his style. What need was there for him to imitate the voice on the sarod and renounce his training?" (Chaubey 1976: 137, quoted in Manuel 1989a: 175).

The claim of orthodoxy on the part of the Lucknow gharānā would seem to lie precisely in the distinction between "traditional" ṭhumrī-based *gat*-s on the one hand and "nontraditional" ṭhumrī-inflected instrumental style on the other. And yet, as cited earlier, Kaukab Khan specifically decries the superficiality of entire rāga-s, irrespective of the quality or authenticity of the repertoire of *gat*-s they contain.[12] In particular, Kaukab Khan lists *Khamāj, Jhinjhoṭī, Bhairavīṅ, Sindhurā, Tilak Kāmod,* and *Pīlū* as examples of rāga-s suitable for the "talent of comic entertainers" (Sharar 2006: 184). Yet despite the aspersions he personally casts on these rāga-s, Kaukab's own catalog of commercial recordings includes *Bhairavīṅ, Khamāj, Pīlū,* and *Zila* (another rāga associated exclusively with light musical forms). The recordings of his son-in-law, nephew, and disciple Sakhawat Husain Khan include *Tilak Kāmod,* as well as other patently light rāga-s such as *Ghārā, Pahāḍī,* and *Zila.* Kaukab Khan's own son, Waliullah Khan, recorded only *Pīlū* and *Mānj Khamāj,* a variation of *Khamāj.* In Ilyas Khan's recordings from the mid-1950s, we hear a dynamic, modern style premised on intense virtuosity and ṭhumrī sensibilities including (but not limited to) the standard list of "light" rāga-s, including *Jhinjhoṭī, Kāfī,* and *Des.*

Finally, Karamatullah Khan's son, Ishtiaq Khan (1919–1967), left a recording from the late 1950s or early 1960s of rāga *Bhairavīṅ* that not only emphasizes the *mukhṛā* from "Bābul Morā" (the ṭhumrī discussed extensively in Chapter 1), but employs a ṭhumrī-style *ālāp* (emphasizing all four of the most common accidentals in the *Bhairavīṅ* scale), and takes an existing *bandish* ṭhumrī ("Kaisī Yeh Bhalāī Re Kanhāī") as the basis for his *gat* (composition), thus participating in the primary practice that defines *gāyakī-aṅg* ("vocal-style" instrumental music explicitly denigrated by the Lucknow gharānā).

What are we to make of these contradictions? McNeil suggests that by emphasizing light repertoire in their recorded output, the members of the Lucknow gharānā were concealing their more cherished patrimony. McNeil notes that not only the recordings of the Lucknow gharānā, but all the early sarod recordings evince a "preference for recording light classical rāga-s," suggesting either an attempt to meet the needs of an uninitiated audience or a "reluctance to record *khās* [special] material" (2007a: 72–73). On the other hand, commercial recordings by Kaukab Khan also included such serious rāga-s as *Bhūpālī* and *Brindābanī Sāraṅg,* while Sakhawat Husain recorded *Mewār* and *Soraṭh.* Further, Ilyas Khan performed extensively for All India Radio in Lucknow, producing an archive of recordings that include such rāga-s as *Alhaiyā Bilāwal, Bihāg, Gauḍ Sāraṅg, Basant, Miyāṅ kī Toḍī,* and other major rāga-s suitable for orthodox treatment. Nevertheless, there is no doubt that the light rāga-s and exciting compositions that characterize the bulk of the commercial output of the Lucknow gharānā were an important part of the family repertoire, and that from the 1950s onward, gharānā members embraced modern musical trends such as evoking a vocal style in their performance.

It would seem that the contradictions of musical modernity as experienced by the Lucknow gharānā are echoed not only in "Bābul Morā" but in the genre of ṭhumrī itself. As the members of the Lucknow gharānā assert, ṭhumrī represents a perversion of the orthodox musical repertoire of Tansen and flourishes only owing to the support of unsophisticated patrons. Three successive generations of musicians of the Lucknow gharānā identify ṭhumrī as inimical not only to orthodox Hindustani music, but to the survival of the gharānā itself. And yet we have seen that ṭhumrī was at the heart of the musical and social changes that propelled the Lucknow gharānā to success. The rejection of ṭhumrī thus exposes a fundamental discomfort with the very basis of the gharānā's own renown. A legacy of recordings prove that successive generations of the Lucknow gharānā—from Kaukab Khan to Sakhawat Husain Khan to Ilyas Khan and Ishtiaq Khan—were expert in the performance of lively, accessible, ṭhumrī-based instrumental music; why then do they deride that very repertoire and insist—to their detriment—on their status as elite bearers of orthodox tradition?

The next chapter begins to answer that question through an alternative interpretation of ṭhumrī. While the term certainly refers to a musical category, it may also be understood as a euphemism referencing the underclass of Hindustani musicians, in particular those associated with female professional courtesans and their salons, where ṭhumrī reigned as the "quintessential" genre of "dance-song" (Walker 2014: 133). Chapter 3 reveals that the Lucknow gharānā considers the classes of musicians that now dominate the Hindustani music scene to be distinctly inferior—musically and socially. Thus, consistent statements of disappointment with and rejection of ṭhumrī/gāyakī express the exasperation and distaste of the Lucknow gharānā with a principal social consequence of musical modernity in the twentieth century: the competition between conflicting classes of musicians within and without the long-standing tradition of hereditary specialization. Chapter 3 picks up this theme and explores the social conflict experienced by the Lucknow gharānā, drawing extensively on tales alive in oral tradition that serve to reorient the historical narrative along the lines of a defunct sociomusical hierarchy still embraced by the members of the gharānā today.

THREE

Rival Tales and Tales of Rivalry

Some three hundred pages into Vikram Seth's epic novel *A Suitable Boy*, a tense scene unfolds within the canteen at an All India Radio facility. The antagonists are Ishaq Khan, a lowly sāraṅgī player, and Majeed Khan, a high-status vocalist who "sat alone at the head of the table by the far wall, musing and stirring his tea" (Seth 2005 [1993]: 320). Breeching the normal decorum, Ishaq Khan and two of his friends seat themselves at Majeed Khan's table, where Ishaq desires to engage "the great musician" and to offer praise for his recent radio performance of the regal rāga *Miyāṅ kī Toḍī* (ibid.).[1] To Ishaq Khan's disappointment, however, Majeed Khan ignores the three men until, overhearing their conversation, he bursts in with an insult to their status as accompanists, declaring, "For a sarangi-wallah no great musicianship is required" (ibid.: 322).

Thus far, the scene from Seth's novel merely depicts a well-known social fact of Hindustani music: entrenched hierarchies allow soloists (such as the vocalist Majeed Khan) to degrade and denigrate accompanists (such as the sāraṅgīya Ishaq Khan). Yet Ishaq Khan's ill-considered retort to Majeed Khan uncovers another dimension to the conflict. Ishaq Khan publicly shames the senior musician when he angrily expostulates that "these are matters about which Khan Sahib has personal knowledge. Perhaps he can elaborate on the uselessness of the instrument" (2005 [1993]: 322). As Seth's omniscient narrator reveals, "It was no secret that Ustad Majeed Khan himself came from a family of hereditary sarangi players" (ibid.). By calling attention to Majeed Khan's own lowly origins, Ishaq Khan attacks the hypocrisy that has allowed many of independent India's greatest soloists to "dissociate [themselves] from the demeaning sarangi tradition and its historical connection with courtesans and prostitutes" (ibid.), while simultaneously looking down their noses at those who remain associated with that tradition.

Ethnomusicologist Adrian McNeil offers a similar argument, highlighting distance and distinction from the world of the courtesans as the preeminent criterion of respectability in modern Hindustani music culture. As McNeil argues, prior to the mid-nineteenth century, North Indian musical specialists occupied a variety of intersecting and polysemic categories, most famously those named *mīrāsī, ḍhāḍhī, kalāwant,* and *qawwāl* (2007b: 46). Significantly, all such musicians ultimately shared a single status as clients: since antiquity, hereditary musicians in India had served specific patron classes by variously "maintaining the genealogy of their patron groups, praising them and their ancestors through song, accompanying them into battle and performing ritual ceremonial or celebratory music for their weddings, births and so on" (ibid.).

However, in the aftermath of the war of 1857–58, which precipitated both the downfall of many regional sources of patronage and the concomitant rise of the "urbanized colonial cities" of Calcutta, Bombay, and Delhi as the new centers of livelihood for Hindustani musicians, the complexity of hereditary musical communities collapsed into a new binary model (McNeil 2007b: 45). During this era, in which Victorian morality was increasingly adopted by the rising Indian middle class, the primary social hurdle for all Hindustani musicians was the stigma associated with the accompaniment of courtesan performers. For a great many musicians, such work provided the best bet for survival in the new colonial centers, yet to attain a modicum of social respectability, musicians were motivated to distance themselves from their real or perceived association with courtesans. Only certain musicians (armored as vocal or, later, instrumental soloists) were able to do so, relying on the newly invented concept of "gharānā" to distinguish themselves from the great majority of musicians who served as accompanists, whether to courtesans or not. Such accompanists were stigmatized as mīrāsī-s, an appellation that branded them as craftsmen rather than artists, and thus marked them as both socially and musically inferior to *gharānedār* performers.

The foregoing understanding is crucial because it suggests that the divisions between musicians are largely ideological; in fact, all hereditary musicians occupied a relatively low social rank within the broader society, despite the existence of a sociomusical hierarchy among them. Nevertheless, as Daniel Neuman and others have powerfully documented, the new division of musicians into two essential categories (gharānedār versus mīrāsī) did not constitute an impenetrable barrier between sociomusical classes. To the contrary, it provided a new mechanism for musicians to raise their status either by claiming a gharānā identity (as in the case of instrumental soloists adopting what had been a preserve of vocalists) or by changing occupational specializations from accompanist to soloist (as in the phenomenon of sāraṅgī players abandoning their instrument and reinventing themselves as vocalists).

The Gharānā Debate

Gharānā, then, would appear to be a distinctly modern adaptive strategy (Daniel Neuman 1990 [1980]: 168–69), a mechanism for the consolidation of reputability in a world where all hereditary musicians were considered potentially impure and possibly inimical to proper morality, especially in the context of the nationalist movement. And yet even if gharānā-s are not the hoary institution they claim to be, strong evidence indicates that they have been around since at least the late nineteenth century (Kippen 2014: 13; Trivedi 2010: 89 n. 175). As defined by Daniel Neuman in his classic text *The Life of Music in North India*, a gharānā constitutes a musical lineage with at least three generations of distinguished artists, a distinct musical style, and no family association with accompaniment (1990 [1980]: 155). This last criterion is highly contested. Indeed, the earliest known use of the term *gharānā* occurs in Sadiq Ali Khan's 1869 Urdu treatise *Sarmāya-i 'Ishrat* in reference to a line of tablā players, thus upending the theory that denies gharānā authenticity to the accompanist class (Kippen 2014). Beyond the issue of accompanists, there also remains significant controversy around the question of instrumental gharānā-s. For instance, Dard Neuman contends that until the 1950s, gharānā-s were the sole province of high-status vocalists, and that instrumental gharānā-s—such as those of sarod and sitar—did not exist until the 1970s (2004: 252). In a recent work, Daniel Neuman states the proposition most starkly, writing, "In 1969–71, the term *gharānā* was used exclusively for vocal traditions, not for instrumental traditions" (2011: 138).

Despite evidence contradicting these broad assertions by Dard Neuman and Daniel Neuman, it is significant that the earliest written source identifying the lineage at the heart of this book as a discrete gharānā dates only from 1976. And yet this lineage is remarkable precisely because of the dense textual record left behind by successive generations of its most renowned stalwarts. The earliest such texts, Karamatullah Khan's book of 1908 and Kaukab Khan's manuscript of 1915, do not employ the term *gharānā* at all.[2] In his 1924 book *Saṅgīt -Samuccaya*, author Lakshman Das Munim notes that he was a student of Karamatullah Khan for some ten years in Allahabad; in the final line of his discussion of Karamatullah Khan, Das Munim states simply that Karamatullah Khan belongs to the "gharānā of Bahadur Sen-ji" (1924: 10–11). This is currently the earliest written reference to a named gharānā associated with the lineage discussed in this book, yet the implication is unclear. Bahadur Sen ("ji" being simply a suffix of respect) was the disciple of Pyar Khan, brother of Basat Khan and Jaffar Khan. All three brothers were court musicians of Wajid Ali Shah in Lucknow, and in this regard, Das Munim's statement supports a consistent thread of claims from 1908 to the present that link the Lucknow gharānā to the "Seniya" traditions of Basat Khan and the Lucknow court of Wajid Ali Shah. However, Bahadur Sen (also known as Bahadur Hussain) is not popularly associated with Lucknow, but instead with Rampur, where he served as a court musician under Nawāb Yusuf Ali Khan (r. 1855–64). His main disciple was the *sursiṅgār* (fretless lute) player Nawāb Haider Ali Khan, who is remembered today as the teacher of Wazir Khan (Brahaspati 2010: 277), discussed extensively later. I have seen no other references that suggest an affiliation of the musicians of the Lucknow gharānā to Bahadur Sen; thus, Das Munim's early statement remains idiosyncratic and mysterious.

Writing in the early 1950s, Sakhawat Husain Khan employs the term *gharānā* in a specific formulation to reference musical lineages associated with particular sites. It is not clear whether he considers these to be proper names, or if he uses the term *gharānā* more generically. For instance, he does not name the "Agra gharānā"; instead, he invokes the *Āgra wāloṅ kā gharānā*, or the "gharānā of the folks of Agra." In a text printed in Devanāgarī and published in 1976 (though written in 1952), Sakhawat Husain Khan additionally lists gharānā-s of the folks of Gwalior and Kālpī (1976 [1952]: 35). Fascinatingly, Sakhawat Husain Khan's unpublished memoirs contain the original draft of the essay handwritten in Urdu. In the handwritten draft, Sakhawat Husain Khan includes, beyond the gharānā-s of the folks of Gwalior and Kālpī, gharānā-s associated with Kirana, Delhi, and Punjab (Khan n.d.: n.p.). Agra, Gwalior, and Kirana are widely acknowledged khyāl gharānā-s; why does Sakhawat Husain Khan also include in his list Kālpī, Delhi, and Punjab? Were these also khyāl gharānā-s in his estimation, or could the last two names instead refer to the celebrated tablā traditions of Delhi and Punjab? Kālpī is not a well-known gharānā today, but was familiar to Sakhawat Husain Khan through his relationship with sitarist Yusuf Ali Khan, who learned from dhrupad singers and bīn and sitar players associated with Kālpī, in present-day Uttar Pradesh.

I believe Sakhawat Husain Khan's invocation of gharānā-s associated with Kālpī, Delhi, and Punjab reflects his understanding (in the early 1950s) that instrumental and even accompanist lineages qualify as gharānā-s. He supports this interpretation when he notes that students in his day might be interested in various gharānā-s' *gāne aur bajāne*, that is, their "singing and playing" (1976 [1952]: 35). Significantly, despite Sakhawat Husain Khan's apparent embrace of instrumental and accompanist traditions as gharānā-s, he stops short of describing his own lineage as a gharānā, and thus does not suggest any particular name for his own tradition. In the 1976 *Golden Jubilee Souvenir* of the Bhatkhande Music College, Sakhawat Husain Khan is remembered as a dedicated professor and representative of the "*Senī* gharānā" (Dadheech 1976: 65). Likewise, in a radio interview recorded in the late 1970s, Ilyas Khan (shown in Figure 3), the primary sitarist of the Lucknow gharānā in the second half of the twentieth century and the son of Sakhawat Husain Khan, is introduced as a "dhrupad-style instrumentalist of the Seniya gharānā." The terms *Seni* or *Seniya*, discussed in depth in what follows, refer to a line of musicians believed to descend from the primary patriarch of Hindustani music, Emperor Akbar's court singer Tansen. As a general claim to authority, many families of instrumentalists have called themselves "Seniya" in the absence of a more specific gharānā title. In this regard, from the recording of the interview with Ilyas Khan, it appears that as late as the 1970s, the sitarist did not strongly identify with a specific named gharānā that signified his own genealogical inheritance.

Similarly, when asked directly about the name of his gharānā in an interview conducted by ethnomusicologist James Kippen in 1981, Umar Khan (elder son of Sakhawat Husain Khan, brother of Ilyas Khan, and father of Irfan Khan) responds by saying that "we are a gharānā of sarodiyā-s."[3] Umar Khan expands on this broad claim to membership in the lineage of Hindustani sarod players by mentioning the birthplaces of two of his line's most prestigious stalwarts: the districts of Bulandshahr and Shahjahanpur. As in the interview with Ilyas Khan, it is not clear that Umar Khan identifies with a named gharānā, though the two places he names have been used as such (for example, the Bulandshahr gharānā and the Shahjahanpur gharānā). Indeed, a few years earlier, Umar Khan himself had penned a short essay titled "Gharānā-s of Sarod" that was published in the 1976 Bhatkhande College *Golden Jubilee Souvenir*. In it, he explicitly cites several different sarod gharānā-s, introducing the phrase *Shahjahanpur gharānā* perhaps for the first time in print (1976: 95). At some point since the 1980s, however, the lineage adopted the name "Lucknow-Shahjahanpur gharānā" to indicate the joining of two strands of the family, one that shifted from Bulandshahr to Lucknow, and another that remained associated with Shahjahanpur. Only since the turn of the twenty-first century has Irfan Khan shortened the name to simply the "Lucknow gharānā." Even now, Irfan Khan regularly employs the name "Lucknow-Shahjahanpur gharānā" when speaking to knowledgeable musicians or music historians. His opinion is that he cannot, properly and technically speaking, claim to belong primarily to the "Lucknow gharānā" when that name is understood to identify the patrilineal tradition traced to Niamatullah Khan. As the grandson of Sakhawat Husain Khan, Irfan Khan's direct male line connects him to the Shahajahanpur gharānā, while he descends from Niamatullah Khan only through daughters, marriages, and disciplineships.

Although we may therefore ascribe a recent vintage to the title "Lucknow gharānā" in reference to the consolidated lineage discussed in this book, there is no doubt that the family itself possesses well-documented historical depth. As genealogical work by Miner (1997 [1993]), McNeil (2004), and Tamori (2008) reveals, and as just introduced by Umar Khan, the Lucknow gharānā was born from the intertwining of two lines of sarod players who trace their ancestry to the districts of Shahjahanpur and Bulandshahr, about 170 kilometers and 400 kilometers northwest of Lucknow, respectively. Both these lineages ultimately lead back to Afghanistan, where their Paṭhān progenitors were players of the Afghani rabāb.

According to their own oral history, the members of the Lucknow gharānā descend from military musicians who served the well-defined role of hereditary specialists for their patrons. McNeil notes, "Music specialists who played the 'rabab or sarod' are listed by Ibbetson [1883] as the mirasis of the Pathans and are named as sarodis" (McNeil 2004: 17). In an essay published in 1976, Umar Khan specifies his family's class origins, noting that when Emperor Babur, founder of the Mughal Empire, first entered India, his forces were led by "Afghani rabāb" players on horseback whose martial music inspired bravery and heroism. Umar Khan specifically describes these martial musicians as "Mīr-s," arguing that within the military structure they were highly respected (1976: 95).

Arriving from Afghanistan in large numbers in the eighteenth century, such musicians were socially distinct from the indigenous musical specialists of North India. As Paṭhān-s, the ancestors of the Lucknow gharānā enjoyed a privileged status as *ashrāf* Muslims, immigrants from Muslim lands, as opposed to converts to Islam from the ranks of low-caste Hindus. The story of the adoption of Hindustani music by the ancestors of the Lucknow gharānā is well known and actively celebrated. None are troubled by the suggestion that prior to the nineteenth century, the lineages that would come to be known as the Lucknow gharānā were not involved in Hindustani music, and thus were not hereditary specialists of rāga music, but were instead essentially mīrāsī immigrants from Afghanistan. However, the descendants of these men clung strongly to their newly adopted identity as authoritative and specifically high-status artists with a hereditary pedigree that distinguished them from the low-status mīrāsī-s who attempted to climb the ladder of sociomusical legitimacy in the twentieth century.

Within the context of a struggle for respectability, the oral histories of the Lucknow gharānā seem to demand rigorous skepticism: they appear to reflect a well-worn strategy among Hindustani musicians—as dramatized by Vikram Seth at the beginning of this chapter—of attacking the origins of fellow musicians, even when those origins may be shared by the attackers themselves. On the other hand, there is no doubt that men such as Irfan Khan and Gulfam Ahmad Khan (the last living concert artists of the Lucknow gharānā) possess credible historical knowledge. In this regard, while I agree that oral history may often deliver psychological truths more accurately than historical facts (Portelli 1991: 51), the oral narratives of the Lucknow gharānā conspire with an archive of historical documents (which themselves warrant critical scrutiny) to evince an undeniable reality to the historical experience of the Lucknow gharānā, even when the messy details of that experience are subject to exaggeration, conflation, selective erasure, or political manipulation both in the present and in the past.

This chapter focuses on historical counternarratives relayed to me by Irfan Khan and Gulfam Ahmad Khan that concern the three dominant instrumental lineages of the present day. Despite the manifest differences among these three lines, the oral history of the Lucknow gharānā depicts them as ultimately sharing a crucial quality: for various reasons they occupy a sociomusical status inferior to that of the Lucknow gharānā. As introduced in Chapters 1 and 2, the musical lineage traced to Niamatullah Khan rose as the elite kalāwant lines of the Mughal courts began to recede. The kalāwant lines had primarily specialized in dhrupad in both its vocal and instrumental dimensions: beyond their renown as singers, the kalāwant-s of the Mughal courts also performed the dhrupad-associated bīn and rabāb. By the nineteenth century, these musical traditions were considered old-fashioned, and were no longer dominant in the famed royal courts of the day, such as that of Wajid Ali Shah in Lucknow.

Before the last generation of great rabābiyā-s faded away, they trained a new cohort of nonlineage disciples in new styles and new instruments. For this reason, the descendants of Niamatullah Khan—a primary recipient of kalāwant instrumental training—claimed not only the musical traditions but the exalted sociomusical status of the kalāwant-s before them. As discussed in Chapter 2, the musicians of the Lucknow gharānā participated in radical reinterpretations of Hindustani instrumental performance; they were famed as performers of high-speed, thumrī-based compositions on new instruments such as the sarod and even the banjo (discussed further in Chapter 5). Yet a century of written and oral discourse of the Lucknow gharānā reveals that in each generation the primary representatives of the lineage saw themselves as stalwarts of orthodoxy, resisting the pernicious onslaught of musical change.

In the writings of Kaukab Khan, Karamatullah Khan, and their primary disciple, Sakhawat Husain Khan, and in the oral narratives of Sakhawat Husain Khan's sons, Umar and Ilyas Khan, the maintenance of orthodoxy is framed in terms of the purity of traditional compositions, and the rejection of new-fangled attempts at vocal imitation. However, I argue in this chapter that such statements may also function as veiled criticisms of social as much as musical change. Significantly, the post-independence period saw the triumphant rise of new classes of musicians with distinctly lower sociomusical status in the eyes of the Lucknow gharānā. Dard Neuman convincingly argues that the rise of the underclass of musicians in the post-independence era ushered in new "heterodox" musical techniques and styles that diverged from the orthodoxy of the dhrupad-associated kalāwant-s and their discipular descendants (2004: 283, passim). Yet, as we saw in the previous chapter, hard and fast distinctions between the new musical fads and the ostensibly orthodox repertoire of the Lucknow gharānā were difficult to substantiate. Thus, to separate themselves from the newly rising heterodox lines, the members of the Lucknow gharānā seized on easily identifiable social distinctions. Through focusing on the sociomusical inferiority of the newly empowered classes of musicians, the latter-day members of the Lucknow gharānā project a historical revision that casts the dominant lineages of the contemporary era as illegitimate usurpers. In this way, the Lucknow gharānā adopts a position not unlike that of the music reformers of the early twentieth century who railed against ostensibly "illiterate" ustād-s who had allegedly appropriated sacred rāga traditions from the temple and sullied them in the court in previous centuries. Significantly, despite claims of lineal superiority, the Lucknow gharānā has in fact receded far into the shadows of contemporary Hindustani music culture while the very families derided for their inferior lines have ascended to heights of renown.

Gharānā Tales

Stories such as those I present in this chapter are characteristic of the genealogical imagination (Shryock 1997). In interpreting them, I dwell in a middle space between positivist history and instrumentalist critique: the stories I discuss in this chapter are presented neither as transparently "true," nor as fictive weapons of the weak, fabricated and lobbed from the margins onto the main stage of contemporary Hindustani music culture. Instead, these stories lie somewhere in the middle, manifestations of the genealogical imagination, passed as oral knowledge from generation to generation, yet simultaneously reflecting the insurgent consciousness of a once-great lineage now pushed to the periphery of the very world it helped to shape. Documenting such stories is vital because despite the centrality of the genealogical imagination to the historical consciousness of lineages of Hindustani musicians, there are few available texts that represent Indian music history from the musician's point of view. Among these few are the writings of vocalists Alladiya Khan (1855–1946) and Vilayat Husain Khan (1895–1962).

In the introduction to Alladiya Khan's memoirs, the text's translators, Das Gupta and Bhirdikar, identify a key feature of Hindustani music's oral traditions: the narrative anecdote. As they argue, anecdotes constitute a basic vehicle for transmission of ideas about musical technique and musicians of the past, but also serve ideological purposes. For these reasons, such anecdotes demand "close and sophisticated scrutiny" (2000: 4). In this regard, the authors make a critical point: because anecdotes are the currency of history among musicians, "There is essentially no difference between what is recounted by the narrator as part of his own experience, and stories that are heard from others" (ibid.: 6). Memory is thus a collective endeavor: whether a narrative is remembered as a personal account of eyewitness, or as a story told by one's elders, the function of memory and of the anecdote is the same.

Despite the insightful identification of the narrative anecdote as a key medium of historical interpretation and transmission within lineages of hereditary musicians, Das Gupta and Bhirdikar do not address the vital role within such anecdotes of rivalries between musicians. While acknowledging the existence of such rivalries, Alladiya Khan himself suggests that "among the elder musicians [. . .] there was never any enmity" (2000: 72). He underlines this point when he documents his own rivalry with Maula Bakhsh of the Baroda court. Alladiya was ready to accept his own mistreatment, but Bakhsh went too far when he "started saying bad things about elders like Behram Khanji, Mubarak Ali Khansahab, Mohammad Ali Khanji, Imratsenji (a descendant of Tansen's daughter)" (ibid.: 76). Here Alladiya Khan suggests that the denigration of specific ancestors is an unacceptable expression of rivalry between musicians.

Vilayat Husain Khan's book, originally written in Urdu, but translated and published in Hindi in 1959, discloses even less of the genealogical imagination than Alladiya Khan's text. Framed as a corrective to the long tradition of writing about music but not about musicians, Vilayat Husain Khan presents thorough discussions of a large number of lineages and their contributions to the history of Hindustani music, including high praise even for rival gharānā-s. Like the writings of Alladiya Khan, Vilayat Husain Khan's text contains explicit tales of musicians confronting, besting, or defeating one another, but does not include defamatory statements that undermine the authority of rival lines.

Yet if public documents do not provide adequate insight into the genealogical imagination, then where is it to be found? As Shryock shows, it is found in specific oral contexts, as communicated from respected elders to junior members of the same tribe. In the case of Irfan Khan and Gulfam Ahmad Khan, I fulfilled the role of the tribal junior, absorbing the history of their lineage as expressed through a variety of anecdotes. As I have organized them here, the anecdotes speak to specific rivalries with competing lineages, targeting for defamation apical ancestors as well as contemporaries. In particular, the stories attack three major gharānā-s, known today as the Maihar gharānā, the Gwalior-Bangash gharānā, and the Etawah or Imdad Khan gharānā, the dominant instrumental gharānā-s of the late twentieth and now twenty-first centuries. The stories in the following sections invert present-day hierarchies of prestige by depicting significant historical figures of today's dominant gharānā-s as inferior musically, socially, or both, emphasizing their subservience to the ancestors of the Lucknow gharānā in the first half of the twentieth century.

The "Two-Streams" Theory

As Daniel Neuman observed nearly forty years ago, the most powerful and prevalent means of asserting authority and authenticity among Hindustani instrumentalists rests on claims of biological or discipular descent from Tansen (1990 [1980]: 107–9). Even when such claims are patently false — as when a lineage is known to have emerged from lowly origins among the subordinated accompanist class — the assertion is made nevertheless. For instance, ethnomusicologist Gerry Farrell notes that even "Vilayat Khan and his family claim descent to Tansen" (2002: 32). While illuminating the strategic imperative of such claims, Neuman himself participates in the politics of Senism. As recently as 2014, Neuman writes, "The last recognized biological descendant — they were known as Seniyas — was Dabir Khan, who died in 1972" (2014: 285). Though he does not spell this out, the reason that Neuman recognizes Dabir Khan as such is that he was the grandson and disciple of Wazir Khan, the towering figure of early twentieth-century Hindustani music universally embraced as the literal and figurative embodiment of the traditions of Tansen.

Within the dominant discourse of Hindustani music history, Wazir Khan (ca. 1861–1926) serves as the principal conduit connecting the legacy of Tansen to the prevailing lineages of the present. Specifically, Wazir Khan is celebrated as the fount of authentic Seniya knowledge propagated by two of the contemporary era's most successful lineages: those established by Allauddin Khan (today known as the Maihar gharānā) and Hafiz Ali Khan (today known as the Gwalior-Bangash gharānā). Wazir Khan was certainly among the most prestigious artists of the early twentieth century, famously serving as chief musician in the court of Rampur under Nawāb Hamid Ali Khan (r. 1889–1930). In Ravi Shankar's first autobiography, *My Music, My Life*, the famed sitarist paints a romanticized portrait of the place of Wazir Khan within the Rampur court, writing that "there were almost five hundred musicians who belonged to the court of His Highness the Nawab of Rampur [. . . .] At the head of all these musicians was the truly great Wazir Khan himself, a member of [. . .] the family of Tan Sen. He was the guru of the nawab and, in his seat next to the nawab's throne, enjoyed a position that was unique at that time" (2007 [1968]: 61). Wazir Khan is also credited as one of the major sources of repertoire documented in V. N. Bhatkhande's compendia of musical transcriptions (see Bor and Miner 2010: 205).

Significantly, Wazir Khan is widely understood to have descended from the lineage established by Tansen's daughter, Saraswati, and her husband, known as Mishri Singh or Naubat Khan. For instance, in Volume 28 of the *Journal of the Music Academy, Madras*, musician and musicologist Birendra Kishore Roy Chowdhury introduces Wazir Khan as "the last jewel among the descendants of Naubat Khan" (1957: 74). Roy Chowdhury specifies that Naubat Khan was "a Rajput prince [originally] named Misri Singh [. . . .] He was known later as Naubat Khan and married the only daughter of Tan Sen, Saraswati" (ibid.: 72). Vilayat Husain Khan presents much the same understanding of the genealogy of Wazir Khan (1959: 58). Likewise, Alladiya Khan in his own memoirs notes that Wazir Khan descended from a "Rajput Brahman," whose "name was Mishri Singh" (2000: 61). In contemporary scholarship the story remains the same. For instance, while including significant caveats in footnotes, ethnomusicologist Stephen Slawek states, "Although documentation is lacking, Hindustani musicians generally recognize Wazir Khan as a direct descendent of Tansen, the legendary court musician of Emperor Akbar, through the *bīnkār* lineage of Tansen's daughter, Sarasvati, and son-in-law, Misri Singh" (1991: 168; see also Nayar 1989: 73). Here Slawek includes the additional ascription of a specific instrumental specialization to the lineage of Tansen's daughter. As introduced in Chapter 2 through Gulfam's lesson in historical organology, the lineage of Tansen's daughter is associated with the bīn, a stick zither prominent in the Mughal court of Emperor Akbar. Significantly, the understanding of a bifurcated tradition from Tansen associated with the lines of his daughter and his son as laid out by Gulfam is widely accepted in the ethnomusicological scholarship. As Slawek writes in his book *Sitar Technique in Nibaddh Forms*, "The Senī gharānā consisted of two schools: (1) descendants of Tansen's son, Bilas Khan, who were known as *rabābiyās* (*rabāb* players), and (2) descendants of Tansen's son-in-law, Misri Singh, who were known as *binkār*-s (*bīn* players)" (2000 [1987]: 17).

However, despite the dominance of the "two-streams" theory today, the earliest known source to mention a lineage descending from Tansen's daughter dates only to the mid-nineteenth century. Written by Muhammad Karam Imam, a courtier of Wajid Ali Shah, and first published in 1925, *Ma'dan al-Mūsīqī* remains the most significant document of musical life of mid-nineteenth-century Lucknow. Yet we have reason to distrust Imam's contentions regarding the earlier history of Hindustani music. Although many twentieth-century texts, such as Vimalakant Roy Chowdhury's *Bhāratīya Saṅgīt Kosh* (1975 [1965]), provide detailed genealogies culled from oral history, and in fact suggest multiple lineage pathways connecting Wazir Khan to Tansen, there is no source in the known annals of Indian music history prior to Imam's mid-nineteenth-century book that mentions any lineage descending from Tansen's daughter (Delvoye 2001: 221).

The two-streams theory was first publicly questioned by musicologist Acharya Brihaspati (1918–1979), who explicitly rejects the narrative of Wazir Khan's descent from Tansen. Brihaspati argues instead that the narrative of two lines from Tansen (a son's line and a daughter's line) was first fabricated in the eighteenth century by the ancestors of Wazir Khan. As I noted, it does not appear in the literature until Imam, who names Tansen's son-in-law as Samokhan Singh, instead of Mishri Singh.

As Brihaspati writes in his 1976 book,

> Linking the traditions of past great men with their own lineages, artists have tried to obtain respect from the people and patronage from royal states. The family tree presented by Wazir Khan is a perfect example of these kinds of efforts. Wazir Khan's ancestors settled in Lucknow during the time of Nawāb Shujauddaula. Shujauddaula died on January 26, 1775. It's possible that during this period, in order to become worthy of reverence in the eyes of Lucknowi people, the story of Samokhan Singh's becoming Muslim and marrying Tansen's daughter and themselves [Wazir Khan's ancestors] being a part of that lineage, was constructed. They certainly benefited from this story and were thereby considered special in comparison to other artists. Muhammad Karam Imam was influenced by this story and he thus also considered them [Wazir Khan's ancestors] to be of the lineage of Samokhan Singh. (Brihaspati 1976: 208)[4]

Although Brihaspati's discussion of Wazir Khan's genealogy contains some questionable leaps of logic and has not been widely embraced within Indian musicology, his interpretation certainly supports claims by latter-day members of the Lucknow gharānā to the preeminence of the son's lineage from Tansen: indeed, Brihaspati suggests that there was no daughter's lineage at all, and that those claiming such descent rely on a tale manufactured only in the late eighteenth century, nearly two hundred years after the death of Tansen. Such an interpretation would appear to reinforce the superiority of the rabāb lineage of Tansen's son. Indeed, this preference is already inherent in the two-streams theory itself. For instance, Jon Barlow writes that Tansen's musical tradition was passed down through "two specialized streams of instrumental training: his son Bilas Khan's rabābiyā line and his daughter Saraswati's beenkar line. Tansen himself played the Indian rabāb while his son-in-law Mishri Singh, the husband of Saraswati, was a beenkar" (2007: 92). Likewise, sitarist Sharmistha Sen writes, "Tansen's family is divided into two groups. The direct descendants of Tansen took to Rabab playing, whereas the descendants of Tansen's daughter popularized the Veena [bīn]" (1988: 63).[5]

Significantly, these statements by Barlow and Sen suggest a qualitative distinction between the bīn and rabāb lines descending from Tansen: both authors imply that the rabāb lineage maintains a closer connection to the traditions of Tansen than does the bīn lineage. Barlow notes, "Tansen himself played the Indian rabab," passing his own tradition to his son, while training "his son-in-law Mishri Singh, the husband of Saraswati" in the bīn. Likewise, Sen describes the rabāb line as the "*direct* descendants of Tansen," while describing the bīn line as "the descendants of Tansen's *daughter*" (emphases added). This is the very distinction emphasized by Gulfam in the introduction to Chapter 2: the members of the son's line may claim a more direct and thus a more authentic connection to Tansen than those of the daughter's line may claim. However, the most recent historical scholarship casts doubt on the story of the son's line as well.

As Katherine Schofield has suggested, claims of descent from Tansen only gained widespread significance in the middle of the nineteenth century (personal communication, December 18, 2014; see also Miner 1997 [1993]: 86). Prior to the massive rupture resulting from the war of 1857–58, the highest-status musicians of North India were the kalāwant-s, the greatest of whom served as chief musicians to the Mughal court from Akbar's time until its final collapse in 1858. It is true that the descendants of Tansen prevailed in such positions until the eighteenth century, but with the triumph of Sadarang in the court of Muhammad Shah (r. 1719–1748), another branch of the kalāwant birāderī rose to prominence. Significant intermarriage between the lineages of Tansen and Sadarang make any simple distinction between the two families impossible, yet it is clear that in the eighteenth century, there was no concerted attempt to claim descent from Tansen by the direct descendants of Sadarang's line. Allyn Miner supports this same point, noting in her book that "Na'mat Khan [Sadarang] was not popularly associated with a Tansen lineage during his own time" (1997 [1993]: 86).

This last point is especially significant because, as Schofield has recently shown, the kalāwant-s of Wajid Ali Shah's court, including Basat Khan—through whom the Lucknow gharānā claims a discipular connection to Tansen—were not direct descendants of Tansen at all (Schofield, forthcoming).

Instead, their lineage was traced through Adarang to his uncle and preceptor Sadarang, himself a sufficiently prestigious ancestor in the first half of the nineteenth century. Thus, it would appear that whether a line claims descent from Tansen through the "son" or the "daughter," both claims are the result of latterday reinvention. Ironically, it would further appear, according to Schofield's research, that all authentic lineages traceable to Tansen ultimately descend from Tansen's granddaughter (not his daughter). That is, although claimants to the "male line" trace their lineage to Tansen's son, Bilas Khan, in fact that very line continues only through the marriage of Bilas Khan's *daughter* to Lal Khan Kalawant, the primary disciple of Bilas Khan. Thus, all Seniyas are ultimately *beṭīwāle*, that is, "of the daughter." However, it is also surely significant that the historical record reveals a documented line of discipular and genetic descent from the dynasty of Sadarang to Basat Khan, and from Basat Khan down to the last remaining representatives of the Lucknow gharānā today. By contrast, there is no available documentation to support claims by discipular descendants of Wazir Khan that connect their lineage to any branch of the Delhi kalāwant birāderī. Indeed, Brihaspati has boldly argued that no such connection exists.

In this regard, discursive attempts by the members of the Lucknow gharānā to undermine the authority of Wazir Khan (along with his legions of discipular descendants) and to instead assert the priority of Basat Khan (and thereby themselves as his discipular descendants) find some support in the historical record. Crucially, however, the present-day context admits no such argument: the story of Wazir Khan's descent from Tansen is firmly undergirded by the dominance of his discipular descendants today, while the counternarratives of the Lucknow gharānā appear by contrast entirely false and easily dismissible. Having now established the ambiguous terrain in which lies this set of Lucknow gharānā counternarratives, I will introduce a number of specific stories, beginning with those that directly address Wazir Khan.

Counternarratives of Wazir Khan

In her book *Khyāl* (1997 [1984]), Bonnie Wade offers an extended translation of a story from Vilayat Husain Khan's 1959 publication concerning a meeting between the Agra gharānā vocalist Ghulam Abbas Khan and Nawāb Hamid Ali Khan, the celebrated aesthete ruler of Rampur and primary patron of Wazir Khan. In the story, the nawāb asks the visiting vocalist, "What sort of bīn player is Ustad Wazir Khan?" Ghulam Abbas Khan responds that there are three types of bīn player: "Real, imitation, and seasonal," noting that Wazir Khan is surely of the first category, a real bīnkār, neither an imitation, nor a seasonal player who performs only at his whim, or at the whim of someone else (Wade 1997 [1984]: 91).

In 2009 Irfan Khan relayed to me a variation on this story in the form of a joke in which Wazir Khan is not the victor; rather, he is the butt. In Irfan Khan's version, the meeting was between bīnkār Rajab Ali Khan[6] and Nawāb Hamid Ali Khan. The background of the joke is that Rajab Ali Khan—a renowned bīnkār and head of the court musicians of Mahārājā Sawai Ram Singh in Jaipur—had traveled frequently to Rampur in order to challenge Wazir Khan to display his legendary skills, but that Wazir Khan had always fabricated an excuse in order not to play. Reportedly, the nawāb asked the visiting bīnkār on one of these occasions how many kinds of bīnkār-s there are. According to the joke, Rajab Ali Khan responded to the nawāb, "Huzūr [Your Highness], there are three kinds: aslī, naqlī, and faslī. Aslī [original or authentic] are those like me. Naqlī [counterfeit] are those who try to copy me. And faslī [of the harvest season] are those who perform only once per fasl [harvest] such as your Wazir Khan!" The implication is that Wazir Khan performed only rarely, perhaps when—as in the harvest season—there was money to be made.[7]

During my first visit with Gulfam Ahmad Khan in Delhi in 2009, I was treated to another such story that emphasized the inferiority of Wazir Khan. Unlike the previous story, however, the one relayed by Gulfam directly juxtaposes the inferiority of Wazir Khan with the greatness of the Lucknow gharānā's ancestor Kaukab Khan. The story is set in the context of a jalsā (musical gathering) in the Banaras darbār (royal court). As Gulfam Ahmad Khan told me,

It happened in the Banaras darbār that there was a jalsā, and many nawāb-s from the region attended, along with their ustād-s. From Lucknow, Kaukab Khan came. He was famous in that time [. . . .] The Nawāb of Rampur—Nawāb Hamid Ali [Khan]—and his ustād, Wazir Khan, also arrived, and the jalsā began. At some point in the evening, Kaukab Khan was performing rāga Shuddha Kalyān. During the performance, Nawāb Hamid Ali Khan of Rampur spoke up, interrupting the performance, saying, "You have not played the main phrase (tān) of Shuddha Kalyān." Kaukab Khan responded, "Sir, I played it; you must not have been paying attention. I will play it again." Just as Kaukab Khan began playing the phrase, the nawāb's ustād, Wazir Khan, spoke up, asking, "Who says this is the main phrase of Shuddha Kalyān?" Very angrily,

Kaukab Khan replied, *Tu jis ghar kā kutta hai, yeh us ghar kī tān hai* [literally, "This phrase belongs to the house (that is, lineage) whose dog you are"].

Hearing Kaukab Khan's gruff rejoinder to Wazir Khan, the whole audience fell silent. All were astonished that such words had been exchanged in the middle of a jalsā. Finally, Kaukab Khan decided to cut his performance short, and prepared to leave. And thus the *mehefil* [musical gathering] of the Banaras mahārāj was ruined. The Banaras mahārāj was also upset with the Rampur nawāb and his ustād, Wazir Khan, but what could he do? He pled with Kaukab Khan to continue his performance, but Kaukab Khan's mood had been spoiled. After packing his things, as Kaukab Khan was about to leave, the Rampur nawāb, Hamid Ali Khan, himself entreated him, "Khansaheb, please come to my court sometime." Kaukab Khan replied, "I will never come to your court. If you are the nawāb of your city, then I am the emperor of my line of work" [*Agar tu apne shahar kā nawāb hai, to main upne kām kā bādshāh hūṅ*]. (interview, March 18, 2009)[8]

In emphasizing the significance of this confrontation between Kaukab Khan and the nawāb of Rampur, Gulfam explained that even his own father, Ishtiaq Ahmad Khan, nephew of Kaukab Khan, had refused to perform in Rampur in memory of the incident. As Gulfam told me,

The nawāb of Rampur, Nawāb Mustafa Khan,[9] invited my father many times. He used to call the radio station to ask permission to hire my father for a performance at his court, but my father always refused. My father knew that his uncle had spoken this way to the nawāb of Rampur at the court of the Banaras mahārāj. Kaukab Khan no longer remained, but my father felt his oath should be honored [that is, that he would never perform in Rampur]. So my father too refused. And the nawāb of Rampur also knew of this [incident between Kaukab Khan and the prior nawāb, Hamid Ali Khan]. (interview, March 18, 2009)

Finally, according to Gulfam, the nawāb appealed in writing to the director of All India Radio in Delhi, where Ishtiaq Ahmad Khan served as a staff artist, promising that Ishtiaq would encounter no disrespect whatsoever in his court. Ishtiaq Ahmad Khan thus finally relented, agreeing to a performance in Rampur in 1961. By Gulfam's account, his father enjoyed his experience there, and returned subsequently for further performances.[10]

In the early twentieth century, Rampur reigned as the most important royal court for Hindustani music. Significantly, the story as told by Gulfam Ahmad Khan depicts a family of musicians so prestigious and self-assured that they could afford to dismiss invitations to perform at the most celebrated court of their day, again turning a now-commonsense hierarchy of prestige upside down: only when the nawāb of Rampur repeatedly implored Ishtiaq Ahmad Khan to visit his court—and only after specifically promising that Ishtiaq Ahmad Khan would certainly not suffer the kind of indignity endured by Kaukab Khan in the previous generation—did Ishtiaq Ahmad Khan deign to accept the invitation.

The story of the meeting between Wazir Khan and Kaukab Khan underscores the extent of divergence of the historical perspective of the Lucknow gharānā from the commonly accepted narratives of Indian music history today. The latter-day members of the Lucknow gharānā have little power to materially enhance their profile in the present. Yet such stories illustrate their ongoing efforts to maintain a self-contained bubble of discourse in which the outside world is turned on its ear. Such stories often concern the authenticity of musical knowledge, as in the dispute over the proper way to play the main phrase of rāga *Shuddha Kalyān*. In this regard, such counternarratives are not merely oral historical tales; rather, they entail embodied dispositions that connect the superiority of lineage ancestors to the value of inherited musical knowledge in the present. The narrative thus works together with the practice to reinforce both the claims to historical truth and the authenticity of present-day performance. At the same time, we have seen that there is strong historical evidence to support the contention of lineal superiority over Wazir Khan and his discipular progeny. Nevertheless, the counternarratives of the Lucknow gharānā ring false today because of the towering ascendance of the lines that claim descent from Tansen through Wazir Khan, and their ability to control both the historical narrative and the criteria for authentic musical performance. In particular, the Lucknow gharānā focuses on two powerful lineages that claim discipleship from Wazir Khan: the Maihar gharānā established by Allauddin Khan and the Gwalior-Bangash gharānā established by Hafiz Ali Khan.

Counternarratives of the Maihar Gharānā

The story of the Maihar gharānā is well known, owing to the global celebrity of its star representative, sitarist Ravi Shankar (1920–2012). As he writes in his first autobiography (2007 [1968]), Ravi Shankar learned sitar from Allauddin Khan, court musician of the mahārājā of Maihar, a small princely state in present-day Madhya Pradesh. While serving the court, Allauddin Khan also trained disciples, including his own son, the late Ali Akbar Khan (1922–2009), whose celebrity could not rival that of Ravi Shankar, but who nevertheless became the most renowned sarod player of his generation. Other celebrated musicians emerging from this gharānā include Annapurna Devi (b. 1927), Nikhil Banerjee (1931–1986), and many more.

Within the historical narrative established by the Maihar gharānā, the pivotal link connecting musicians such as Ravi Shankar to the authority and authenticity of the traditions of Tansen rests on the discipleship of Allauddin Khan to Wazir Khan. According to Ravi Shankar, "Wazir Khan promised that he would consider Baba [Allauddin Khan] as his foremost and best disciple outside his own family, and said he would teach him all the secrets of the art of music that the members of Tan Sen's family possessed" (2007 [1968]: 62). Shankar recounts that Wazir Khan, on his deathbed, "blessed him [Allauddin Khan] before he died, saying that Baba's [Allauddin Khan's] name and the names of his disciples would live forever and carry on the great tradition of the Beenkar *gharana* and the glory of Mian Tan Sen" (ibid.). In his later autobiography, Shankar discusses a "radio feature which I produced on the life of Mian Tan Sen" (1999 [1997]: 118). The feature was especially significant to Shankar because, as he writes, "Baba's final guru, Ustad Wazir Khan, was a direct descendant of Mian Tan Sen, and I had therefore been fortunate enough to learn the Senia Beenkar style, as it is known, from Baba" (ibid.: 119).

The phrase "Baba's *final* guru" clearly suggests that Wazir Khan was not Allauddin Khan's only teacher. As Sulochana Brahaspati writes, "According to the people of Rampur, the credit for Allauddin Khan's training goes to Ahmed Ali Khan, Abid Ali Khan, Chamman Saheb, and other great men of Rampur. Although Allauddin Khan had formally become Wazir Khan's disciple, he had the opportunity to learn from other maestros as well" (2010: 280). Building on the notion of Allauddin Khan's hunger to learn from a variety of sources, Irfan Khan contends that prior to seeking out sarod instruction either from Ahmed Ali Khan or Wazir Khan, Allauddin Khan first sought training in sarod from Kaukab Khan. In this regard, Irfan Khan suggests a priority of greatness favoring Kaukab Khan over Wazir Khan much like that communicated in the narrative just discussed by Gulfam Ahmad Khan.

Irfan Khan laments, however, that Kaukab Khan refused to accept Allauddin Khan as a disciple; had Kaukab Khan not refused, Irfan Khan reasons, the legacy of the Lucknow gharānā would have been yoked to that of Allauddin Khan, likely resulting in much greater recognition for the Lucknow gharānā today. Yet, as Irfan Khan explains, Kaukab Khan rejected Allauddin Khan as a student because the latter was a mere "common man," whereas Kaukab Khan was accustomed to teaching, beyond his own family members, only "nawāb-s and mahārājā-s" (interview, February 21, 2009). Here Irfan Khan refers to Allauddin Khan's lowly social rank, and reinforces the notion that Kaukab Khan was a member of the musical aristocracy who served powerful and high-status patrons, and who took as disciples wealthy and socially prestigious individuals.

However, the animosity directed by Gulfam and Irfan toward Wazir Khan is not echoed in their depictions of Allauddin Khan. In general, Irfan Khan frames Allauddin Khan as a simple and respectful man who was a devoted and influential teacher. As Irfan Khan stated, "All that you see these days of people playing sarod, it's all thanks to Allauddin Khansaheb. Whoever is now playing, it's due to him. Because he was not miserly with his knowledge. Whoever came, he taught them. And that's why his name is still there. People will remember him 'til eternity" (interview, May 2, 2010). Irfan Khan further asserted that Allauddin Khan always remained a respectful friend and admirer of Kaukab Khan's descendants, including Kaukab Khan's son-in-law (and nephew), Sakhawat Husain Khan. Because Allauddin Khan traveled regularly to both serve as an examiner at the Bhatkhande College and to perform at the All India Radio station in Lucknow, he used to visit frequently with Sakhawat Husain Khan. As Irfan Khan relays, on these visits to Lucknow, Allauddin Khan was known to carry his sarod covered in a simple cloth, and to travel on foot from his accommodations to the radio station. On the way, he would stop at the home of Sakhawat Husain to "pay his respect and to take Sakhawat Khansaheb's permission" (ibid.).

According to Irfan Khan, the intimacy between the two musical families continued into the next generation: Irfan Khan's father (Umar Khan) and Allauddin Khan's son (Ali Akbar Khan) were close friends. According to Irfan Khan, "Ali Akbar Khan used to come in his car and pick up my father. Sometimes he would come in the evening, stay, and drink. Or he would pick up my father and go driving and drink in the car, and throw the bottle, like all wild people do" (interview, February 21, 2009). Emphasizing this brotherhood, Irfan Khan told me of a concert in Allahabad in which both Umar Khan and Ali Akbar Khan performed. After Umar Khan's performance, according to Irfan

Khan, "Allauddin Khan got onstage and declared 'You are both brothers! And you should never ever fight. He is Kaukab Khansaheb's grandson: Grandson of a Tiger!'" (ibid.).

These stories of Allauddin Khan do not contain the rancor and resentment brimming in the narratives concerning Wazir Khan. Having undermined any claims to "Seniya" knowledge by the Maihar gharānā, the counternarratives of the Lucknow gharānā present Allauddin Khan and Ali Akbar Khan as generous and respectful musicians who accepted the greater authority of the Lucknow gharānā, and cherished their connection to the lineage that produced Kaukab Khan, Sakhawat Husain Khan, and many more. Beyond the attack on the Maihar gharānā's claim to Seniya discipleship through Wazir Khan, these narratives do not attempt to defame the Maihar gharānā in any way; to the contrary, Irfan Khan admits great admiration for the global influence of Allauddin Khan as a visionary and prolific teacher. The narratives in the following section—those that address the lineage of Hafiz Ali Khan—are not so tame.

Counternarratives of the Gwalior-Bangash Gharānā

The narratives in this section address the lineage established by Hafiz Ali Khan (1888–1972), a contemporary of Sakhawat Husain Khan, and also a celebrated sarod maestro with a genealogy, like that of Sakhawat Husain Khan himself, that places him at the center of the story of the sarod. Speaking at the Ustad Hafiz Ali Khan Memorial Music Festival in 1973, Birendra Kishore Roy Chowdhury discussed the rise of Hafiz Ali Khan to preeminence among sarod players in the first half of the twentieth century. In particular, Roy Chowdhury noted, "After the death of Asghar Ali Khan, people had become despondent regarding the sarod" (1973: n.p.). In the absence of Asghar Ali Khan, who passed away in the early twentieth century, Roy Chowdhury pointed to two sarod players who were "sort of holding the fort for sarod" (ibid.). These were Ahmed Ali Khan (best known in the present for being one of Allauddin Khan's earliest teachers) and Hafiz Ali Khan. Roy Chowdhury clearly expresses the widely agreed proposition that by the middle of the twentieth century, there were really only two sarod players dominating the field: Hafiz Ali Khan and Allauddin Khan, described by Roy Chowdhury as "the two Supermen of the sarod" (ibid).

In the same publication, famed sarod player Radhika Mohan Maitra reflects another widely held understanding: that Hafiz Ali Khan descends from the most historically significant lineage of sarod players. As Maitra writes,

It is generally believed that it was his family who, through subsequent generations[,] actually developed the Afghan type of Rabab into what is known as
Sarode today. The first member of Khan Saheb's family to settle in India was
Mian Gulam Bandegi Khan Bangash, who had come from Afghanistan primarily as a horse-trader, but who was also a Rabab player of no mean order.
His reputation as a unique player of Rabab reached the ear of His Highness
the Maharaja of Rewa, who was himself a very good musician and a great con-
noisseur of music. The Maharaja invited the Khan Saheb to his Durbar and
appointed him as one of his court musicians. Later on Mian Gulam Bandegi
Khan Saheb started learning Indian Music from one of the descendants of
Mian Tansen of hallowed memory. Thus began the dynasty of Sarodias about
250 years ago, which produced a host of great Sarode players including Ustad
Hafiz Ali Khan Saheb. It is said that Ustad Gulam Ali Khan, one of the greatest Rababiyas of his days and a court musician of His Majesty the King Wazid
Ali Shah of Oudh, was the first man to give Sarode its present form by changing gut-stings to steel-made strings, wooden plates to steel plates and adding
a few more strings for Tarafs and Chikari. (Maitra 1973: n.p.)

Son of Hafiz Ali Khan, the superstar celebrity sarod player Amjad Ali Khan
tells a slightly different version of the early history of the family (for instance,
in Amjad's telling, Ghulam Bandegi Khan was appointed by the mahārājā of
Rewa not as a court musician but as a "Risaldar in the State cavalry," that is, as
a military officer), but his narrative of his father's musical inheritance is much
the same. As Amjad Ali Khan specifies, Hafiz Ali Khan was inducted into the
"Swami Haridas school of Mathura" by Ganeshi and Chukha Lal, who "belonged to the eleventh generation of descendants from Swami Haridas" (Malhotra 1973: 18). Here Amjad Ali Khan notes that beyond his father's descent from
an illustrious Paṭhān lineage, Hafiz Ali Khan is believed to have learned from
significant teachers outside his family.

In his "final" interview, Hafiz Ali Khan himself notes that in his twenties he
left home "in quest of more knowledge" (Khanna 1973: n.p.). Hafiz Ali Khan
continues, stating that his quest led him to "Vrindavan to the feet of Pandits
Chukkhalalji and Ganeshilalji. They sang in the Dagar Vani style, pure pristine
tradition of Swami Haridasji" (ibid.). As discussed in Chapter 2, Swami Haridas is believed to have been Tansen's primary teacher, and thus the primor-
dial source of orthodox rāga tradition, though the relationship between the two
lacks documentation. Later, when Hafiz Ali Khan's travels took him to the court

of Rampur, he performed before the nawāb. As he states, "Well, it seems by the blessing of Allah, that my performance must have displayed some unusual talent, for, after a short conversation, Ustad Wazir Khan agreed to accept me as his pupil" (ibid.). Hafiz Ali Khan reports that "Ustad Wazir Khan Saheb taught me the pure framework of Raag—its rigid rules—and directed that not even by a whisper must these rules be transgressed" (ibid.).

In addition to his lineage and his *talīm* from authoritative sources outside his family, Hafiz Ali Khan is remembered as a performer with nearly superhuman power. Indeed, as already noted, Birendra Kishore Roy Chowdhury refers to Hafiz Ali Khan as one of the two "Supermen of the sarod." Supporting such legends of his own near-miraculous musicianship, Hafiz Ali Khan recalls a musical duel that led to the death of his opponent in the midst of performance. As he narrates the incident,

> I had been playing very vigorously for well over four hours with Shambhu Singh accompanying me on the Pakawaj, and having raised the speed to a tremendous pitch I finished off my recital for the evening. I was quite tired. The cognoscenti of Calcutta were there and acclaimed the performance most flatteringly. Darshan Singh had been listening. I had played very seldom with him, and he was perhaps a little peeved because of this and wanted to test my stamina. He came up to me even while everyone was congratulating me, and asked me to play with him. I said I had finished for the evening, but he kept importuning me and indeed provoking me with a hint of challenge in his tone. I was young then and my temper was high and I decided to show him my capabilities which he seemed to question. Taking Allah's name I picked up my instrument and began playing at the tremendous speed at which I had ended the evening's performance earlier. Although Darshan Singh was fresh it was not an easy pace to maintain—and the recital had taken on the flavor of a contest. My practice was at its highest pitch. I was able to play thunderous rhythms at breath-taking pace. Suddenly after about 30 minutes, Darshan Singh slumped forward on his pair (of Tablas) dead! I was left speechless with horror. I could not eat for four days, so great was my shock and sorrow at his tragic end. (Khanna 1973: n.p.)

In his own narrative of the incident, Amjad Ali Khan states, perhaps more bluntly, "the challenger fell flat on his face across the *tabla* and died of a heart attack" (Malhotra 1973: 19).

Having read this section in the manuscript that would become *Lineage of Loss*, Irfan Khan noted that the narrative concerning the death of Darshan Singh upon his tablā is accurate, yet the powerhouse sarod player who gave a heart attack to his accompanist has been misidentified. Over the phone Irfan Khan commented, "It was not Hafiz Ali Khan; it was Karamatullah Khan." As evidence, Irfan Khan directed me to an article titled "The Great Masters I Have Heard" by Dhurjati Prasad Mukherji (1894–1961). A longtime professor at the University of Lucknow, D. P. Mukherji is recognized as among the founding fathers of Indian sociology (Mukherji 2006: 2). His essay was included in an educational and promotional booklet announcing the second annual Radio Sangeet Sammelan, a series of concerts and live broadcasts held November 10 to 15, 1955. Mukherji's essay, the final substantive item in the booklet, offers a ten-page reflection on the author's experience with past masters of Indian music.

Mukherji plays somewhat fast and loose with his spelling of Muslim names—even referring to the infamous nawāb of Lucknow as Wajid Ali Khan instead of Wajid Ali Shah—but his ranking of "undisputed masters" of the sarod of "the last few decades" is nevertheless easy to interpret. As Mukherji writes, "Fida Husain of Rampur, Karamat Hussain Khan of Calcutta, Allauddin Khan of Maihar and Hafiz Ali Khan of Gwalior would belong to the top rank of instrumentalists in any part of the world" (1955: 65). The second name on his list refers to Karamatullah Khan, who settled in Calcutta after the death of his brother in 1915. Mukherji goes on to present a specific anecdote concerning "Karamat Khan" (now with the erroneous middle name expunged) that took place "the last day of December one year when we wanted to ring out the old" (ibid.: 66). Significantly, both Hafiz Ali Khan and "Karamat Khan" were present, and both performed in the course of the evening.

As Mukherji writes,

Both were in excellent form, but at two in the morning Karamat Khan began to play a rare *raga* (*Kusum*) which, as I learnt later, was a specialty of his *gharana*. I lost all consciousness in listening to it. This is one of my richest experiences in life. Usually he (and his brother Katub [*sic*] Khan, the famous banjo player) used to play in very fast tempo. Darshan Singh, the one-eyed *tabaliya* of Gaya, was his favourite accompanist. I was a witness to that dramatic and tragic incident when Darshan Singh collapsed on his *tabla* while accompanying Karamat Khan on a[n] extremely fast *dhun* [tune]. As far as I am concerned, Karamat Khan's compositions and *gats* still remain unequalled. (Mukherji 1955: 66)

Within the discourse of the Lucknow gharānā, Mukherji's recollections of this incident (documented more than fifteen years earlier than those of Hafiz Ali Khan) are accepted as fact. The appropriation and rearrangement of the story by Hafiz Ali Khan, Irfan Khan argues, was only possible in the 1970s, long after the deaths of Kaukab Khan, Karamatullah Khan, Sakhawat Husain Khan, and of course D. P. Mukherji himself. While rejecting the veracity of the story as reimagined by Hafiz Ali Khan, Irfan Khan points to the very fact of the appropriation as evidence of the injustice that has propelled Hafiz Ali Khan's lineage to dominance while burying Karamatullah Khan and his progeny under the sands of time.

Indeed, as already illustrated, dominant narratives of Hafiz Ali Khan position him as the most authoritative and virtuosic sarod maestro of his generation, far eclipsing any potential rivals among the Lucknow gharānā. In a frequently cited interview, Amjad Ali Khan notes that his own lineage shares an important characteristic with the Maihar gharānā, discussed earlier. As Amjad Ali Khan states, he and other famous musicians such as Ali Akbar Khan and Ravi Shankar possess musical educations "derived from the *Senia* school." However, he appears to specifically slight the Lucknow gharānā when he continues, mentioning "yet another gharānā, that of Ustad Karamatullah Khan of Calcutta from whom Ishtiaq Ahmad, Ilyas Khan and Umrao [*sic*] Khan of Lucknow learnt" (Malhotra 1973: 24).[11] While Amjad Ali Khan is ready to name many individuals of the Lucknow line, he does not acknowledge that both Karamatullah Khan and his brother, Kaukab Khan, learned from their father, Niamatullah Khan, who himself learned from Basat Khan, widely embraced as a descendant of Tansen from the "male line." Nor does Amjad Ali Khan mention that Niamatullah Khan remains a strong contender for the title of "inventor of the sarod," a distinction Amjad Ali Khan ascribes to his own great-grandfather (ibid.: 18). As Amjad Ali Khan narrates, it was "Ghulam Ali Khan Sahib who really converted the *rabab* into the *Sarod* as we know it today" (ibid.). As one might expect, Amjad Ali Khan's sons, Amaan Ali Khan and Ayaan Ali Khan, present much the same understanding in their own book, reporting that "the sarod originated in Afghanistan from an Afghan folk instrument called the rabab. In time, it was modified in India by Ghulam Ali Khan Bangash (who happens to be one of our forefathers)" (2009: 13).

Beyond dismissing Hafiz Ali Khan as an unscrupulous person and an over-rated performer, an even more damning attack on the man and his legacy targets his claims of elite musical descent. When I spoke with Irfan Khan's aged mother, Shahjahan Begum (1926–2016), in December of 2012, she recalled that in Shah-jahanpur there was a sarod player named Abdul Aziz Khan, whose daughter married Hafiz Ali Khan. The marriage stood out in Shahjahan Begum's memory because it was controversial: the clan objected to the marriage on the grounds that Hafiz Ali Khan was an outsider, not the true son of their kinsman, Nanhe Khan. As Shahjahan Begum stated, "They say instead he was the son of a mīrāsī" (interview, December 20, 2012).

As suggested by Irfan Khan's mother, it is an accepted truth within the Luck-now gharānā that Hafiz Ali Khan was not himself born into the illustrious lin-eage to which he would lay claim. The lineage includes Ghulam Ali (d. ca. 1850), considered by many to be the inventor of the sarod, and certainly the main chal-lenger to Niamatullah Khan's claim of that distinction. In the dominant under-standing, Hafiz Ali Khan is known to be the son of Nanhe Khan, himself the son of Ghulam Ali. The Lucknow gharānā, however, remembers otherwise. In making his case, Irfan Khan cites a book by Harendra Kishore Roy Chowdhury from 1929 that states, "Nanneh married in Nika form a Domni, the mother of Hafezali Khan[,] when Hafezali was a boy of three years of age. The Domni, in her professional career, was in the employ of His Highness the Nawab of Ram-pur as a player on the Harmonium. It is said Hafezali was born of a Pathan father" (1929: 48–49).[12]

The term domnī refers to a female singer-entertainer who, unlike the tawāif of North India, was "not a sexual entertainer" (Brown [Schofield] 2000: 19; see also Qureshi 1981: 46). Thus, the reference to Hafiz Ali Khan's mother as a domnī does not, in itself, condemn her as a woman of low morals. The statement that she married Nanhe Khan in nikāh form—that is, through a binding marriage agreement within Islamic law—further emphasizes the legality of the wedding, distinguishing it from the "temporary" or so-called fixed-time marriages some-times associated with courtesanry.[13] Yet Harendra Kishore Roy Chowdhury's statement also suggests that Nanhe Khan's bride was a widow, had been di-vorced, or was otherwise not a virgin. The last point is especially emphasized, as she is said to have already given birth to Hafiz Ali Khan three years before her marriage to Nanhe Khan.

This story attacks the link between Hafiz Ali Khan and his illustrious ances-tors, positing that he was not their genetic descendant at all. Thus, beyond the assault on Hafiz Ali Khan's claims to Seniya discipleship (through undermining Wazir Khan as a representative of that tradition), such counternarratives actively excommunicate Hafiz Ali Khan (and all of his descendants) from the prestigious Bangash lineage from which the Lucknow gharānā asserts descent. Most significantly, Hafiz Ali Khan is framed not only as an illegitimate son, but as an offspring, perhaps, of a mīrāsī father.

Counternarratives of the Etawah Gharānā

The concluding counternarratives I will discuss in this chapter concern the sitar lineage established by Imdad Khan (1848–1920). Widely deemed the most influential and prolific sitar lineage of the twentieth century, the Etawah or Imdad Khan gharānā grew from the adoption of the sitar by Imdad Khan's father, Sahabdad Khan, whose progeny "in each of the five generations," from his time to the present day, rose to "the front ranks" among India's topmost sitar players (Dard Neuman 2000: 4–5). Imdad Khan's sitar style revolutionized the music world through the proliferation of his 78-rpm recordings in the early decades of the twentieth century. Imdad Khan's son, Inayat Khan, himself "developed a style that musicians of his generation would come to emulate" (ibid.: 9). Inayat Khan's own son remains a towering figure of sitar musicianship in the twentieth century: the late Vilayat Khan (1928–2004), who himself further revolutionized sitar technique and repertoire, creating a style known as gāyakī-aṅg (discussed in Chapter 2) that has proliferated in the present day. Vilayat Khan's son, Shujaat Khan, remains one of the leading lights of his generation, an embodiment of the ongoing primacy of hereditary musicianship today. In this regard, Shujaat Khan is reported to have declared, "I am Indian culture" (Qureshi 2009: 166). Though dominant in the world of instrumental music today, the lineage descending from Sahabdad Khan is widely known to have lowly sociomusical origins. Indeed, Sahabdad himself was originally a sārangī player, and was thus marked as a member of the subordinated classes of accompanists.

Emphasizing this last point, both Irfan Khan and Gulfam Ahmad Khan relayed stories that aimed to establish the superiority of their family's musical heritage over that of the Imdad Khan gharānā. Gulfam, for instance, told me that just as Allauddin Khan had sought—and been denied—discipleship under Kaukab Khan, Vilayat Khan himself had sought to learn from sitarist Waliullah Khan, son of Kaukab Khan. In Gulfam's telling, Vilayat Khan came daily to Waliullah Khan's house in Calcutta for "seven to eight years" asking to become his disciple. Waliullah Khan, however, refused to teach Vilayat Khan, owing to his status as a mīrāsī (personal communication, April 1, 2009).[14] Despite this refusal, according to Gulfam, Vilayat Khan succeeded in obtaining material from Waliullah Khan. Gulfam described a personal meeting with Vilayat Khan in 1989 in the home of patron and producer Naina Devi: according to Gulfam, Vilayat Khan revealed in this meeting that he had in his possession "one hundred and fifty gat-s [instrumental compositions] by Kaukab Khan, transcribed by Waliullah Khan" (personal communication, April 1, 2009).

The stories of the Lucknow gharānā that pertain to the Imdad Khan gharānā generally depict a close relationship between the two families, emphasizing the great esteem in which Vilayat Khan and his kinsmen held the Lucknow musicians. Another such story pertains to the close relationship between Vilayat Khan's father, the legendary sitarist Inayat Khan (1895–1938), and Sakhawat Husain Khan. According to the story, when Inayat Khan died, his widow brought both of her two young songs—Vilayat and Imrat Khan—to live with Sakhawat Husain Khan in Lucknow. As Irfan Khan recounts, all three remained under his grandfather's roof for six months, during which time Vilayat Khan received tālīm (training) from the sarod patriarch (interview, February 21, 2009). The three departed, however, when Sakhawat Husain Khan rebuffed the suggestion by Vilayat and Imrat Khan's mother that her two sons should be married to his own two daughters. The implication is that the low social status of Vilayat and Imrat Khan marked them as unsuitable matches for the daughters of the great sarod gharānā. Just as Irfan Khan regrets Kaukab Khan's rejection of Allauddin Khan as a suitable student, he likewise laments his own grandfather's pride in turning down the marriage proposal offered by the mother of Vilayat and Imrat Khan. Had they married into the family, Irfan Khan reasons, the brothers might have raised the profile of the Lucknow gharānā and shared the limelight with its latter-day members.

In a variation on the theme of reverence for the Lucknow gharānā by the Imdad Khan gharānā, Gulfam relayed a story that simultaneously illustrates the great respect for sarodist Karamatullah Khan (Gulfam's grandfather) by sitarist Inayat Khan (Vilayat Khan's father) and also aims to reassert the sitarist's low social rank. According to the story, Karamatullah Khan was performing in Allahabad when Inayat Khan entered the hall. Seeing the renowned sitarist in the back, Karamatullah called out to him, inviting him to assume a position of respect by sitting in the front, where he and the artist would be in close proximity.[15] In the story, however, Inayat Khan chose to remain in the back of the room, crouching near the collection of sandals and shoes deposited by the concert listeners, and replying to Karamatullah Khan's invitation, "In this house, this is the most appropriate place for me" (personal communication, April 1, 2009).

Because, in India, footwear is considered dirty and defiling, and is often removed before participation in a musical event, such a statement would suggest that Inayat Khan had adopted a posture of extreme subservience in the presence of Karamatullah Khan. In effect, this story is similar to the account of Kaukab Khan's meeting with Wazir Khan; for anyone—especially a renowned musician—to remain in the back of the hall near the collection of footwear represents an act of supreme humility—indeed, an artist would elect to occupy such a position only if his status were precisely a "dog of the house" of a great musician. Although this account sounds most improbable, it powerfully reflects the Lucknow gharānā's sense of historical priority over the gharānā of Imdad Khan.

Irfan Khan elaborated on the manner by which the Imdad Khan gharānā rose to such great prominence. As he explained,

> You see all their ancestors were sārangī players . . . and before that they were Hindus. They converted. Sahabdad Khansaheb used to play sārangī. Imdad Khansaheb also used to play sārangī. Half his life he was playing sārangī with two *bāījī*-s [courtesans] called Atani and Chavani in Calcutta. And then there was Sajjad Husain Khan, Ghulam Muhammad Husain's son. He used to play surbahār. So Imdad Khan became the disciple of Sajjad Husain. Not a formal *shāgird* [disciple], but he used to go there and listen, and listen, and he picked up the technique. And then he started playing surbahār and sitar. They didn't learn from anybody. They knew the rāga-s. Sārangīya-s know so many rāga-s because they are accompanying a lot of musicians. And in those days there were good vocalists, people who knew rāga-s. So he knew the rāga-s. All he needed was the technique and he did it. And the greatest thing about that family is they are great *riyāzī*-s. They practiced like mad from morning to evening, evening to morning, around the clock. It is said that when Inayat Khansaheb or Imdad Khansaheb used to travel, even on the train they would take out their instrument and sit on the floor and practice. That is why they can play so well. Practice is the secret. But they have no Seniya connection as such. (personal communication, May 4, 2010)

Here Irfan Khan praises the tenacity and dedication of Imdad and Inayat Khan, but simultaneously asserts their sociomusical inferiority, emphasizing

Imdad Khan's own continued work as a sāraṅgī player in the company of two well-known courtesans of Calcutta, and their willingness to sit and practice on the polluted floor of a moving train car. Most centrally, however, Irfan Khan rejects the authority of the Imdad Khan gharānā in the realm of rāga, mastery of which requires, according to Irfan Khan, extensive, formal tālīm from a Seniya or a discipular descendant of the family of Tansen.

Irfan Khan interprets the great renown of Vilayat Khan in a similar vein:

> But they worked hard; they acquired it. And Inayat Khansaheb went on to become one of the leading sitar players of his time. There is no doubt about it. No one can deny it. But as far as rāga and tālīm and 'ilm [training and knowledge] are concerned, they were very limited. That's why you'll find Vilayat Khansaheb or anyone [in their family] playing just a few rāga-s: always Yaman, Mālkos, Bāgeshrī, Rāgeshrī, Darbārī, sometimes maybe Sohnī, and lighter rāga-s: Pīlū, Khamāj, and Mānj Khamāj. In afternoons sometimes Shyām Kalyān, and also not correctly. Puriya, Purva, Puriya Kalyān. I mean, those rāga-s which are very easy to play. (personal communication, May 4, 2010)

Significantly, the enmity between the Lucknow gharānā and the Imdad Khan gharānā is not entirely one-way. Amaan Ali Khan and Ayaan Ali Khan write in their book, for example, that "Ustad Enayat Khan [also spelled Inayat Khan] had a strong rivalry with a sarod player of his time called Sakhawat [Husain] Khan" (2009: 56). Amaan and Ayaan Ali Khan go on to discuss a famous recording of rāga Khamāj by Inayat Khan, who, following common practice of the time, verbally announces his own name in the final moments of the recording. In this particular recording, however, Inayat Khan offers more than merely his name. Instead, he states "Enayat Khan, Sakhawat kā bāp," identifying himself as the "father" of Sakhawat Husain Khan, and thus emphasizing his superiority over the sarodist. Amaan and Ayaan Ali Khan add, "Apparently, Sakhawat [Husain] Khan had[, in response,] filed a defamation case against Khan sahib [Inayat Khan], so he [Inayat Khan] renamed one of his sons Sakhawat for a while" (2009: 56).

———

The recording of rāga Khamāj by Inayat Khan constitutes a valuable historical document: it attests to a significant rivalry between two renowned musicians of the early twentieth century. Yet in the present day, only the descendants of one of these men remain important and respected performing artists. The descendants of the other—the present-day members of the Lucknow gharānā—have only their inherited musical repertoire and their accumulated knowledge of the family history as evidence of their descent from a significant musical lineage. Yet there is simply no doubt that Niamatullah Khan, Kaukab Khan, Karamatullah Khan, and Sakhawat Husain Khan were among the most celebrated and influential instrumentalists of their day. For example, in his 1959 book, Vilayat Husain Khan discusses the most famous instrumentalists of the first half of the twentieth century, beginning his list with three sarod players: Hafiz Ali Khan, Sakhawat Husain Khan, and Allauddin Khan. From this order, it is clear that Vilayat Husain Khan placed Sakhawat Husain Khan among the top three sarod players of the day (1959: 214).

In the intervening years, however, Sakhawat Husain has been nearly forgotten, and the other two—both claiming a connection to Tansen through their discipleship under Wazir Khan—have been ensconced as the only two relevant sarod players of the early twentieth century. Likewise, Ravi Shankar's narrative of his own discipular descent from Tansen through Wazir Khan remains unquestioned in the popular imagination. For example, the authors of the undergraduate survey text *What in the World Is Music?* introduce Tansen as "an important composer and singer in the development of the classical tradition whose continuing influence may be heard in the artistry of Pandit Ravi Shankar" (Arnold and Kramer 2016: 131).

Like Sakhawat Husain Khan, Karamtullah and Kaukab Khan have also begun to fade from the collective memory of Hindustani musicians today. In his influential book on ṭhumrī, Peter Manuel includes a large block quote from the writings of Kaukab Khan as published within Sharar's famous book, *The Last Phase of an Oriental Culture* (2001 [1975]). Yet Manuel introduces Kaukab Khan merely as a "writer" whose statements index changing musical tastes: Manuel argues that "Kaukab's confusion" in his alleged misuse of the terms *dhrupad* and *horī* indicates that such austere and orthodox genres had fallen into "obscurity" by the time of Kaukab's writing (Manuel 1989a: 67 n. 2).[16] To extend the formulation, Manuel's own statement—informed by extensive fieldwork among musicians in North India in the 1980s—indexes the extent to which Kaukab Khan and his gharānā had fallen into obscurity by the late twentieth century.

Today only two men—Irfan Khan and Gulfam Ahmad Khan—retain significant memories and musical motifs of their once-proud ancestors. The stories documented in this chapter illustrate the workings of the genealogical imagination in a context of gradual but inevitable historical erasure. Significantly, the visions of music history relayed by Irfan Khan and Gulfam Ahmad Khan turn the tables on the dominant musical families of the present day through the reassertion of old-fashioned paradigms of musical hierarchy and social superiority. And yet such narratives do not merely expose a politics of resentment;[17] they illuminate a sense of decorum, hierarchy, and superiority that is anachronistic today. We may bid good riddance to such outmoded and caste-like structures of social constraint, but they offer value beyond their extension of largely vanished sociomusical mores into the present. The stories narrated by Irfan Khan and Gulfam Ahmad Khan sustain the living memories of Kaukab Khan, Karamatullah Khan, and Sakhawat Husain Khan, towering figures of Hindustani music history fading fast from the collective consciousness as their descendants recede from the main stage of Hindustani musical culture.

And yet competing hereditary lines were far from the only challenge faced by the Lucknow gharānā in the twentieth century. For at the same time that rival clans of musicians were ascending to the status of elite soloists, another constituency set out to reinvent the culture of Hindustani music as a national tradition for the rising Hindu bourgeoisie.

FOUR

The College and the Ustād

In November of 1952, Lucknow's Marris College of Hindustani Music celebrated its Silver Jubilee, marking twenty-five years as India's preeminent institution of music education. The president of India, Dr. Rajendra Prasad, attended the opening ceremonies and enjoyed a concert arranged in his honor at the residence of the Uttar Pradesh state governor. At the concert, the chief minister of Uttar Pradesh, Govind Ballabh Pant, introduced the assembled artists to the audience and announced the first performance of the evening: a duet by Sakhi-Sakha, the affectionate name given to the duo of sarod player Sakhawat Husain Khan and pakhāwaj drummer Sakharam Ramchandra, two illustrious artists who were also senior professors at the Marris College (Khan 1986: 47; see also Mutatkar 2001: 29). According to the recollections of Sakhawat Husain Khan's son, after the concert the president of India remarked on the significance of Sakhi-Sakha, who were known to perform as a pair in weekly concerts at the college itself (Khan 1986: 47; see also Misra 1985: 34).

We do not know why the president of India chose to remark on the significance of Sakhi-Sakha, or what he actually said. However, it is not far-fetched to suppose that the president believed the image of a Muslim soloist (Sakhawat Husain) and a Hindu accompanist (Sakharam) performing together under the banner of the state deserved particular celebration. In 1952 the savagery of partition was only five years in the past, and the two new nations of India and Pakistan had already fought their first war. Within India, the period between 1950 and 1952 saw seventy bloody clashes between Hindus and Muslims—so-called communal riots—in which 184 lives were lost (Gayer and Jaffrelot 2012: 327). President Rajendra Prasad and the other prominent politicians present at the concert—including the governor and the chief minister of Uttar Pradesh—were all stalwarts of the Indian National Congress, the avowedly secular political party that led the struggle for independence and governed the Republic of India nearly continuously from 1947 to 1989.[1] In this context, the performance of Sakhawat Husain Khan and Sakharam Ramchandra presented a powerful rebuttal to the forces of communalism (identity politics dividing Hindus and Muslims) as well as an opportunity for leaders of the Congress Party to extoll the performance of Hindustani music as a primary exemplar of India's traditions of tolerance and syncretism.

This anecdote places Sakhawat Husain Khan—the preeminent representative of the Lucknow gharānā from the 1920s to the 1950s—at the center of a vital but largely overlooked dimension of Hindustani music history in the twentieth century: the nexus of nationalist ideology, institutional education, and hereditary musicianship. From outward appearances, the scene just described may be read as evidence of the absence within North Indian music of communal animosity, despite its prevalence in the society at large. However, a closer look at the relationships between nationalist ideologues, music institutions, and ustād-s reveals a political terrain laced with obstacles against the robust perpetuation of hereditary musical dynasties such as the Lucknow gharānā. For while the college depended on Muslim hereditary practitioners as its earliest professors, the ideology shaped within the institution alienated and eventually dispossessed those very musicians; similarly, even the most stridently secular Congress politicians—including all those present at Sakhi-Sakha's concert in November of 1952—embraced a vision of Hindu nationalism that ultimately drove Muslims from the party, resulting finally in the partition of British India and the birth of Pakistan as a homeland for India's Muslims.

In pursuing the connections between Hindu nationalism and the Marris College, this chapter explores the role of communalism within Hindustani music history. Scholars of Indian music have rightly noted that naked communal antipathy does not characterize the world of Hindustani music, where Hindus and Muslims accompany, teach, and even—most remarkably—marry one another. Yet, as we will see, Hindustani music's reformers (especially V. N. Bhatkhande) propounded a vision of musical modernity with unmistakable overtones and implications of communalism. This chapter continues the story of the Lucknow gharānā and its struggle with musical modernity through a focus on the relationship between Bhatkhande's flagship institution (established in Lucknow in 1926) and Sakhawat Husain Khan. Like his forebears, Sakhawat Husain Khan set down his life experiences and opinions in his own writings, the bulk of which were never published and have never been accessed for scholarly purposes until now. One of the earliest instructors in the Bhatkhande Music College, Sakhawat Husain publicly documented his pride and humility as a supporter of Bhatkhande's vision of a reformed musical tradition and, indeed, participated directly in it as a classroom teacher from 1927 until his death in 1955. This chapter also shows, however, that the everyday operations of the college promoted a distinctly Hindu-centric nationalism invested in Muslim oral musical traditions, but not in Muslims themselves.

As suggested in the anecdote that begins this chapter, the college did not operate in a vacuum, but was connected in a variety of ways to the state, first as part of the effort to consolidate a national culture in the late colonial era, and then as a government institution serving the independent Republic of India. Investigating the relationships between the state, the college, and the Lucknow gharānā, this chapter sketches a historical counternarrative in which educational institutions such as the Bhatkhande College (see introduction, n. 7, on college names) played a significant but entirely overlooked role in shaping the Hindustani music tradition in the twentieth century. In particular, I argue that the college propagated underlying ideologies of Hindu nationalism, thus contributing to a reinterpretation of Hindustani music as a Hindu cultural practice, and ultimately reducing the prestige of such lineages as the Lucknow gharānā in a process I call institutional communalism.

The Shift

This chapter brings together two dimensions of Hindustani music history that have proven problematic in the literature: institutions and religion. Citing the inability of schools and colleges to produce professional performing artists, scholars have generally dismissed the role played by educational institutions within Hindustani music history. If institutions have been disregarded, the significance of religion has been rigorously denied. As shown in Chapter 3, a small number of high-profile Muslim hereditary professionals flourish in the upper echelons of Hindustani music culture today, yet in general, Muslim musicians have endured a drastic decline in patronage over the past century, pushing many hereditary musical families into the economic and cultural margins. Indeed, no one denies that there has been a marked shift in the population of performing artists in Hindustani music from a Muslim majority to a Hindu majority over the past one hundred years (see Manuel 2007 [1996]: 123; Peterson and Soneji 2008: 7–8; Powers 1980: 27; Qureshi 1991: 162; Slawek 2007: 507).

How do scholars explain such a shift from Muslim to Hindu predominance while minimizing the significance of religious identity? The most convincing arguments, advanced independently by ethnomusicologists Regula Qureshi and Peter Manuel, have leveraged Marx's theory of mode of production to explain the changing demographics of Hindustani music (Manuel 1986, 1987, 1989a, 1989b, 1991, 2000, 2001, 2002, 2007 [1996], 2008; Qureshi 2000, 2002, 2006).[2] Briefly summarized, Qureshi argues that prior to the mid-twentieth century, Hindustani musicians were essentially feudal servants beholden to powerful landed patrons. The patron class appropriated the cultural capital produced from musical performance through their ownership of the means of production: the venue in which the performances took place (2002). From the sixteenth to the mid-twentieth centuries, the great majority of such patrons were Muslim, and thus, Qureshi contends, "their hereditary servants were naturally Muslim" (1991: 161). With independence in 1947, however, the feudal system began to crumble, replaced by capitalism; concomitantly, the old feudal patrons were replaced by the new bourgeoisie. For a variety of reasons, the new patron class was largely Hindu, and thus impelled the rise of a parallel constituency of middle-class Hindu performing artists. Manuel offers a similar analysis, while emphasizing the musical over the social consequences of the shift from feudalism to capitalism. Focusing on the music's ability to weather broad social changes resulting from the shifting mode of production in India, Manuel notes that "Hindustani music successfully underwent the transition from Muslim feudal patronage to predominately Hindu bourgeois patronage" (2007 [1996]: 125). Like Qureshi, Manuel suggests that this transition produced as a secondary effect the shift from Muslim to Hindu majorities among performers, an unintended consequence of patronage by the new bourgeoisie, which, Manuel notes, "happened to be predominately Hindu" (2008: 396).

Beyond the realm of music, strife between Hindus and Muslims has been a central point of political friction for over one hundred years, yet there remains in the scholarship a reluctance to identify the politics of communalism in the heart of the Hindustani music tradition. Manuel encapsulates the prevailing perspective when he writes that North Indian music has "evolved as an inherently syncretic and collaborative product of Hindu and Muslim artists and patrons" (2007 [1996]: 120), thus describing Hindustani music culture as "a resilient island of communal harmony more or less impervious to the antagonisms polarizing society at large" (2008: 381). In this chapter, I offer an alternative interpretation, suggesting that communalism operated to the detriment of Hindustani music's Muslim hereditary practitioners even in the absence of outward and aggressive exclusion and prejudice. Understanding how this may be possible requires a new approach to thinking about communalism in India.

Communalism

Invented in the eighteenth century by India's British rulers to advance their colonial policy of divide and rule, the notion of communalism asserted that conflicting religious identities prevented peaceful coexistence between Hindus and Muslims, and thus functioned as a justification for colonialism itself (Pandey 1996 [1990]: 10).[3] Yet what began as an orientalist myth "became a modern institutional reality" (Ludden 2007 [1996]: 11; see also Gould 2012: 34). As many recent scholars have convincingly demonstrated, one enduring result of the colonial construction of communalism was the invention in the late nineteenth century of "Hinduism" as a monolithic and pan-Indian religious tradition (Dalmia 1997; Hansen 1999; Ludden 2007 [1996]; Pandey 1996 [1990]; Sarkar 2007 [1996]). The orientalist notion that Indian civilization emanated from an ancient and unitary Hindu culture provided the foundation for early nationalists such as Swami Vivekananda (1863–1902) to argue that India possessed a unique national character premised on the contrast between its own spirituality and the materialism of the West (Hansen 1999: 68–69; see also Jaffrelot 2007: 6; Van der Veer 1994: 20). Similarly, Swami Dayananda Saraswati (1824–1883), founder of the Arya Samaj, propelled a reform movement that advocated Hindu practice and tradition against the onslaught of Western culture and religion (Jaffrelot 2007: 8–10), promoting an all-India Hindu community and a Sanskritized Hindi as the "common national language" (Hansen 1999: 73). The growing impulse for such movements—including a countrywide proliferation of Hindu *sabha*-s, or associations—was ultimately anticolonial, yet the increased investment in Hindu identity politics produced grave consequences for Muslims. By the 1890s, for example, the Arya Samaj and other Hindu reform or revival organizations precipitated widespread violence against Muslims as part of the Cow Protection Movement (Ludden 2007 [1996]: 13; Pandey 1996 [1990]: 200).

By the 1920s, the discourse of Hindu nationalism was firmly established by groups such as the Hindu Mahasabha and the Rashtriya Swayamsevak Sangh (RSS)—Association of National Volunteers—which developed a fierce militancy, arguing for "India as essentially the land of the Hindus" (Pandey 1996 [1990]: 260; see also Hansen 1999; Sarkar 2007 [1996]). Vinayak Damodar Savarkar (1883–1966), president of the Hindu Mahasabha, was the leading theorist of "Hindutva," a Hindu essence "shared by all Hindus" that excludes Muslims (and Christians) from the imagined nation (Hansen 1999: 77; see also Savarkar 2003 [1923]). Significantly, religion was not important for Savarkar; an avowed atheist, he drew on European theories of nationalism to define the Hindus as a national ethnic group (Jaffrelot 2007: 15).

The story of communalism in India is usually told through a focus on the rise of overt and assertive brands of Hindu nationalism propounded by the groups just introduced. Moreover, the theory of Hindu nationalism is frequently correlated with the political reality of communalism through a focus on violent clashes—"communal riots"—with the catastrophic partition of the country along religious lines as the most egregious such example. The study of postcolonial communalism has focused on the role of a consortium of Hindu nationalist organizations known as the Sangh Parivar, comprising the aforementioned RSS, the Vishva Hindu Parishad (World Hindu Council), and the Bharatiya Janata Party (Indian People's Party). In the 1990s the Sangh Parivar succeeded in pushing Hindu nationalism into the political mainstream, ultimately capturing a majority in the national government, and propelling the most horrific scenes of anti-Muslim violence since the partition of the country in 1947 (Bose and Jalal 1998: 227–29; Hansen 1999; Jaffrelot 1996; Metcalf and Metcalf 2002: 260–95; Van der Veer 1994; Varadarajan 2002).

It is true that Hindu nationalist groups have had little presence within the mainstream culture of Hindustani music. Yet historians such as William Gould argue persuasively that it is a mistake to limit our understanding of communalism to the politics of organizations that explicitly advocate Hindu supremacy (2004: 33) or to focus excessively on instances of riots and pogroms (2012: 80). Dominant historical narratives embrace precisely these assumptions, thus depicting the mainstream forms of Indian nationalism, especially as propounded by the Indian National Congress, as inherently secular. Congress nationalists such as Jawaharlal Nehru (independent India's first prime minister) made the case themselves, arguing that communalism was the enemy of true nationalism—which was by definition modern and thus free of religious bias. However, as historian Sumit Sarkar has noted, "It has often seemed important for even the most secular nationalists to derive sustenance and authenticity from an image of subcontinental unity [. . .] extending back into a glorious past [. . . .] And then it becomes difficult [. . .] to resist the further slide toward assuming that that unity, after all, has been primarily Hindu" (2007 [1996]: 275). Anthropologist Thomas Hansen pushes this notion further, contending that "the public spheres in secular India remained full of religious signs and practices, packaged and represented as culture, making up a nationalized cultural realm represented as unpolitical, pure, and sublime" (1999: 53). Indeed, Sarkar dismisses the naiveté of scholars who posit nationalism and communalism as incommensurable, writing, "The enormous overlap in personnel, assumptions, and symbols between mainstream Indian nationalism and Hindu communalism is too obvious to need much elaboration" (2007 [1996]: 271).

If we are to understand the ways that communalism may operate in the absence of overt animosity and public violence, however, such overlap deserves a bit of elaboration. As I argue in this chapter, we require a more finely crafted lens if we seek to identify communalism as a subtle and institutional phenomenon. Gould's work in particular helps us reframe Hindu nationalism: instead of seeing it as nurtured only within a group of "relatively powerless" hardline communal organizations, Gould illuminates the "persistent use of a Hindu idiom within mainstream nationalism" (2004: 265; see also Hasan 1982).

Institutional Communalism

As already noted, communalism is most often discussed in terms of political strategies and the brief, explosive moments of violence that they engender. By contrast, the notion of a low-level, continual, everyday communalism—an *institutional communalism*—has been scarcely theorized. Broadening our understanding of communalism, sociologists Patricia Jeffery and Roger Jeffery direct our attention to the "grinding and routinized aspects of communalism that pervade people's daily lives" (1998: 123), arguing that "normal and apparently gender- and community-blind institutional procedures can dramatically signal inequalities of opportunity and result in structured inequalities. Such institutional sexism or communalism is deeply embedded in the daily workings of many social institutions, including the state apparatuses" (ibid.: 125). While such everyday communalism proves difficult to identify in individual cases, the recent Sachar report on the *Social, Economic and Educational Status of the Muslim Community of India* (Sachar et al.: 2006) employs "large-scale empirical data" to confirm that India's Muslims—some 150 million people, or 13.4 percent of the entire population—suffer disadvantages at every turn (Basant 2007: 829;

see also Basant and Shariff 2010).[4] As Hansen notes, the Sachar report power-fully documents "decades of systematic neglect, non-action, and open exclusion of Muslims from virtually every facet of life in the country" (2007: 50).

The dynamics are akin to the persistence of a structural form of disadvan-tage in the United States today, an "institutional racism" that is "covert" and not easily "identifiable in terms of specific individuals"—rather, it operates through "established and respected forces in the society" (Ture and Hamilton 1967: 4). Institutional racism thus proves difficult to track and attack: it is sus-tained through the everyday functioning of society, allowing its beneficiaries to "absolve themselves from individual blame" (ibid.: 5). Several scholars have recently described institutional racism as invisible, silent, or hidden (Brown 2002; Shapiro 2004; Trepagnier 2006). In his influential text on the present-day functioning of institutional racism, George Lipsitz elaborates on this notion, writing, "As the unmarked category against which difference is constructed, whiteness never has to speak its name, never has to acknowledge its role as an organizing principle in social and cultural relations" (2006: 1). By no means has anti-Muslim communalism remained a silent, unspoken force. However, following scholars of institutional racism, I maintain that if we identify com-munalism only where it loudly announces itself, we risk overlooking those sites where it operates silently.

My argument is that educational institutions, and especially music schools, are key sites of ideological production that have effected widespread change with deleterious effects for Muslims, but without calling attention to them-selves, and thus without attracting ideological critique. That is to say, unlike racism in America, communalism in India has not been effectively theorized in terms of institutions. Following Louis Althusser's suggestion that educational institutions are the primary sites of ideological indoctrination in the modern era (2006 [1970]: 103; see also Katz 2012), in this chapter I focus on one particu-lar school of music, the Bhatkhande College of Music, arguing that its ideologi-cal connections to the broader nationalist movement entailed the cultivation of an institutional communalism antagonistic to the continuity of Muslim heredi-tary musicianship on which the Hindustani tradition was based.

A Brief History of the College

As Regula Qureshi has noted, Lucknow's "preeminence in music [. . .] became enshrined institutionally" with the establishment in 1926 of "one of India's premiere music colleges," today known as the Bhatkhande Music Institute University (2007: 16). Though the college bears the name of its primary intellectual inspiration—V. N. Bhatkhande—he was not the only important founder of the institution. Bhatkhande, in fact, had originally desired not a local, independent college in Lucknow, but a national academy of music in the capital city of Delhi. The idea for such an academy was first proposed by social activist Atiya Begum Fyzee Rahamin at the first All-India Music Conference, organized by Bhatkhande himself, and held in Baroda in 1916 (Report 1917: 24; see also Bakhle 2005: 182; Singh 1952: 1). The proposal envisioned a national institution that would offer instruction in Hindustani music in a systematic and modern manner. Bhatkhande embraced the plan, and was joined in his effort by Thakur Nawab Ali Khan, taluqdar (large landholder) of Akbarpur, who served as the president of the 1916 conference. Thakur Nawab Ali Khan had become interested in Bhatkhande's project of music reform a few years earlier, and apparently sent his own court musician, Kale Nazir Khan, to Bombay to learn about and report on Bhatkhande's "work in music" (Ratanjankar 1967: 35). According to Ratanjankar, Kale Nazir Khan was "very much impressed" with Bhatkhande: his report to Thakur Nawab Ali Khan intrigued the taluqdar so much that he aligned himself with Bhatkhande's goals, eventually producing his own version of Bhatkhande's texts in Urdu, the *Ma'ārif-ul Naghmāt* (*Knowledge of Melody*) (ibid.: 35–36).

At the Second All-India Music Conference, held in 1918 in Delhi, Rai Umanath Bali, taluqdar of Daryabad (in the Barabanki District, near Lucknow), made a competing and more modest appeal for a college of music at Lucknow. The president of the conference, Nawāb Hamid Ali Khan of Rampur, supported Bali's proposal, but neither Bhatkhande nor Thakur Nawab Ali Khan was interested, focused as they were on the establishment of a truly "national" institution in Delhi as proposed by Atiya Begum Fyzee Rahamin (Singh 1952: 1). At the third conference, held in Banaras in 1919, the establishment of a national academy was again pursued vigorously by Bhatkhande and his supporters, and thus Rai Umanath Bali's repeated proposal for a music college at Lucknow was again denied (ibid.; see also Bakhle 2005: 199). Plans for the national academy, however, were unrealistically grand, and by 1920 hopes for such an institution had collapsed (Singh 1952: 1; see also Bakhle 2005: 198).

In November of 1922, Bhatkhande met with Rai Umanath Bali in Lucknow, where Bhatkhande composed a new vision of a smaller-scale college, and hatched plans for the Fourth All-India Music Conference, to be held at Lucknow

(Singh 1952: 1; see also Bakhle 198–99). The conference was convened in January of 1925, and resulted in a resolution to establish an All-India College of Music in Lucknow (Singh 1952: 1; see also Bakhle 2005: 200; Report 1925: 96).[5] Bali would serve the college as honorary secretary and oversee its day-to-day functions for some three decades.[6] Bhatkhande himself organized the curriculum, and remained in Lucknow, giving lectures at the college from July 1926 until March 1927. Thereafter, he visited the college twice a year until 1933, when he took a fall in Bombay and as a result was "bed-ridden for a full three years" until his death on September 19, 1936 (Ratanjankar 1967: 50; see also Singh 1952: 2).

The College and Nationalist Ideology

The connections between the All-India College of Music and the nationalist movement for independence from British rule were apparent from the beginning. But do such connections necessarily argue for the presence of institutional communalism within the college? Once again, I want to emphasize the point that the college never operated on an overtly anti-Muslim basis. Yet, as Gould writes of the "looser forms of Hindu nationalism," even ostensibly secular political platforms shared "some important basic premises" with hardline communalists (2004: 7). For this reason, manifestations of Hindu nationalism in mainstream nationalism "are more problematic to define but more significant" (ibid.) precisely because they were hidden at the very heart of India's most successful anticolonial party.

The ideological underpinnings of the college shared many features with the Congress, and were voiced with uncanny and explicit conviction in speeches and writings emerging from Bhatkhande's All-India Music Conferences.[7] The perspective invoked repeatedly by the conference organizers focused on the great continuity of Indian music from antiquity through the eighteenth century, the importance of the Hindustani tradition as an aspect of national cultural heritage, and the detriment to Indian musical culture of British colonialism. As Rai Umanath Bali declares in an appeal for funds for the Fourth All-India Music Conference in 1925, "Culture is the foundation of nationalism. The achievement of our race in the past is the basis of our faith in our future and our spiritual heritage of art and science, philosophy and literature, is the true spring of our national self-consciousness" (Report 1925: 7). Bali goes on to emphasize the great continuity of the national cultural tradition of music, proclaiming that "the story of [music's] developments may be traced in a continuous line from the Vedic times [ca. 1500–500 BCE] to the spacious days of Akbar and his magnificent successors [1556–1707 CE]" (ibid.). The reason Bali does not draw this line of continuity up to his own time is that he intends to argue that music is in need of resuscitation: it has suffered as a result of British rule, a process that began with the fall of the Mughal Empire in the early eighteenth century. Bali reinforces the point regarding the deleterious effects of foreign rule upon Indian music when he writes, "Music is essentially a part of our national culture," explaining its alleged downfall by noting that "except in Native States which are still the repositories of this our ancient heritage, there is not much scope for the free development or diffusion of the national art in British India" (ibid.: 155).

In his writings and speeches, Bali suggests that the college should fulfill both nationalist and anticolonial ends. However, despite his embrace of the Muslim Mughal period as part of the Golden Age, Bali additionally insists on the liberation of the knowledge of Hindustani music from the grip of its traditional performing artists, the largely Muslim hereditary musicians. In a letter dated January 21, 1926—some six months in advance of the college's grand opening—Bali discusses this aspect of his goals for the college. Addressing his remarks to the secretary of the department of education, Bali writes in request of government funds for a proposed "All India Music College" in Lucknow. The goals of the proposed college were "to (1) revive old and ancient art of music and to introduce it to high society, which from the last 60 years has fallen in the hands of illiterates; (2) to arrange for new Raga productions on scientific and systematic lines and (3) to collect and preserve the great master pieces of the art now in the possession of illiterates" (Bali 1926a: 2).[8]

In a College Progress Report from 1931 summarizing the effects of its first four and a half years in operation, Bali writes, "In short this institution is meeting the keenly felt need of turning out properly and scientifically trained music teachers from amongst the respectable classes" (ca. 1931: 111). In these statements, the co-founder of the college does not directly mention religion or "community." Yet he does establish the intention of the college to produce a new class of music teachers and to thereby create a new class of music lovers, listeners, and performers. He is clear that this means retrieving the art from those who currently hold a monopoly on its performance and pedagogy, to whom he refers as "illiterates."

As Justin Scarimbolo asks in his critique of my article on institutional communalism (Katz 2012), who were these illiterates (2014: 405)? How reliable is my implication that "illiterate" was meant as a euphemism for "Muslim"? A fairly uniform set of statements by Bhatkhande and his supporters, as well as many other music reformers, defamed hereditary musicians as premodern obstacles to music's modernity. We know that the great majority of such hereditary musicians were Muslim. But does this mean that the effort to appropriate musical knowledge away from hereditary musicians for the benefit of the "respectable classes" was necessarily communal in nature? In his book *Hindu Nationalism and the Language of Politics in Late Colonial India*, Gould reminds us that political language can be "related to forms of political action that could not have been guessed from language itself" (2004: 13). Thus, interpreting nationalist discourse requires the study of "both intention and context," such that even statements lacking explicit communal bias may communicate such within a context that "historically acquired a communal dimension" (Gould 2002: 622). In this regard, it is not necessary to prove that Bali had Muslims in mind when he spoke against music's illiterates. Rather, the analysis requires evidence of a pervasive Hindu-centrism in which such statements may have reasonably been interpreted as a reclamation of musical knowledge for the Hindu nation.

This context was conditioned in part by the precipitous rise in communal riots in Uttar Pradesh during the years leading up to the founding of the college. Though there are inherent problems in imputing religious causes to such violent confrontations, they were certainly framed as religious conflicts at the time. As Gould documents, the official colonial record shows, in Uttar Pradesh alone, "ninety-one reported 'serious' Hindu-Muslim clashes between 1923 and 1927 inclusive. Again, the majority of these conflicts were related to music before mosques and cow-slaughter controversies" (2012: 107). As suggested by Gould, music was at the heart of a great many communal clashes throughout the 1920s. For example, in September of 1924, one such clash occurred in the center of Lucknow, where a Hindu *ārtī* ceremony (which can include singing, bells, and blown conch shells) interrupted prayer at a nearby mosque (Gould 2012: 108). The operational premise of the Bhatkhande College—with Muslims teaching "Hindu" music—would appear to thwart the dynamics that pit Hindus against Muslims, especially in the realm of music. Yet ideology operates on subtle levels, and thus even the willingness of Muslim musicians to participate in the propagation of a Hindu national culture may have contributed to the marginalization of those very musicians.

Another objection may be raised: because many of the earliest instructors at the college were Muslim hereditary musicians, is it not possible that Bali included such individuals within his category of "the respectable classes"? Could it be that the renowned Muslim teachers and performing artists of the era were exempt from the ascription of illiteracy? The willingness of Bhatkhande and Bali to employ and patronize many such Muslim musicians would appear to argue for this interpretation. But if the one hundred high-profile performing artists present at Bhatkhande's Fourth All-India Music Conference (held in Lucknow in 1925) were embraced as respectable representatives of the Hindustani tradition, then how could the speakers at the conference, such as Sir William Marris—namesake of the Marris College, president of the conference, and governor of Uttar Pradesh—reasonably claim that "this ancient and honourable art has in these times fallen upon evil days" (Report 1925: 49)?[9] The ideology cultivated within the All-India Music Conferences, and upon which the college was founded, did not permit the celebration of music's traditional performing artists as its rightful bearers. Thus, despite the immediate and manifest presence of a large contingent of the nineteenth and twentieth century's greatest musicians, reformist discourse—inspired by mainstream Indian nationalism—insisted that Hindustani music was in immediate need of rescue. Marris continued: "The practice of music has fallen nowadays into the hands of [a] special class, lacking social status or enlightenment who cannot be expected to realize the potential wealth of their inheritance, and simply have not got it in their power to reclaim the art from its less reputable concomitants, to call forth all its latent virtues and to seat it again upon a throne of honour" (ibid.).

The prevailing ideology blinded the founders and supporters of the college to the immediate facts on the ground. For instance, the leaders of the Fourth All-India Music Conference publicly disparaged not only contemporary professional musicians—the expert musicians on whom they relied as their primary musical informants and instructors—but the musical atmosphere of Lucknow itself. As Bali declared, "At one time Lucknow was prominent as a centre of music and song and although to-day it has fallen on evil days, the voice of its master singers is still and the springs of charity of their cultured patrons have run dry—Lucknow still boasts of a public which is keenly interested and highly appreciative" (Report 1925: 9). Thakur Nawab Ali Khan, chairman of the reception committee of the same conference, echoed Bali's statement, announcing that "Lucknow particularly, the seat and centre of that glory[,] has faded much, and, I am afraid, little now remains of its past glory in music except a highly appreciative and keenly interested public" (ibid.: 46).

Such comments by the leaders of the conference present an absurd inversion: they argue that although musicians and their patrons have slumped into oblivion, at least a hungry and engaged music-loving public remains. In fact, Lucknow of 1925 was, as Qureshi has written, "India's acknowledged center [. . .] of feudal patronage for literature and music" (1999: 325–26; 2010: 223). Moreover, the primary purpose of the conference, as noted earlier, was to rally support for the establishment of a major institution in Lucknow with the raison d'être of rectifying the lack of awareness of and interest in music by the general public.

One more consideration remains: even if the founders of the college ascribed illiteracy and degeneracy to the greatest performing artists of their day, how could musicians such as Sakhawat Husain Khan (an author and a descendant of a manifestly literate musical lineage) possibly have been deemed less than respectable? It is not my intention to argue that Bali or Bhatkhande had Sakhawat Husain Khan in mind when they spoke of retrieving the knowledge of Hindustani music from its illiterate and illegitimate usurpers. Nor do I contend that Sakhawat Husain Khan felt threatened by such statements—in his mind, they must have obviously been meant for someone else. Yet the theory of institutional communalism suggests that neither the reformists' intentions nor the ustād-s' interpretations determine the material consequences of an ideology built into the structure of a network of institutions. The world was changing before Sakhawat Husain Khan's eyes. As we will see, he believed strongly in Bhatkhande's vision, and Bhatkhande likely respected him in turn, yet the college could not but undermine the power and prestige of Hindustani music's hereditary lines of Muslim performing artists.

A National Academy of Music?

The college established by Bhatkhande and Bali in Lucknow in 1926 rapidly became the leading music institution in the country. For instance, in a 1934 article in the *Calcutta Review*, author Dhurjati Prasad Mukherji (famed professor of sociology at Lucknow University introduced in Chapter 3) notes that "the taste for classical music is spreading among our people," and thus "young men and women are eager for *ustads*" (1934: 63). Mukherji further specifies that when "such [ustād-s] are not available in Bengal," students "knock at the gates of the Marris College of *Hindusthani* Music at Lucknow" (ibid.). Much of the practical work of raising the profile of the college was accomplished by Bhatkhande's prestigious disciple, Shrikrishna Narayan Ratanjankar. Ratanjankar served as principal of the college from 1928 to 1957; in the last year of his service, he was awarded one of India's highest civilian honors—the Padma Bhushan. He is also widely celebrated as a master performer, having learned from one of the most renowned vocalists of the twentieth century, Faiyaz Khan (Mutatkar 2001: ix).[10] Under the directorship of S. N. Ratanjankar, by the 1950s the college had grown to an institution not only of national repute, but of political significance. Moreover, the success of the college coincided with the reopening of the proposal to establish a national academy of music, now under the auspices of the central government of independent India.

On October 15, 1950, a large conference was held in New Delhi for the purposes of establishing the constitution of the National Academy of Hindustani Music; it was attended by representatives of the national government and many state governments, and by individual musicians and musicologists as well. For reasons both financial and political, the academy was never established, but the large files of documents and correspondences on the academy housed at the National Archive in New Delhi—files as yet unexplored in the literature—reveal important insights into the state of Hindustani music education at midcentury, and the preeminence of the Bhatkhande Music College in Lucknow.[11] For instance, many state governments refused to participate in the development of the national academy, explicitly stating that Hindustani music was not offered at their flagship colleges and universities, and that they therefore could not send a representative to the General Council. Among these were Hyderabad, Orissa, and Gujarat. In addition to state governments, representatives of specific universities also responded to the invitation of the central government to join the coalition to create the national academy. Representatives of Calcutta University, University of Bombay, Gauhati University, Muslim University of Aligarh, and University of Delhi all responded that Hindustani music education was not offered at their institutions.

It is clear that by 1950, Hindustani music was scarcely embraced within the academic institutions of the country. By contrast, Lucknow held an unrivaled position as the historical cultural center for Hindustani music and the most prestigious center for music education at the time. Throughout the collected documents relating to the establishment of the National Academy of Hindustani Music, Lucknow is repeatedly invoked as the long-standing musical capital of India, and as the location of choice for the establishment of the national academy. For instance, at the October 15 meeting in 1950, the chairman of the conference, Dr. Tara Chand, explicitly instructed the committee that "the Government of India had already decided to establish the headquarters of the

Academy at Lucknow and recognise the Marris College as the first constituent college of the Academy."

The Marris College in Lucknow was not chosen merely by default, however. Several other institutions and state governments vied for the honor, responding to the initial proposal with enthusiasm for the establishment of a national academy, along with reminders of their own important contributions to the cause of Hindustani music education. The influential musicologist B. R. Deodhar, for instance, wrote to the minister of education of the central government in a letter dated October 31, 1950, arguing for greater recognition of V. D. Paluskar's competing model for Hindustani music education. Deodhar states that "the graduates of the Gandharva Maha Vidyalay Mandal are recognized as equivalent to the graduates of the Marris College of Music, Lucknow, in all parts of the country." We should not underestimate the significance of the phrase *equivalent to*, suggesting as it does that there was no question of claiming superior status to that of the college in Lucknow. Another well-known music teacher and performer, Omkarnath Thakur, principal of the College of Music and Fine Arts at Banaras Hindu University, wrote also to the minister of education in a letter dated November 15, 1950, arguing for the primacy of his own institution. Similarly, an impressive rejoinder came from Shri P. C. Gupta, deputy secretary to the government of Madhya Bharat, Gwalior. In a letter dated January 9, 1951, Gupta presents an extensive history of music and musicians in Madhya Bharat (later Madhya Pradesh) together with a request that his state government be given, for this reason, greater representation on the General Council of the academy. Significantly, among these most vociferous claimants, only Omkarnath Thakur directly states that the academy should be established in a location other than Lucknow, and even he tempers his position by acknowledging that "the choice of the Marris College of Music (Bhatkhande University)" is "quite understandable because of the long standing of the institution."

And yet the Bhatkhande College had been in existence for only twenty-four years by 1950, while Paluskar's competing Gandharva Mahavidyalaya system had been established for forty-nine years by that time. Thus, beyond "the long standing" of Bhatkhande's college, the discussion of the establishment of a national academy emphasizes once again the musical and cultural primacy of Lucknow itself. In 1952, when plans to establish the academy were crumbling, Sri Krishan Chand, additional secretary to the government of Uttar Pradesh, wrote several letters to the Ministry of Education of the Government of India, in which he reasserted that throughout the campaign to establish the academy, "there was no question of having the headquarters anywhere except at Lucknow," owing to "the long standing and pre-eminent position which Lucknow occupies in the world of music" (August 18, 1952). Though the national academy was never established, the reputation of Bhatkhande's college continued to grow. In 1952, the president of the managing committee of the Marris College of Hindustani Music wrote, "It is no exaggeration to say that the lead the Marris College has given in the revival of Hindustani music has been followed heartily throughout the Northern India and the Marris College is looked upon today as a centre of musical culture for guidance" (Singh 1952: 2).

The Ustād

From the 1920s to the 1950s, one of the college's most prestigious instructors was Sakhawat Husain Khan. In his own writings, Sakhawat Husain Khan acknowledges that his role as professor at the college reflects the long-standing relationship between his gharānā elders and Bhatkhande himself. We do not know the nature or extent of this relationship in great detail, but as we will see in Chapter 5, both Karamatullah and Kaukab Khan were engaged in the discussion of Bhatkhande's ideas and met with him in person on at least two documented occasions. Further, Sakhawat Husain Khan's own sons would follow in his footsteps as professors at the college, one of them serving from 1955 (when Sakhawat Husain himself passed away) until 1982. In this section I discuss Sakhawat Husain Khan's understanding of the relationships between the national cause, the college, and his own lineage, as documented in his handwritten memoirs, as well as in writings published by the college. These writings reveal that Sakhawat Husain Khan embraced the reformist vision of a modernized Hindustani tradition, and participated in it fully as an educator and author while also championing his own lineage and extolling its ongoing vibrancy. Was there no contradiction for him?

Looking closely at Sakhawat Husain Khan's handwritten memoirs, one finds that the notebook is divided roughly in half: the first half contains his own handwritten Urdu; the second includes brief passages and numerous musical compositions in Devanāgarī script, written apparently by his student, Devrani Chatterjee. The last section of text written by Sakhawat Husain Khan serves to frame a series of compositions in Urdu musical notation. Here, Sakhawat Husain Khan provides an unusually evocative and novelistic narrative of the sights, sounds, and smells of India during the rainy season and suggests a direct connection between the rāga tradition and the very soul of the Indian people. He begins this remarkably populist endeavor by painting a portrait of

a hamlet of very poor farmers who work hard all day in the fields along with their bullocks, slaking their hunger with raw seeds of millet, and washing them down with gulps of sugar-sweetened water. Eating the poorest of food, they give thanks to *Bhagwān* [a Sanskrit word for the Divine], lie down on coarse beds, and drift off into a sound and sweet sleep. Today, in these farmers' little huts, the songs of *Sāwan* [the fifth month of the Hindu lunar calendar, associated with the arrival of the annual monsoon] can be heard; the poor girls of this village make a swing on the branch of a banyan tree, singing as they swing. A poor farmer sits beneath a tree puffing on his hookah. Looking over his small fields of rice, corn, and millet (*dhān, makka, jawār, bājre*) he feels peace in his heart, and hearing the *Sāwan* songs of the nearby girls he is transported into a world of spiritual joy (*wajdānī kaifiyat mahsūs karnā*). He offers silent praise to the ancestors who have composed these songs. (Khan n.d.: n.p.)

From the picturesque village, Sakhawat Husain Khan conducts his readers to the city, where he reveals that cultivated scholars and musicians also revel in *Sāwan* melodies, taking us right into the concert hall of the Bhatkhande College and leading us through a series of performances by various master musicians who unite the music, the audience, and the rain as one through their mastery of monsoon rāga-s, especially emphasizing Mirabai's *Malhār*, a rāga ascribed to the widely revered sixteenth-century poet-saint. Walking back from the concert hall, Sakhawat Husain Khan directs our attention to "the sounds of song and music coming from an apartment up above," and then leads us upstairs to a meeting with "Muhammad Umar Khan, the elder son of Professor Sakhawat Husain Khan," who is playing a beautiful rendition of the monsoon rāga *Miyāṅ kī Malhār* on sarod. "After him, his younger brother Muhammad Ilyas Khan played the *ālāp* of [another monsoon rāga] *Gauḍ Malhār* first and then a *gat* of *Gauḍ Malhār* with such beauty that the gathering resounded with cries of '*wāh-wāh*'; the rise and fall of the *tān*-s [melodic runs], the twists and turns, created a wonderful feeling. This too ended and we all returned to our homes" (Khan n.d.: n.p.). At each point of arrival in his narrative, Sakhawat Husain Khan includes notated musical compositions, thus supplying an imaginary context for each piece, and writing his own sons into his fictive musical travelogue of India in the rainy season.

Through this narrative, Sakhawat Husain Khan implies a Nehruvian conception of essential unity, a nationalist vision that unites town and country—poor and elite—in musical continuity. Indeed, in his memoirs Sakhawat Husain celebrates his acquaintance with Nehru himself. For instance, upon returning to India in 1938 after several years touring with Madame Menaka, the troupe arrived in Bombay, where they were welcomed by Congress Party leader Jawaharlal Nehru. Sakhawat Husain recalls that, as the leader of the show, he was privileged to personally garland Nehru and other political figures such as the mayor of Bombay. Sakhawat Husain Khan further notes that after his own sarod solo, "the Prime Minister came onto the stage himself, garlanded me, and said that he was very happy that I had been able to display my art and skill around the world, bringing fame and glory to India" (Khan n.d.: n.p.). Emphasizing the parallel relationship between his own lineage and that of the first family of nationalist leaders, Sakhawat Husain Khan offers high praise for Motilal Nehru, Jawaharlal's father, who patronized Karamatullah and Kaukab Khan and sponsored their visit to the exhibition in Paris in 1900 (discussed further in Chapter 5) (ibid.).

Returning for a moment to Sakhawat Husain's fictive monsoon travelogue, we should not overlook the significance of his choice to invite his readers into the concert hall of the college established by V. N. Bhatkhande. Indeed, among all his exploits, Sakhawat Husain Khan appears proudest of his long-standing service to the Marris College, writing that his position at the college has allowed him to pass his musical gifts to "the mothers, sisters and brothers of my land," while emphasizing the point that "at this time there is no one who is able to play this instrument like my family or the students of my household" (Khan n.d.: n.p.). This last statement folds the students of the college—"the mothers, sisters and brothers of my land"—into his own lineage, suggesting a pivotal role for the Lucknow gharānā in the story of the nation; amplifying this point, he proclaims, "As long as I am given life, I shall continue to serve in this manner, and my two sons, Muhammad Ilyas and Muhammad Umar, shall do so after me" (ibid.). Sakhawat Husain Khan embraces the notion that his own family's role in propagating the heritage of the nation would scarcely be possible without the institutional structure of the Marris College. Sakhawat Husain Khan thus saves his most glowing words of praise for V. N. Bhatkhande himself, writing,

I had the opportunity to meet Panditji at music conferences in Delhi, Banaras, and Lucknow. He came across as extremely good-natured and well mannered, and conversed with great affection; while listening to him, one wanted only that he go on speaking. He had a close association with the elders of my family, and he used to love me very much; because of this, upon opening his college, he summoned me and installed me as a servant at the college, where he would listen to my sarod with extreme interest and love; he used to give me blessings. Today, since his passing, we are all extremely sad and sorrowful. Fine, it is the will of God. (Khan 1976 [1952]: 34)

The Singing Camera

In particular, Sakhawat Husain Khan focuses his praise on Bhatkhande's system of musical notation, a revolutionary and now-ubiquitous contribution to the history of Indian music. The 1976 *Golden Jubilee Souvenir* publication of the Bhatkhande College, celebrating the fiftieth anniversary of the founding of the institution, includes the reprinting of an essay by Sakhawat Husain Khan in which he addresses this aspect of Bhatkhande's career. The essay, a transliteration and partial translation into Hindi of a handwritten section of Sakhawat Husain Khan's Urdu journal writings, is titled "The Singing Camera: Notation."[12] Sakhawat Husain Khan begins his essay by stating that the principal of the college, S. N. Ratanjankar, had asked him to contribute a piece of writing on Bhatkhande to mark the anniversary of the establishment of the college, thus suggesting an original date of 1952, in which year the college celebrated its twenty-fifth anniversary.[13]

Sakhawat Husain Khan begins by characterizing Bhatkhande as a great savior of Hindustani music, supporting the notion that before his epochal intervention, music had been on the verge of extinction. In this regard, Sakhawat Husain Khan describes Bhatkhande as "a music lover of the highest order," who was "obsessed by the idea that a method should be born through which this music, which enchants and intoxicates the hearts of India, and which the hands of time have begun to gradually erase, should in some way or another be saved" (1976 [1952]: 34). Comparing Bhatkhande's quest to that of a mystic in pursuit of union with God, Sakhawat Husain Khan presents Bhatkhande's system of melodic notation as a revelation of sorts. As he writes,

> After sacrificing the most valuable years of his life in this very quest, relying on his intelligence and perseverance, he ultimately discovered a new method. Just as a spiritual seeker through his own practice and effort attains God, Panditji,

through his hard work and striving, ultimately discovered this method, and wherever in India the experts of the art of music existed, with great respect he presented to them his idea, hearing which, every just-minded person was appreciative. That method, which renders a very complex thing easy, and which creates an exact picture of every movement of the throat, is like a camera invented by Panditji, for which he is worthy of congratulations. And the name of this camera is the "singing camera," meaning notation. (Khan 1976 [1952]: 34)

Here, Sakhawat Husain Khan compares Bhatkhande's transcription method to a camera capable of creating "an exact picture of every movement of the throat." Yet by midcentury, when he composed his essay, sound recording technology had been available in India for some fifty years. Why would a professional musician such as Sakhawat Husain Khan continue to extol the outmoded and incomplete method of textual notation when musical sound could be captured directly on disc? Sakhawat Husain Khan's use of the metaphor of a singing camera helps to answer this question: in his essay, Sakhawat Husain Khan specifically praises Bhatkhande's method as a form of visual representation, a method that allows the student to *see* the musical details of important compositions and styles. For Dard Neuman, the visual conception of rāga practice reflects the "modernist ethic of perfection and efficiency" of the musicologist (2012: 437), as against the "body knowledge" cultivated by hereditary musicians (ibid.: 440). In this regard, Sakhawat Husain Khan's praise for Bhatkhande's system of musical notation further aligns the ustād with the reform movement and its modernizing agenda. Indeed, Sakhawat Husain Khan—a preeminent beneficiary of the "body knowledge" developed through hereditary discipleship—is inspired, not threatened, by such new approaches to musical pedagogy.

In the next section of his essay, Sakhawat Husain Khan enlarges on this point, arguing that "the experts of the art" appreciated Bhatkhande's new method of musical transcription. As he writes,

When this method reached its final stage, [Bhatkhande] had the honor of the experts of the art—those who were the very best performers of their era—becoming his disciples. And with this singing camera he took pictures of their singing and of their ancient compositions and he put over these a "light shade" of pleasing color; thus, we all received in our hands something like an album whose every photo and their embellishments are so clear and bright that every sound-minded lover of music even today obtains the pleasure and enjoyment they offer. In those pictures are captured what was available in the ancient singers and players, thus those pictures do not represent the face of any human or animal, but rather they represent the delicate and fine rays that—born in the heart and mind—became manifest in the throat, though the individuals who originally manifested them no longer exist in the world today. But because of Panditji's mental effort—which produced the singing camera—snapshots of the ancient styles of singing and their compositions are echoing in our eyes and ears today. When any one of his pictures is presented before us, spontaneously from our hearts emerges the sound of blessings for the invention of Panditji's singing camera. May God grant a place in heaven to Panditji. (Khan 1976 [1952]: 34–35)

Written for publication by the college itself, this essay may reflect a degree of uncritical veneration of the beloved founder. But Sakhawat Husain Khan surely chose the topic himself, thus thwarting latter-day interpretations of notation as necessarily counterposed to hereditary musical knowledge. Dard Neuman, for instance, argues that "while musicology enabled a wider audience to take pleasure in this tradition[,] it did so through a medium that also served as a mode of inspection and humiliation. Theory was deployed as both a mode to mock the ustad's pride in his musical authority and a means to appropriate that authority" (2004: 123–24). Dard Neuman is surely correct that the methods of "musicology" offended some hereditary ustād-s. For example, Qureshi introduces the sāraṅgī player Yaqub Husain Khan, who tells a fascinating story of several hereditary musicians hired as instructors in the early years of Bhatkhande's college. According to Yaqub Husain Khan, they summarily resigned from their positions when they learned that their musical heritage would be transcribed—captured in notation—and spread liberally to "outsiders"—that is, students unconnected to their family traditions (Qureshi 2007: 195).

And yet Sakhawat Husain Khan (along with his gharānā predecessors, as we will see in Chapter 5) thwarts the assumption of a binary opposition between hereditary musicians and modern music theory, suggesting instead a potential partnership between Bhatkhande's reformist program and hereditary musicians such as himself. He argues for the vital role of Bhatkhande's singing camera in propagating the heritage of hereditary musicians, however, he does not suggest an awareness of the threat to those very musicians posed by Bhatkhande's larger Hindu-centric program of music reform. We do not know whether Sakhawat Husain Khan consciously sought to reconcile his own gharānā priorities with those of Bhatkhande, or if he was simply resigned to the new national context, but his writings clearly reflect his great admiration for the Muslim contributions to music history, while also supporting and celebrating the role played by Bhatkhande in shaping a new musical modernity. As he writes,

> When the sun of music, Ustād Faiyaz Khan Saheb, was alive the opportunity to hear the singing style of the gharānā of the folks of Agra used to be available. Today, since he has passed away, if we want to know the method of that gharānā, we will have to listen to those records or those disciples who are still available. As for those who have neither record nor disciple, how should we assess their gharānā's style? For them we will have to take up our Panditji's singing camera, and in the album of pictures, among the pictures of every house we will find a few—which through extreme dedication and hard work Panditji prepared through his singing camera, and which are of such use to us today—and from them we can comprehend that this was the method of such and such a gharānā. This was their singing. This was the good work done by [Bhatkhande], and as long as the world remains, none of us music experts will ever forget his benevolence. (Khan 1976 [1952]: 35)[14]

The Congress and the College

As documented in his essay "The Singing Camera" and in his private memoirs, Sakhawat Husain Khan was a devoted servant to Bhatkhande's vision, teaching hundreds of students as a professor at the college from 1927 until he passed away at age eighty in 1955. In this same year, both of Sakhawat Husain Khan's sons—Ilyas and Umar Khan—took up positions as instructors at the college. Following in his father's footsteps, Ilyas Khan remained on the teaching staff for over twenty years, retiring in 1982 and thereafter continuing his service intermittently until his death in 1989. Umar Khan, however, resigned his position shortly after his father's passing. As Umar Khan explained to ethnomusicologist James Kippen in a 1981 interview, the great musicians of Lucknow were not sufficiently patronized and respected by the Bhatkhande College. To support this point, Umar Khan invokes the khalīfā of the Lucknow tablā gharānā, Afaq Husain Khan (1930–1990), arguing that he was unable to obtain a position at the college, owing to the control of the institution by state-level politicians who stacked the roles with instructors from Banaras, a city 300 kilometers southeast of Lucknow famous as a Hindu pilgrimage site. In particular, Umar Khan names Uttar Pradesh chief minister Sampurnanand, stating that "he brought all the Banarasi musicians" into the college staff (interview by James Kippen, August 11, 1981). Finding the political atmosphere of the college untenable, Umar Khan resigned his post after only a short service.

Who was Sampurnanand, and why does Umar Khan name him specifically? Is it possible that we may learn something about the experience of Muslim teachers at the college through a study of Sampurnanand's career? A representative of the city of Banaras, Sampurnanand was a powerful figure in the Congress Party of Uttar Pradesh from the 1930s through the 1950s; he was active in the anticolonial struggle and also in the government of independent India. Significantly, he was a staunch secularist and socialist from the left wing of the Congress Party. Yet historian William Gould focuses on Sampurnanand as a primary example of the high-profile combination of avowedly secular politics with elements of Hindu communalism (2004: 166). In the twentieth century, Uttar Pradesh became "the crucible of the Congress movement," itself the dominant nationalist institution in the anticolonial struggle. Though the Congress claimed to represent all Indians irrespective of caste, class, or religion, Gould shows through his focus on Congress politicians in Uttar Pradesh that elements of Hindu nationalism pervaded its ostensibly secular vision, and that "by the 1930s at least, the working out of communal relations in Uttar Pradesh had a huge impact on other parts of the subcontinent" (ibid.: 2–3). Standing at the heart of Uttar Pradesh, the Bhatkhande College was thus established in the midst of a vital struggle over the nature of Indian nationalism as defined by the Congress and as embodied by Congressman Sampurnanand. Serving first as education minister in Uttar Pradesh, and subsequently as chief minister of the state from 1954 to 1960 (ibid.: 169, 180), Sampurnanand "persistently championed the causes of Hindi versus Urdu, Hindu social reform, Hindu cultural revivalism and Congress socialism" (ibid.). Indeed, Sampurnanand's "political and religious works were inextricably linked, drawing upon Hegel, Marx and the Arya Samaj" (ibid.: 170). Sampurnanand's philosophical stance insisted that India's rational, scientific, and secular socialism was itself a result of ancient Hindu tradition; he was thus "able to maintain direct contact with Hindu communal organisations in the belief that a rejuvenated Hindu society could have radical political implications" while entirely overlooking the possibility that Muslims may have been alienated by such a conflation of socialism with Hindu nationalism (ibid.: 173). In this regard, the career of Sampurnanand presents the opportunity to explore the question of intention versus consequence. One may argue that by appointing his own constituents to posts at the Bhatkhande College, Sampurnanand was merely playing to his voter base in his home city of Banaras. In this interpretation, the Hindu identity of those musicians may not have constituted the primary reason for their appointment. But does that mean their appointment was not read as communally motivated by musicians such as Umar Khan?

The discussion thus returns to a consideration of an institutional communalism that does not depend on outward anti-Muslim animus. Adapting a well-worn formulation, this analysis shifts the site of inquiry from communalism "with a snarl" to communalism "with a smile," highlighting an ideology with laudable goals (the defeat of British colonialism) that was nevertheless built on a foundation of Hindu-centrism that devalued the contribution of Muslims to Indian history, culture, and society. Gould's work demonstrates that such institutional communalism was not isolated in schools such as the Bhatkhande College, but suffused a broad spectrum of nationalist politics and institutions. In this regard, Gould's statement about Sampurnanand might apply equally well to Bhatkhande: though he was "conscious of the 'Hindu' orientation of his ideas about the nation, its culture and religious traditions," he was "relatively unaware of the communal consequences" such an orientation produced (2004: 175). As I have noted, my concern in this chapter is to illuminate the consequences rather than to demonize the orientation.

One of the ways we see this institutional communalism in action at the college is through its attempt to promote a unified vision of Indian music. For instance, one of S. N. Ratanjankar's goals for the college in the years after Bhatkhande's death was to cultivate a "national integration," thus proving "the underlying unity of Indian music" (Mutatkar 2001: 27). Predictably, his method of doing so relied on an assumption of Hindu religious universality: as Ratanjankar's student Sumati Mutatkar recalls, the college organized "special musical activities" for Hindu holidays such as Janamasthami, the birth of Lord Krishna, wherein students from the various regions of India[15] would sing "songs relating to Krishna" in such languages as "Punjabi, Sindhi, Marathi, Bengali, Gujarati, Telugu, Sanskrit, Malayalam and Assamese" and then "explain the theme in Hindi or English" (ibid.). Such programs drew not only community members, but also important politicians, including "Govind Ballabh Pant and his family, A. G. Kher, Dr. B. V. Keskar, Kamladevi Chattopadhyaya, Harindranath and others. The Uttar Pradesh Chief Minister, Dr. Sampurnanand, usually managed to be present in the early hours of the last day" (ibid.: 28). As noted in the opening of this chapter, events such as the college's twenty-fifth anniversary celebration included the participation of President Rajendra Prasad, Uttar Pradesh chief minister G. B. Pant, and Uttar Pradesh governor K. M. Munshi.

The Disappearing Muslims

Beyond the manifest connections between the college and the broader Hindu-centric nationalist ideology of the Congress Party, what evidence suggests the presence of institutional communalism at Bhatkhande's flagship school? Answering this question requires a return to the earliest days of the college. When it opened its doors in July of 1926, the college employed seven instructors, and served only thirteen students (Bali 1926b, 1940). By the second semester of its first year of operation, the student population of the college had increased more than tenfold, from the initial 13 to 134. Though the global depression of the 1930s brought a reduced enrollment, the college continued to attract large numbers of students. In a College Progress Report of 1931, for instance, Rai Umanath Bali, honorary secretary of the college, documents 121 enrolled students for the year. Of these, Bali estimates that 50 were "bound to take up music as profession; for they are doing no other work and are devoting the whole of their time in the study of the subject" (ca. 1931: 107). By December of 1939, there were thirty-one instructors, and as many as 622 students (Bali 1940: 9). By this time, 236 students had finished a three-year course and passed their "Intermediate in Music" exam, 83 had finished an additional two-year course and passed their *Saṅgīt Vishārad*, or bachelor of music, and more than 125 were employed at various music "institutions and film studios" around the country (ibid.: 2). By August of 1940, the college was attended by 708 enrolled students, a cohort made up of individuals from Punjab, the United Provinces, Bihar, Orissa, Assam, Madras, Bombay, Sindh, Bengal, Delhi, "Indian States" (meaning those still ruled by native royalty), and Ceylon (Bali 1941: 2). We do not have data on the backgrounds of all of these students, but the College Progress Report covering the period from August 1926 to December 1939 includes a section titled "Statements about the activities of passed Students" containing a list of 74 students who had already graduated (Bali 1940: 6–8). Of these 74, only three Muslim names are to be found.

Although the proportion of Muslim students was minuscule, from its very inception the college relied heavily on Muslim teachers. When classes began in 1926, three of the college's seven teachers were Muslim hereditary professional musicians: vocalists Murad Khan and Munne Khan, and tablā player

Abid Husain (Bali 1926b), a legendary patriarch of the Lucknow tablā gharānā.[16] The remaining teachers included M. K. Joshi (the college's first principal), S. N. Ratanjankar, G. N. Natu, and V. N. Bhatkhande himself (ibid.). By January of 1927, there were still only seven teachers on the college payroll, but both Bhatkhande and Murad Khan were no longer listed, having been replaced by two more Muslim musicians: vocalist Ahmad Khan (1887–1964) and Bagar Ali, the latter described by Bali in a handwritten note as "a local sarangi player with the good knowledge of the art" (1927). In her text on the renowned teachers in the early years of the college, Misra cites a letter written by Bhatkhande to Bali on February 28, 1927, in which Bhatkhande notes that the other newly hired teacher, Ahmad Khan, "belongs to a Dhrupad gharana and may turn out to be a good teacher. He is a willing hand, and energetic too" (quoted in Misra 1985: 37).

In July 1927, the college acquired as an instructor yet another Muslim hereditary musician, the famed Lucknow gharānā sarod player Sakhawat Husain Khan (Bali 1928: 69). As already discussed, the musicians of the Lucknow gharānā were deeply intertwined with Bhatkhande's new institutional structure for much of the twentieth century, yet they were far from the only high-profile Muslim hereditary artists who labored on behalf of the college. In August of 1931, the college hired its first sitar teacher, the well-known Muslim hereditary musician Hamid Husain (Bali 1941: 20), whose book *Aslī Tālīm Sitār (Authentic Sitar Training)* was a required text at the college (ibid.: 7; see also Misra 1985: 42–43; Miner 1997 [1993]: 143). In August of 1933, the college hired another Muslim musician, Mahmud Ali (Bali 1941: 20), a sārangī player described by Misra as "a regular and sincere teacher who worked inconspicuously throughout his long tenure on the staff" (1985: 39). In August of 1935, the college hired Muslim vocalist Mohammad Usman, once a student of the college. Though born into a musical family, Usman had initially joined the college as a student in order to learn from the vocalist Nasir Khan, "one of the famous representatives of the Tanras Khan gharānā of Delhi" (ibid.) who taught at the college briefly in the early 1930s (Bali 1931: 104).

By the end of the academic year in 1941, the teaching staff had grown to thirty-five, yet the only Muslims among them were the four just discussed — Hamid Husain (sitar), Sakhawat Husain Khan (sarod), Mahmud Ali (sārangī), and Mohammad Usman (vocalist) — along with Abdul Rahman, a vocal teacher hired in August of 1940 (Bali 1941: 20). Thus in hardly four years, we see a radical shift in the ratio of Muslim to Hindu teachers. By the time of Ilyas Khan's retirement some forty years later in 1982, the college had trained hundreds of musicians and teachers, many of whom became instructors at the college itself.[17] Indeed, by 1986, sixty years after its founding, the college employed a staff of sixty-seven teachers and accompanists. Among these were four Muslims, including two teachers (sitarist Tajammul Khan and tablā player Ahmad Miyāṅ) and two sāraṅgī accompanists (Yaqub Husain Khan and Muhammad Khan). Today the college boasts a total of one hundred seventy-five faculty and staff, with only one or two Muslims among them. The enrollment has swollen to over thirteen hundred students, including only a small handful of Muslims. The college's department of sitar and sarod—founded and cultivated by such master musicians of Lucknow as Sakhawat Husain Khan, Hamid Husain, and Ilyas Khan—today features four sitar teachers and one sarod teacher, all Hindus, all hailing from middle-class families, and none from a family of musicians.

The Lucknow gharānā, by contrast, has very nearly ceased to exist, and one can scarcely find a single hereditary sitar or sarod player of consequence in the city today. Despite its dependence on Muslim teachers from the moment of its founding, the college never sought to protect its prized instructors as privileged culture bearers, or to preserve their family-based traditions as national cultural monuments. The marginalization of Muslim hereditary musicians and the ennobling of middle-class Hindus, I argue, was a nearly inevitable consequence of the ideological basis on which the college was founded, and thus should not be ascribed to the bias or prejudice of any specific individual. Indeed, the college was born in the context of a heated struggle for national independence from British colonialism, and operated in tandem with a great many institutions of civil society to project a new form of identity for the colonized subjects of British India. Unfortunately, the newly crafted image of Indian subjectivity required the effacement of elements of the colonial society that appeared archaic, outmoded, or premodern, including the dominant class of hereditary—predominantly Muslim—musicians.

––––––

The notion that the Hindustani tradition has historically included both Hindus and Muslims is surely important, yet overemphasis on this point leads to an excessively rosy view of Hindustani music culture in the twentieth and twenty-first centuries. Likewise, the study of religious riots and anti-Muslim pogroms in Indian history serves vital purposes, yet a focus on communalism as defined solely by direct violence and personal prejudice threatens to elide the persistent presence of institutional or structural forms of discrimination and oppression. In this chapter I have endeavored to bring both of these points of view together, arguing for increased attention to the ideological work accomplished by the institution and its connections to the broader nationalist movement.

I have argued that there was an identifiable anti-Muslim dimension to the re-form movement, yet musicians' identities were (and are) complex, and thus we cannot assume that professional musicians (who were predominately Muslim) were sidelined primarily because they were Muslim. Moreover, the principal architects and administrators of Bhatkhande's college did not explicitly deni-grate Muslims qua Muslims. Instead, they made statements against "illiterates," and thus replicated criticisms of professional performing artists that date back to seventeenth-century Mughal texts (discussed further in Chapter 5). Yet this chapter has argued for the power of ideology to marginalize Muslims even in the absence of explicit statements of religious bigotry.

What then may serve as evidence of an anti-Muslim ideology at work? Like institutional racism, institutional communalism is exceedingly difficult to iden-tify and critique, precisely because it does not rely on outward bigotry. This being the case, my analysis is certainly open to the criticism that it does not present direct proof of an anti-Muslim agenda within the college. The same argument could be made of mainstream nationalist politics of the time: the Congress Party did not propound an explicitly anti-Muslim agenda. However, if it is possible that an ostensibly secular political movement contributed to the alienation of Muslims and thus ultimately to partition and the creation of Paki-stan, then there is reason to consider that an unspoken or even unintentional ideological preference for a Hindu-centered national culture produced ma-terial effects that marginalized Muslim musicians from the newly constructed Indian public sphere. At the Bhatkhande Music Institute University today, the Lucknow gharānā is entirely unrepresented, and as we have seen, the lineage is fading fast. As the gharānā disappears, so too do its collective memories, along with the critiques and counternarratives they contain. Was there an alternative to the nationalist musical modernity realized in the Bhatkhande College? As I explore in the next chapter, there certainly was: in the early decades of the twen-tieth century, when the soul of the nation and its music remained precariously undefined, the brothers Karamatullah and Kaukab Khan offered a template for music's modernity that married gharānā traditions to nationalist pride, em-bracing a vision of broad inclusion, while retaining an emphasis on the Muslim contributions at the heart of the Hindustani tradition.

FIVE

Voices and Visions
from the Archive

For six days in March of 1916, musicians, politicians, scholars, princes, and the general public gathered in Baroda for the first All-India Music Conference. The mastermind of the conference, V. N. Bhatkhande, offered a speech on the opening day that framed the collective endeavor: it was time to both revive and modernize the ancient art of Indian music through a judicious combination of Sanskritic textual authority and modern scientific inquiry. The conference featured moments of conflict, controversy, and contention, yet one underlying assumption remained nearly unquestioned: the music itself—"our ancient music"—originated in Hindu antiquity. A lone voice contradicted this view. On the second day of the conference, the renowned Urdu novelist, essayist, poet, historian, and translator Abdul Halim Sharar (1860–1926) offered a paper titled "The Persian Influence on the Music of Hindustan" (Report 1917: 18; see also Bakhle 2005: 192–93; Naqvi 2010: 15–18). In his Urdu essay, which was read aloud in English translation by a professor of the local college, Sharar argued for the hybrid origins of Hindustani music, and for the relevance of musicological works of extra-Indian origin. Yet Sharar was neither a musician nor a music scholar. How did he come to his radical ideas regarding the history of North Indian music?

Sharar's most enduringly influential writings concern the history of Lucknow, his beloved birthplace and home throughout his career. As I have noted, the English translation of Sharar's collected essays on Lucknow, first published in 1975 as *The Last Phase of an Oriental Culture*, remains among the most commonly cited sources on the colorful details of the royal city prior to its collapse in the wake of the 1857 uprising. Significantly, Sharar's knowledge of the musical history of Lucknow was obtained largely from his correspondence with "an expert and a noted professor of music," none other than "Asad ullah Khan Kaukab" (Sharar 2001 [1975]: 135). I cannot prove that the writings of Kaukab Khan (1915), or those of his brother Karamatullah Khan (1908), supplied Sharar with the radical premise he publicly promulgated before the conference attendees in Baroda. Yet when we turn to the writings of the brothers Khan—eminent representatives of the lineage known today as the Lucknow gharānā—we find two unprecedented examples of scholarly works by professional musicians that argue explicitly for the Muslim contributions to Hindustani music history.

This chapter focuses on the writings of Karamatullah Khan (1848–1933) and Asadullah "Kaukab" Khan (ca. 1850–1915), pictured together in Figure 11. The brothers were leading sarod players of the early twentieth century who established music schools, performed in Europe, trained large numbers of disciples, and served powerful patrons. Most significantly for present purposes, both brothers also authored treatises of music theory that reveal their own self-consciously modern orientation and document their participation in vital debates about the modernity of Hindustani music raging in the early decades of the twentieth century, while simultaneously drawing on a six-hundred-year legacy of Islamicate texts on Indian music. This chapter thus engages textual documents to reconstruct the historical experience and perspective of the Lucknow gharānā. However, in contrast to Diana Taylor's characterization of the archive as a "permanent and tangible resource of materials" (2003: 191), the texts by Karamatullah and Kaukab Khan discussed in this chapter have been virtually forgotten. Karamatullah Khan's book has been out of print for more than a century; it was never reprinted, edited, or translated, though it has been accessed and cited by a small number of historians of Indian music (McNeil 2004; Miner 1997 [1993]; Naqvi 2010; Tamori 2008; Trasoff 1999). Even more obscure, Kaukab Khan's book consists of an unfinished manuscript that was never published and has not been the subject of extensive investigation until now.[1]

As introduced in Chapter 1, the story of the Lucknow gharānā is tied to the story of the city of Lucknow itself. Following their migration from Afghanistan to India, Irfan Khan's rabāb-playing forbears ultimately arrived at the lavish court of Lucknow—capital of the kingdom of Awadh—where they encountered the orthodox kalāwant-s and participated in the proliferation of new musical forms and compositions for which the Lucknow court remains famous

today. With the ouster of the king in 1856, many court musicians relocated to Wajid Ali Shah's new court-in-exile. One of these was Basat Khan, along with his disciple Niamatullah Khan, Irfan and Idris Khan's great-great grandfather.

Prominent as a performing artist, Niamatullah Khan was also an author who began writing a manuscript he could not complete before his death. His eldest son, Karamatullah Khan, completed the text and published it in 1908 under the title *Isrār-e Karāmat urf Naghmāt-e Niamat*. The title itself evokes the relationship between father and son. Their given names—Niamatullah and Karamatullah—employ a common convention of Muslim naming whereby a significant noun is attached to the suffix "of God." For instance, the name Habibullah results from combining *habīb* (beloved) with *ullah* (of God) to form "Beloved of God." In the case of Karamatullah and Niamatullah, their names mean "excellence" (*karāmat*) of God, and "beneficence" (*niamat*) of God, respectively. To craft the title of his book, Karamatullah Khan employed the two basic names (Karamat and Niamat) and combined them with two other words: *isrār* and *naghmāt*, meaning "mysteries" and "melodies," respectively. The two parts of the title are separated by *urf*, meaning "otherwise known as." One translation of the title could thus be *The Mysteries of Excellence, Otherwise Known as the Melodies of Beneficence*. But understanding that Karamat and Niamat also refer to the names of the authors, the title could also be rendered as *The Mysteries of Karamat, Otherwise Known as the Melodies of Niamat*. Despite their equal invocation in the title, however, the book is written from the point of view of Karamatullah Khan (the son). We do not know which portions may have been completed by Niamatullah Khan himself; despite Karamatullah's statement that his father labored for thirty years in research and writing before his death, authorship is ascribed to Karamatullah Khan alone (Khan 1908: 2).

In the final lines of his book, Karamatullah Khan invokes his younger brother, Asadullah "Kaukab" Khan, proclaiming that both sons are the recipients of their father's knowledge, and that both have now completed their written works: Karamatullah Khan notes that Kaukab Khan's *Jauhar-e Mūsīqī*, "which is truly a gem of music, written with extreme diligence of research, will soon be published for the viewing of the general public" (1908: 278). Unfortunately, that book—*Gems of Music*—was never published. In *Lucknow: The Last Phase of an Oriental Culture*, Sharar specificaly laments, "It is sad that the professor is no longer in this world, otherwise I should have been able to get much more help from him especially as he wished to have his new book, an excellent exposition of musical science, printed by our press" (2001 [1975]): 135).[2] In his reference to the death of Kaukab Khan in the November 1915 issue of *Dil Gudāz*, Sharar specified that the *a'lā darje ke sāhib-e-'ilm ustād*—the "supremely knowledgeable ustād"—passed away only a few days prior, thus providing reliable evidence that Kaukab Khan died in 1915, and not in 1919 as has been previously understood (Sharar 1915: 261).[3] Kaukab's half-finished book is also dated 1915. Since that time, the sole draft of the incomplete manuscript has remained in the possession of his descendants and is the property of Irfan Khan today.

A Confluence of Discursive Flows

The texts of Karamatullah Khan and Kaukab Khan reflect the confluence of two major discursive flows. The first is the nationalist argument for music reform propagated from the mid-nineteenth century by English-educated, middle-class activists, especially in Maharashtra and Bengal. The second is the legacy of Indo-Persian literature on Hindustani music, a literary tradition originating with the writings of Amir Khusrau in thirteenth-century Delhi, which itself draws on multiple streams of knowledge: comprising texts in Persian and later

Urdu language, the Indo-Persian discourse on Indian music interprets the long-standing succession of Sanskrit music treatises while simultaneously accessing the practical knowledge of contemporary artists, all framed within a Greco-Arabic epistemology. The principal contribution of Karamatullah and Kaukab Khan lay in their ability to draw on the Indo-Persian tradition to both participate in and critique the nationalist effort to shape musical modernity in their own time.

As discussed in a number of recent works, the late nineteenth and early twentieth centuries saw a powerful and concerted effort to recast elite forms of Indian music and dance (in both north and south) as national classical traditions available to the burgeoning middle class (Allen 1997; Bakhle 2005; Kobayashi 2003; Peterson and Soneji 2008; Qureshi 1991; Soneji 2012; Subramanian 2006; Weidman 2007 [2006]). This reform movement sought most centrally to modernize the practice and pedagogy of the Indian performing arts, envisioning a musical modernity of rational, systematic music education grounded in public institutions. In the north, this effort was led by several key figures, including Sourindro Mohun Tagore, Maula Bakhsh, and Vishnu Digambar Paluskar, yet the dominant intellectual figure of the movement was Vishnu Narayan Bhatkhande (1860–1936), credited by Sanskrit scholar Emmie te Nijenhuis with starting "the renaissance of traditional Indian music" (Nijenhuis and Delvoye 2010: 35). Bhatkhande organized four All-India Music Conferences (1916–1925), developed a now-ubiquitous system for musical notation, transcribed and published volumes of compositions, collected and published dozens of rare Sanskrit manuscripts, consolidated and updated a system of typology for the panoply of North Indian rāga-s, and helped to establish a new paradigm of music education premised on a systematic syllabus that allowed public access to musical knowledge long held only by hereditary performing artists and their disciples.

In a radical historical intervention, Bhatkhande disproved the assertion of an unbroken continuity connecting contemporary Hindustani music practice with the ancient and medieval Sanskrit treatises. In his speech on the first day of the first All-India Music Conference in 1916, Bhatkhande cast doubt on the relevance of the *Nāṭyaśāstra* and the *Saṅgītaratnākara*—the most revered of Sanskrit treatises on music—stating that such texts have become "inapplicable to the current practice" (1974: 34). Some fourteen years later, after the establishment of his flagship institution in Lucknow, Bhatkhande published an article in the first issue of his college's own journal reasserting the obsolescence of music texts dating earlier than the fifteenth century, specifically describing the *Nātya-*

śāstra and the *Saṅgītaratnākara* as "perfectly unintelligible" and thus "outside the sphere of study of the ordinary music student" (1930: 13).[4]

However, despite his modernizing zeal, Bhatkhande insisted that the reform of Hindustani music required a return to the Sanskritic tradition, prescribing the study of eighteen Sanskrit texts from the fifteenth to the eighteenth centuries, and declaring that despite manifest changes to music's theory and practice since its origins in antiquity, "there is no such fundamental alteration in it as to make the modern music an essentially different thing" (1930: 8).[5] In this regard, all of Bhatkhande's contributions were predicated on his assumption that the Hindustani tradition was necessarily rooted in an ancient Hindu culture to which it rightfully belonged.

Bhatkhande imbibed and propagated a broad sense (especially within Maharashtra) that the art of Hindustani music had been misappropriated and sullied by Muslim musicians since the advent of Muslim rule in India. This view was spelled out as early as 1849 by social reformer Gopal Hari Deshmukh, who wrote that "Muslims got this knowledge [of music] from Hindu people and Hindu people have forgotten it," characterizing professional musicians as "stupid," as having "bad manners," and as "users of *bhāng* [cannabis]" (quoted in Rosse 2010: 313, brackets added; see also Rosse 1995: 65–66). Charles Capwell uncovers a similar attitude in Bengal motivating the work of early music reformist Kshetra Mohan Goswami (the chief instructor at S. M. Tagore's Bengal Music School), whose *Saṅgītasāra* (1869) argued that the "great intellectual tradition of Sanskrit learning in music died out with the usurpation of musical practice by Muslim ustads" (Capwell 2010: 297; see also Rosse 1995: 33–34).[6] Thus, despite Bhatkhande's acknowledgment that the only relevant Sanskrit treatises date from "the period when the country was under the influence of Mohammedan rulers" (1930: 9), the nationalist imperative to consolidate and enshrine the Hindustani tradition as a classical musical system necessarily threatened the centrality of its largely Muslim hereditary performing artists.

Yet the reform movement did not announce itself as a program to cleanse Muslims from the Hindustani tradition and thereby reinvent the music as a Hindu cultural practice. Instead, the movement was premised on a widely shared—though empirically incorrect—perception that the art music traditions of India were in a state of decline and required immediate intervention before they were lost entirely. As demonstrated by David Trasoff, the proceedings of Bhatkhande's own All-India Music Conferences document the participation of dozens of "artists who were or would be considered among the greatest and most influential of the late-nineteenth and twentieth centuries" (2010: 351). While there was clearly no shortage of master musicians, the leaders of the reform movement presented the case that those musicians were illegitimate and undeserving bearers of a national culture struggling to be free. For instance, on the first day of Bhatkhande's first All-India Music Conference, the president of the conference, Thakur Nawab Ali Khan, announced in his opening speech that "no one will deny that the Music of the country is at present in the hands of an ignorant and illiterate class and that it is essential to rescue it from the possibility of complete destruction and place it on a scientific basis" (Report 1917: 10). Yet if the target of Thakur Nawab Ali Khan's criticism was "an ignorant and illiterate class," and if the speaker himself was a Muslim, how then can the reform movement be interpreted as having posed a threat to Muslim musicians per se?[7]

The ethnomusicologist Justin Scarimbolo approaches this question through a fine-grained analysis of more than two hundred years of published statements about Muslim musicians in India. Against Bakhle (2005) and others who argue for a direct discursive connection between eighteenth-century colonial scholarship and the twentieth-century reform movement, Scarimbolo shows that colonial authors (for example, Augustus Willard) drew on both European and Indian discourses that positioned bearers of oral tradition — "professionals" or even "ustād-s" — as illiterate usurpers, yet did not necessarily imply that such musicians were Muslims (2014: 292–363; for a similar review of Bengali writings, see Williams 2014: 257–77). Indeed, Katherine Schofield positions Willard not as a colonial orientalist, but instead as the "last great Indo-Persian theorist of Indian music history" (2010: 509). Earlier colonial writers (such as William Jones) certainly blamed the alleged downfall of Hindu civilization on Muslim rulers, yet Jones also emphasized and celebrated the "syncretic Indo-Persian traditions" characteristic of Indian civilization (Scarimbolo 2014: 300) and, as Schofield has argued, "held up Muslim cultures [. . .] as the yardstick for European aesthetic theory" (2010: 505). It was only in the Indian reformist writings of the mid-nineteenth century that a consolidated narrative emerged that specified Muslim *musicians* as perpetrators of music's decline and, by extension, as obstacles to its modernity. Encapsulating the narrative, Scarimbolo writes,

> Improper patronage by Muslim rulers caused music's theory to become separated from its practice; the practice of music then became dominated by Muslims, many of whom were previously Hindus either forced, tricked or encouraged to convert to Islam; Hindu musicians declined in number either because

they feared associating with Muslims, deplorable as they were, or because Muslim musicians were unwilling to share with them their hereditary knowledge. (Scarimbolo 2014: 353)

The earliest known statement that touched all the main points of this narrative was authored by S. M. Tagore and published in 1872;[8] the narrative was subsequently reproduced with variations by prominent reformist writers and activists, and employed as the motivation and justification for the project to reinvent Hindustani music as a modern, systematic, publicly accessible yet ancient and national tradition.

While documenting the relative ubiquity by the late nineteenth century of the narrative of Muslim musical intransigence, Scarimbolo reminds us that it was not the only available discourse for reformist writers, and that criticisms of "professionals," "ustād-s," or "illiterates" even into the twentieth century are potentially separable from the anti-Muslim element of the reform movement. Indeed, Muslim musicians, writers, and activists (such as Thakur Nawab Ali Khan, quoted earlier) were often at pains to embrace the modernizing vision of the reform movement—complete with its disdain of the uneducated performing artist—while implicitly rejecting the movement's communitarian dimension. Pursuing this phenomenon, a number of scholars have documented direct participation in the reform movement by Muslim musicians: Bakhle (2005) emphasizes the work of Maula Bakhsh (38–40) and Abdul Karim Khan (231–40) in establishing and operating modern schools of music, and shows that Agra gharānā vocalist Tassaduq Hussain Khan was an outspoken proponent of "the reform and uplift of Indian music" (192). Kobayashi (2003) also discusses Abdul Karim Khan's contributions to the reform movement, as well as the personal support offered to Bhatkhande's mission by vocalist Vilayat Husain Khan and sārangī player Bundu Khan (204–5). Rosse (1995) contributes an extensive discussion of the life and works of Maula Bakhsh, noting that he wrote a "three-and-a-half page endorsement" of Kshetra Mohan Goswami's system of notation and included an explicit appeal for adoption by both Hindu and Muslim musicians (139).[9] As Kippen succinctly notes, "one can [. . .] think of many instances where Muslim scholars and performers participated fully and enthusiastically in the nationalist endeavour" (2006: 181).

However, Muslim scholars and performers rarely offered counterarguments that specifically undermined the validity of the music reform movement's Hindu-centricity; instead, their resistance to the anti-Muslim dimensions of the movement remained merely implicit.[10] This is why the texts by Karamatullah and Kaukab Khan are especially valuable: they present a contemporaneous critique of the reform movement that both envisions a robust musical modernity and explicitly emphasizes the rightful place of Muslims and streams of knowledge from the Islamicate world in the history of Hindustani music. In part the brothers do this through the very performance of their scholarship, thus undermining persistent stereotypes of Muslim musicians as uneducated, backward, and premodern anchors preventing the progress of Hindustani music. That is to say, beyond the content of their work, the very form it takes—that of the scholarly treatise—participates in the argument against the nationalist construal of Muslim hereditary musicians as obstacles to musical modernity.

More significantly, the Khan brothers document their own contributions to and participation in the sociomusical transformations of the twentieth century, and specifically address the project to systematize, institutionalize, and make widely available the knowledge of music. Kaukab Khan in particular labors to demonstrate his scientific, skeptical, and systematic approach to Hindustani music theory and history, indicating his full immersion in the concerns of the reform movement. Indeed, at many points in Kaukab's manuscript, his perspective appears in perfect congruence with that of Bhatkhande, yet it derives from an alternative epistemological basis.

Here both Kaukab and Karamatullah make their most profound intervention in the debate over music's modernity. Instead of drawing on orientalist-inspired understandings of the fall of Indian music from a mythical Sanskritic Golden Age, the brothers present a genealogy of Indian music that highlights the origins of "musical science" ('ilm-e-mūsīqī) not in ancient India, but instead in ancient Greece. Both brothers argue that the transformative work of the Arab scholar al-Kindi in the ninth century provided a conduit transmitting the ancient Greek science of music to medieval India. As this chapter reveals, Karamatullah and Kaukab Khan participated in an Islamicate stream of knowledge that traces itself to Pythagoras of Samos, while simultaneously engaging early twentieth-century debates over the ownership of music and the place of Muslims at the heart of Indian national culture. Their genius was to agree with the basic claims of Bhatkhande—working alongside him to create an ennobled, systematic, and national tradition—while simultaneously rejecting the Hindu-centricity of Bhatkhande's vision, propounding instead a worldview premised on an Indo-Persian epistemology.

While both brothers drew on a shared epistemology, it is also clear that they pursued distinct goals for their respective books. As discussed by Naveena Naqvi, the Indo-Persian musicological tradition did not itself advance the notion that music in India developed as a hybrid practice. Instead, Indo-Persian authors accepted Sanskrit texts as the foundation of elite court music. Kaukab Khan, in his manuscript, remains largely inside this tradition, citing Sanskrit treatises and Persian works premised on the Sanskrit canon, while simultaneously arguing against contemporary attempts to defame Muslim musicians and Muslim contributions to Indian music history. Karamatullah Khan's book, on the other hand, attempts to circumvent the Sanskritic tradition entirely by arguing that "an understanding of Arabic and Persian musicology was the key to properly understanding the music that Muslim musicians in Hindustan presently practiced" (Naqvi 2010: 47).

The clues to the shared epistemology advanced by both Kaukab and Karamatullah Khan are revealed at the beginning of Karamatullah Khan's book, when he describes the origins of his father's quest to reinvigorate the ancient science of music, centering the story on the family instrument, the sarod. As Karamatullah Khan narrates, the story begins one day in Nepal, where he lived as a young man and where his father served as a court musician. Listening to his father play the sarod, Karamatullah posed his father this question: What is the linguistic origin of the word *sarod*? Niamatullah Khan answered simply, "Farsi." In the same vein, the young Karamatullah asked about the names of three more instruments: the *cang* (harp), rabāb (short-necked lute), and *nafir* (fife), to which his father responded that the names are all either Farsi or Arabic.[11] Finally, Karamatullah Khan arrived at the question that he claims inspired his father's research into the origins of musical science: How it is that instruments designed to accommodate Indian rāga-s would not have indigenous Indian names? The suggestion is that the science of music cannot be assumed to have exclusively Sanskritic origins, and that the Persian and Arab contributions to Indian music history are evident in the very names of India's musical instruments (Khan 1908: 5).

The Indo-Persian Musical Theoretical Tradition

Scholars of Indian music are familiar with a long succession of Sanskrit treatises on music theory that provide a chain of citations reaching back to the *Nātyaśāstra*, dating to roughly the first century of the Common Era. With the writings of Amir Khusrau in thirteenth-century Delhi, however, a new tradition of music scholarship was born that drew on Sanskritic predecessors, but also on streams of knowledge from West Asia and included direct observation of contemporaneous musical practice (Nijenhuis and Delvoye 2010: 46). This new tradition employed Persian and later Urdu language instead of Sanskrit, and constituted its own Indo-Persian musical theoretical tradition, yet produced few volumes (as far as we know) throughout the thirteenth, fourteenth, fifteenth, and sixteenth centuries. It was not until the seventeenth century, and especially during the reign of the last of the Great Mughals, Aurangzeb (r. 1658–1707), that Indian music was indigenized in the Mughal court to the extent that musicians and nobles were particularly concerned that the practice should not drift away from the original theory as documented in Sanskrit texts (Brown 2003: 45). As Katherine Schofield (formerly Katherine Brown) observes, the "upsurge in Indo-Persian musical treatises during Aurangzeb's reign seems to reflect an unprecedented interest among the general Mughal élite in understanding the intellectual, emotional, and philosophical underpinnings of the Hindustani tradition" (ibid.).[12]

The seventeenth-century proliferation of Indo-Persian music treatises in the Mughal court coincided with the court's adoption of a medical system that had flourished in Islamicate India from the thirteenth century, but originated in the contact between the early Islamic empires and the intellectual traditions of Greek antiquity (Alavi 2008 [2007]: 18; see also Attewell 2007). Such contact initially took place as the Islamic realm expanded under the Umayyad dynasty (661–750), encountering medical texts and practices in Persia and Byzantium premised on the writings of Plato, Aristotle, Hippocrates, and Galen (Alavi 2008 [2007]: 18–20). Under the Abbasid dynasty (750–1258), a library and research center (the *Bayt al-ḥikma*, or House of Wisdom) was established in Baghdad for the translation into Arabic of texts in Greek, Persian, Chinese, and Sanskrit; the medical system that grew from this confluence of traditions combined "ideas of Islamic cosmology and procreation with [. . .] Graeco-Roman and Sanskritic cosmological frameworks" (ibid.: 25). Known as Unani—"Greek"—this medical tradition constituted a vast and sophisticated epistemology that had a "profound bearing on the fabric of society" in North India from the seventeenth through the nineteenth centuries (ibid.: 1). Brown convincingly argues that throughout this same period, the main source of "attributions of emotive and supernatural properties to the *rāgas* was their seventeenth-century incorporation into the Unani medical system" (2003: 188).

The incorporation of Hindustani music into the Unani system, with its links to ancient Greece, forged a complex series of associations between music, mathematics, and astrology, and led some authors of the Indo-Persian tradition to celebrate Pythagoras and Plato as "founding fathers of Hindustani musical science" (Schofield 2010: 497). Pythagorean thought in particular came to India largely through translations and later recensions of the ninth-century writings of al-Kindi (d. 870), a philosopher prominent at the *Bayt al-ḥikma*, who "established in Islamic intellectual history the Greek tradition of discussing music as a mathematical science" (Shehadi 1995: 15). Though not often referenced directly, texts such as those of al-Kindi contributed to a shared historical imagination among the authors of Indo-Persian music scholarship from the seventeenth century onward.

Pythagoras, al-Kindi, and the Lucknow Gharānā

Karamatullah and Kaukab Khan are unusually forthright in their explicit citations of al-Kindi, and in their forceful arguments that the Pythagorean science of music came to India only through the work of Muslim scholars and musicians. Karamatullah Khan's book achieves this end by asserting that Hindustani music as practiced in his time is a result of the Muslim cultivation of scientific discoveries that date back to Pythagoras. Despite this continuity, Karamatullah Khan argues that a renewed connection must be forged between contemporary practice and the ancient Pythagorean principles. As Karamatullah Khan recounts, his own father set out to revive this connection through obtaining and translating into Urdu a copy of the Arabic writings on music of al-Kindi and then using al-Kindi's interpretations of ancient Greek music theory to compose his own treatise (Khan 1908: 2–3). Having imbibed the knowledge made available by his father, Karamatullah Khan confidently declares, "Seven-thousand six-hundred and two years have passed since the death of Pythagoras and the same knowledge has been in practice amongst the Muslims ever since" (ibid.: 10). Pythagoras (ca. 570–495 BCE) would have been dead closer to 2,400 years at the time of Karamatullah's writing, yet the intention is clear: in a mirror-image of Bhatkhande's insistence on a Sanskritic genealogy for music, Karamatullah Khan maintains that the Pythagorean science of music has been kept alive in India entirely by lineages of Muslim musicians (including his own).

Connecting the origins of musical science in ancient Greece to his own family's role in the history of Indian music, and simultaneously performing cosmopolitan sophistication, Karamatullah Khan argues that the sarod itself was originally invented by Pythagoras (1908: 159), citing as evidence Longfellow's 1845 poem "To a Child." The poem contains these lines:

As great Pythagoras of yore,
Standing beside the blacksmith's door,
And hearing the hammers, as they smote
The anvils with a different note,
Stole from the varying tones, that hung
Vibrant on every iron tongue,
The secret of the sounding wire,
And formed the seven-chorded lyre. (Longfellow 2000: 42)

Karamatullah Khan readily acknowledges, however, that the "sarod" invented by Pythagoras is not the same instrument played by the author; here he leverages the multiple meanings of "sarod" to intertwine and conflate the Lucknow gharānā with the lineage of Greco-Arabic scholarship descending from Pythagoras. Despite his insistence on the anqituity of his own tradition of musical knowledge, Karamutallah Khan does not focus the weight of his argument on the past. In bringing such knowledge into the present, he aims instead to prove that he and his family thrive at the cutting edge of musical modernity.

The Spirit of Invention

After the sitar, the sarod is the most prestigious and widely played stringed instrument in Hindustani music today. As discussed in Chapter 2, the instrument developed in India from early forms originating among the Paṭhān-s of eastern Afghanistan. Yet grasping the transformation of the Afghani rabāb to the present-day sarod is complicated by overlapping terminology, because the early sarod in India appears to have been a slightly modified version of the Afghani rabāb, which itself varied in size and shape (Trasoff 1999: 224). Even until the 1860s, the early sarod still featured a wooden fingerboard and double courses of gut strings, though it evidenced a shallower and more rounded body than that of the Afghani rabāb (ibid.: 227, 236). Miner agrees that the sarod of the late 1850s most likely resembled the Afghani rabāb with wooden fingerboard, gut strings, and tied frets (1997 [1993]: 67), though she suggests that it was 50 percent larger (2010: 382). Even today, Indian musical instruments are handmade and thus relatively unstandardized, yet it is not difficult to identify the key changes marking the transition from the early sarod to the more familiar instrument known by that name today: the incorporation of single-course steel strings and a steel plate in place of the gut strings and wooden fingerboard (Trasoff 1999: 212).

In his book, Karamatullah Khan lays out in detail the process of the transformation. As he writes, "it has been fifty years since my father became the disciple of Ustad Basat Khan in Matiyaburj," noting that this was "the very period in which the sarod was invented," thus referring most likely to the late 1850s or early 1860s (1908: 160–61). Karamatullah Khan continues, "Originally, the sarod had a wooden fingerboard and strings made of intestine. But the wooden fingerboard was replaced with a steel plate, and the gut strings were replaced with stronger brass and bronze strings, and he [Niamatullah Khan] is the one who actually authored these changes. Earlier, there used to be two gut frets on the sarod, but he removed those as well. As the saying goes 'all that is new is delicious,' and everyone started copying his new invention" (ibid.). Though Karamatullah Khan's narrative of this transformation is certainly the earliest, the struggle over conflicting accounts of the "invention" of the sarod remains significant today, as discussed in Chapter 3. For present purposes, however, the significant point is that Karamatullah Khan celebrates his father not as an orthodox traditionalist, but instead as an innovator, a musician positioned on the cusp of modernity, pioneering a new instrument that would come to redefine instrumental music across North India in the late nineteenth and early twentieth centuries.

Significantly, the spirit of invention in the Lucknow gharānā does not end with Niamatullah Khan. Though neither brother documents the episode in his book, family oral history indicates that Kaukab Khan followed in his father's footsteps by inventing an instrument of his own, the "Kaukab" banjo. Drawing on a 1977 interview with Umar Khan (Kaukab Khan's grandson and Irfan Khan's father), Allyn Miner offers a condensed version of the story of the invention that took place during a visit by Karamatullah and Kaukab Khan to Paris: "The story goes that Kaukab Khan's *sarod* was broken on the trip [to Europe], and when he got to Paris he was given a Western banjo. He removed the frets, put a metal plate over the fingerboard, and played it like a *sarod*. His success on the new instrument was such that he continued to play it even upon his return to India. He became more famous on the banjo than on the *sarod*" (1997 [1993]: 154; see also Sen 1992: 114). Famed vocalist Alladiya Khan writes in his memoirs of having met "the banjo player Asadullah [Kaukab] Khan" in Nepal, and reports seeking him out subsequently for a meeting in Calcutta (2000: 93).

Alladiya Khan clearly admired Kaukab Khan, describing him as "a good banjo player," and remarking, "I was very pleased to see him" (ibid.). Until recently, Kaukab Khan's original banjo remained in the possession of the family; Gulfam Ahmad Khan—grandson of Karamatullah Khan—reports that it clearly bore the mark "Made in U.S.A., City of Chicago" (interview, April 1, 2009). Beyond the prototype instrument, however, family oral history further contends that a "Kaukab Patent Banjo" was manufactured in Calcutta and became the instrument of choice for many of Kaukab Khan's students. Within the gharānā it was played and taught by Karamatullah Khan's son, Ishtiaq Ahmad Khan (1919–1967), and by Ishtiaq's eldest son, Mukhtiyar Ahmad Khan (1941–1994). Figure 12 shows Mukhtiyar Ahmad Khan playing the Kaukab banjo sometime in the late 1950s or early 1960s. It is the only known photo of the instrument.

The banjo also plays a role in the earliest sound recordings of the Lucknow gharānā. Though neither brother discusses this fact, Kaukab Khan was one of the earliest instrumentalists to produce commercial recordings in India, some of which are still in circulation (McNeil 2004: 117; Sharma 1993: 198). From information offered by Michael Kinnear (a specialist in the early recording industry in India), Adrian McNeil suggests that Kaukab Khan made all of his recordings (a total of three double-sided, 78-rpm discs) in 1912 (2007a: 64). I have been able to inspect only one of the original discs, a recording of *Bhairavīn* on one side, with *Zila* on the other. Kaukab Khan's instrument is listed as simply "Banjo" (spelled in English, Hindi, and Urdu), as shown in Figure 13. The spirit of instrumental invention in these two generations of the Lucknow gharānā, and especially the willingness of Kaukab Khan to participate in the recording industry in its earliest years in India, indicates an embrace of new materials and technologies that highlights the forward-looking orientation of the lineage.

Institutions and Education

Both Kaukab and Karamatullah Khan celebrated their own contributions as educators who sought to disseminate the knowledge of music among nonhereditary students. Specifically, both brothers taught extensively at music schools, the establishment of which was a core tenet of the reform movement. One of the earliest such schools was Sangeet Sangha, established in 1911 in Calcutta by Lady Pratibha Chowdhury (1865–1922), a Bengali aristocrat; Kaukab Khan was the founding principal of this school, though little else is known about it (McNeil 2004: 118–19; Sharma 1993: 198, 266; Rosse 1995: 52). Evidence suggests

FIGURE 12 Mukhtiyar Ahmad Khan.
Courtesy of Gulfam Ahmad Khan.

FIGURE 13 Kaukab Khan's gramophone recording of *Bhairavīṅ*, played on banjo.

that Kaukab Khan's residence in Calcutta was itself a result of an invitation by Sourindro Mohun Tagore, a patron, educator, and musicologist who founded the first school of music in Calcutta in 1871 (Chatterjee 1996: 208, 269). Among Kaukab Khan's many nonhereditary students was "Dhirendranath Bose, the first Bengali to become a recognized performer of the sarod" (McNeil 2004: 119; see also Chatterjee 1996: 269).[13]

While specializing in sarod and banjo, Kaukab Khan also trained eminent disciples in both sitar and surbahār, including Jnaanada Prasanna Mukherji,

Harendra Krishna Sheel, Shivkumar Thakur, Hiralal Haldar, and Kaukab Khan's own son, Waliullah Khan (1892–1951) (Chatterjee 1996: 269). Waliullah Khan extended the sitar tradition within the gharānā, training his own son, Noorullah Khan (1939–2008), in sitar as well. The diversified skill that allowed Kaukab Khan to teach sarod, banjo, sitar, and surbahār to his students was likely a consequence of the wide range of his own training. In addition to his father, Kaukab Khan learned from a famed sitar and surbahār player, but it is not clear whether this person was Sajjad Mohammad—described by Miner as the "single most outstanding influential instrumentalist of later nineteenth-century Calcutta"—or Ali Mohammad Khan, the elder son of Basat Khan (Miner 1997 [1993]: 150; see also Chatterjee 1996: 269; McNeil 2004: 136 n. 30).[14]

Karamatullah Khan established his own music school in the city of Allahabad, writing in his book, "Nowadays a lot of people (those who sing and play various instruments) know that I have been their ustād. The school has been established for a long time, and with God's grace it has been successful. God is keeping it alive because He wants this knowledge to stay alive" (1908: 166). According to family history, Karamatullah Khan remained in Allahabad until 1915 when, upon the death of Kaukab Khan, he relocated to Calcutta to continue the instruction of his brother's students. Karamatullah Khan documented his own experience with a variety of instruments far afield from his own gharānā traditions: in addition to learning to sing dhrupad, baṛā khyāl, and choṭā khyāl, he lists bīn, sāraṅgī, sitar, rabāb, sursiṅgār, taus, harmonium, piano, and tablā among his specialties (ibid.: 161–62). This is an extraordinary list of instruments, containing the most prestigious (bīn and sursiṅgār), the least prestigious (sāraṅgī and tablā), and foreign instruments (piano and harmonium), thus indicating a catholic and wide-ranging musical appetite that defies stereotypical assumptions of rigid specialization on the part of gharānā musicians. In this regard, Karamatullah Khan provides evidence for his open-mindedness and his freedom from the constraints often attributed to Muslim hereditary artists. Moreover, he specifically notes that his experience with such a range of instruments served primarily to benefit his students, thus further emphasizing his role as a teacher and eager propagator of musical knowledge. Through celebrating his own role as an educator and founder of a music school, Karamatullah Khan powerfully thwarts the core claim of reformist discourse that Muslim hereditary musicians hoarded musical knowledge and revealed it only through an arduous and premodern process of discipleship.

National Pride

The reform movement embraced Hindustani music as a classical musical tradition that proved both the ancient roots and the modern sophistication of the incipient nation, and thus served as evidence of the illegitimacy of British rule in India and of the necessity of national independence. As Karamatullah Khan shows in his book, he and his brother were themselves important players in the nationalist movement: they were embraced as exemplary purveyors of Indian musical traditions by the early nationalist leader Motilal Nehru, father of India's first prime minister, Jawaharlal Nehru. In 1900 the senior Nehru lobbied the British government for a change to laws of emigration such that he might take a delegation of Indian performers to the international exhibition at Paris (Lunn 2014). To represent Hindustani music, Motilal Nehru chose Kaukab and Karamatullah Khan, who performed at the exhibition (see Bakhle 2005: 111; Barlow 2007: 99; Umar Khan 1976: 95; McNeil 2004: 118; Miner 1997 [1993]: 154; Misra 1991: 88; Sen 1992: 114).[15]

Karamatullah Khan wrote about the visit to Europe in his book, stating that he was selected to represent India (*Hindustān*) at the international exhibition in Paris, where he played his *qaumī bājā* and was appreciated by the upper echelons of French and British society (1908: 162). The phrase *qaumī bājā* is highly significant: *bājā* clearly means "instrument," but the term *qaumī*—the adjectival form of *qaum*—requires some interpretation. As given in Platts's *A Dictionary of Urdu, Classical Hindi, and English* (2004 [1884]), the Urdu word *qaum* (derived from Arabic) is defined as "A people, nation; a tribe, race, family; sect, caste" (796). We may understand Karamatullah Khan to mean that he played the instrument that represents his own *qaum*, thus referencing his identity as a Muslim, Paṭhān, or descendant of the Bangash clan of Afghani rabāb players. I believe, however, that Karamatullah Khan employed the word *qaum* to mean "nation" in the modern sense, thus extending a definition of the term established as early as 1884 by Sir Sayyid Ahmad Khan, India's leading Muslim political figure of the second half of the nineteenth century. Though remembered today as a reformer and modernizer of Islam—and even as the grandfather of the Muslim separatist movement that would culminate in the birth of Pakistan—Sir Sayyid (as he was widely known) explicitly defined *qaum* as the plural Indian nation, stating in an Urdu speech on February 3, 1884, "By the word *qawm* I mean both Hindus and Muslims. That is the way in which I define the word nation (*qawm*) [. . .] all of us, either Hindus or Muslims, live on one soil, are governed by one and the same ruler" (Mujahid 1999: 88).

The Urdu scholar C. Ryan Perkins cautions that in the late nineteenth century, the word *qaum* bore contradictory and overlapping meanings. As Perkins argues, "When [Abdul Halim] Sharar or Sir Sayyid addressed Muslim audiences, the *qaum* generally referred exclusively to Muslims. When addressing an audience of both Hindus and Muslims the *qaum* generally referred to all the inhabitants of Hindustan" (2011: 65). The possibility thus remains that Karamatullah Khan meant to claim the sarod for the Muslim community. But given his evident pride in representing *Hindustān* abroad, and given the ostensibly wide audience for his book, there is little doubt that Karamatullah Khan considered the sarod the national instrument of India.

Moreover, Karamatullah Khan suggests a pivotal place for his own family in the story of the emerging nation when he notes that "the very instrument my father invented is the one I played there, and the one I continue to play" (1908: 162), thus identifying the sarod as both the national instrument of India and as the invention of his father, and thereby further emphasizing the role of his family in connecting an ancient Greek past to an Indian national future.

Bhatkhande and the Lucknow Gharānā

The preceding sections have emphasized Karamatullah Khan's efforts to document the contributions of his family to a few of the primary structures of musical modernity, including their invention of the sarod, their establishment of educational institutions, and their participation in the nationalist cause. In all of these areas, Karamatullah Khan debunks common misconceptions that allowed the reformists to exclude Muslim hereditary musicians from their vision of musical modernity. Yet the clash between the Lucknow gharānā and the politics of the reform movement was not entirely discursive.

Janaki Bakhle reveals a fascinating meeting between Karamatullah Khan and Bhatkhande in Allahabad in 1908 or 1909. As documented in Bhatkhande's own travel diaries (anonymously hand-copied and finally translated from Marathi to English by Bakhle), the meeting did not go well. Already prejudiced against professional musicians, Bhatkhande was especially appalled by Karamatullah Khan's contention that Hindustani music could have origins outside India and that treatises in Arabic and Persian could serve as authoritative documents of

Indian music theory. Karamatullah Khan explored such Islamocentric ideas at length in his own book, which he gave to Bhatkhande in the course of their meeting. Adamant that Indian music was the product of a Hindu civilization and that Sanskrit was its only language of authority, Bhatkhande terminated the conversation in disgust (Bakhle 2005: 110–11).

From our brief survey of the relevant passages of Karamatullah Khan's book, it should be clear that he chafed against the implication that as a Muslim, he was not the rightful owner of the practical traditions of his lineage. Yet where Karamatullah Khan's critique of the anti-Muslim dimension of the reform movement relies on his insistence on a Muslim genealogy for music, and on his depictions of his own family's contributions to musical modernity, his brother Kaukab Khan attacks the issue directly. In the following sections, I focus on Kaukab Khan's writings, and especially on his direct engagement with the concerns and objectives of the reform movement as represented by V. N. Bhatkhande. Family oral history indicates that Kaukab Khan was personally acquainted with Bhatkhande, and that they exchanged extensive correspondence concerning music theory, yet in Kaukab's manuscript he does not mention Bhatkhande by name, instead referring to him obliquely as "a Panditji in Bombay" (1915: 149). Nevertheless, as illustrated in what follows, it is clear that Kaukab was on familiar terms with Bhatkhande's work and with the larger vision for a nationalized Hindustani music he represented.

Bhatkhande was motivated to systematize the theory of Hindustani music such that it could be easily taught, and such that professional performers would not have a monopoly on determining the correct rules and regulations for the music's many rāga-s. In his desire to unite theory with practice, in his dismissal of professional musicians who lacked theoretical knowledge, in his skepticism of ancient texts, and in his fear that Indian music was losing its purity and authenticity, he and Kaukab Khan were in concert. Yet one fundamental disagreement remained: Bhatkhande believed that Hindustani music was ultimately rooted in an ancient Sanskritic tradition and was thus foremost a product of a Hindu civilization.

In his writings Kaukab signals his modernity, his sophistication, and his vital awareness of the struggle over the future of Hindustani music as defined by Bhatkhande. Moreover, on the surface, Kaukab appears to agree with Bhatkhande's basic binary understanding of the roles of Hindus and Muslim in the history of music: Hindu scholars who read and write Sanskrit but have no practical knowledge of music are counterposed to Muslim professional musicians who lack formal textual knowledge but carry embodied oral traditions. One of Kaukab's primary arguments is that both of these groups share responsibility for the problems facing Indian music, asserting that they should unite: authentic textual knowledge should be available to musicians, and musicians should take an interest in such knowledge (Khan 1915: 129). Like Bhatkhande, Kaukab singles out "professionals" for heavy criticism, describing them as largely uneducated and noting that in their ignorance, "people such as these can be the most dangerous enemies of this honorable art" (ibid.: 120). As discussed earlier, in the lexicon of the music reform movement, "professional musicians" were often assumed to be Muslims who were borrowers or even usurpers of an essentially Hindu practice.

Kaukab Khan, however, inverts this stereotype: "from the time of Tansen this knowledge has been passed down generation to generation [. . . .] Truth be told, music is wholly indebted to the Muslims alone, whom the Hindu gentleman must acknowledge and give thanks" (Khan 1915: 133). Like his brother, Kaukab Khan offers in his book a genealogy of the science of music that originates in ancient Greece, and comes to India through Arabic texts (ibid.: 4). In introducing various theories of the origins of musical pitch, Kaukab notes that there are several different mythologies corresponding to several different ancient civilizations, all of which have compelling claims to the first discovery of the science of music. In this context, Kaukab Khan emphasizes the idea that *sur* or pitch was practiced for three thousand years in the Arab world, thus declaring "the Hindu claim that Muslims obtained this knowledge in Hindustan is completely wrong" (ibid.: 13).

By agreeing with Bhatkhande's core propositions, yet asserting the preeminence of Islamicate contributions to music history, Kaukab Khan signals a radical intervention in the debate over music and modernity. As numerous scholars have shown, the anticolonial nationalist movement in India was led by the English-educated middle class and drew heavily on ideas and scholarship crafted by the British themselves (Chatterjee 1993 [1986]; Cohn 2002 [1996]; Pandey 1996 [1990]; Prakash 1990; Van der Veer 1994). By drawing instead on the Indo-Persian intellectual tradition, Kaukab offers an implicit critique of the prevailing trends of nationalist modernity, showing that a progressive program of music reform and national pride is available through an indigenous intellectual tradition that does not threaten the preeminence of the established lines of hereditary musicians. Indeed, for Kaukab and his line, the struggle over the place of Muslim hereditary artists in the rapidly changing world of Hindustani music was not only a matter of academic debate, but an existential crisis. Though Kaukab's attempt to perpetuate his own family's centrality within the reconfigured world of music was ultimately a failure, his writings suggest that in the early twentieth century, he believed they had a fighting chance.

In part Kaukab Khan thwarts the anti-Muslim claims and contentions of the reform movement by demonstrating his agreement (as a Muslim) with the larger goals of the movement. This strategy is unveiled at the beginning of Kaukab's manuscript, where he establishes his investment in textual knowledge, providing a numbered list of thirteen major sources, including works in Persian, Sanskrit, Gujarati, Marathi, and English (1915: iii). The first three sources on the list are easy to identify, as they are the most influential Persian texts on Hindustani music of the seventeenth and eighteenth centuries: (1) *Uṣūl al-Naghmāt-i Āṣafī* by Ghulam Raza Sabir Ali (1793), (2) *Tuḥfat al-Hind* by Mirza Khan ibn Fakhruddin (ca. 1675), and (3) *Shams al-Aṣwāt* by Ras Baras Khan (1698). Produced in the Lucknow court of Nawāb Asafuddaula, it is not a surprise that *Uṣūl al-Naghmāt-i Āṣafī* should come first on Kaukab's list, though it is based nearly entirely on the earlier *Shams al-Aṣwāt* (Brown [Schofield] 2003: 78).[16] The next five sources listed by Kaukab Khan are familiar Sanskrit treatises: (4) *Saṅgītaratnākara* by Sharngadeva (ca. 1250), (5) *Saṅgītadarpaṇa* by Damodara (ca. 1625), (6) *Saṅgītapārijāta* by Ahobala (ca. 1650), (7) *Rāgavibodha* by Somanatha (ca. 1609), and (8) *Nāradīyaśikṣā* by Narada (ca. first millennium CE). For source number 9, Kaukab lists *Saṅgīta-Kalpadrū*, apparently a reference to *Saṅgīta-Rāgakalpadrūma* (1842) by Krishnananda Vyas. Number 10 on the list, *Cintāmani*, has proven difficult to identify. Widdess documents a Sanskrit treatise titled *Saṅgīta-Cintāmaṇi* written by Jagajjyoti Malla (the king of Bhaktapur, Nepal, from 1614 to 1637) (2013: 45). Another candidate would be the *Saṅgīta-Cintāmaṇi* of Vemabhupala, a well-known fourteenth-century Sanskrit text. However, because Kaukab specifies that his *Cintāmani* is a Gujarati—not a Sanskrit—treatise, I have not been able to definitively identify it. The last three items in Kaukab's bibliography are again easily identified: (11) *Kalādh* refers to *Saṅgītakalādhar*, a Gujarati treatise by Dahyalal Shivram, court musician of the Mahārājā of Bhavnagar, first published in 1901 (see Miner 2010: 385); (12) *Saṅgīta-Bālbodh* (in Marathi) was authored by Vishnu Digambar Paluskar and published in three volumes in 1901, 1902, and 1903, respectively; and (13) *The Music and Musical Instruments of Southern India and the Deccan* was authored by Charles Russell Day and published in 1891.

The very length and diversity of Kaukab's bibliography would appear to effec-

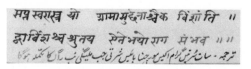

FIGURE 14 Manuscript excerpt
from *Jauhar-e Mūsīqī*.

tively undermine the ascription of illiteracy to Muslim hereditary musicians. However, one may wonder: Could Kaukab really read Sanskrit (along with Gujarati, Marathi, and English), or did he merely include such a list to answer misperceptions such as those of Bhatkhande, who claimed that he could not name a single Muslim "who understood a Sanskrit music *grantha* [treatise]" (quoted in Bakhle 2005: 121)? Though political strategy may have played a role in Kaukab's decision to begin his manuscript with a consolidated list of sources in a diversity of languages, there is no doubt that he consulted and comprehended them as well. Beyond his initial list of sources, Kaukab includes detailed bibliographic references, as when he notes that he employs the edition of the *Saṅgītaratnākara* published in Pune and edited by Mangesh Ramakrishna Telang, which includes Kallinatha's fifteenth-century commentary on the original thirteenth-century text (Khan 1915: 41). This edition of the *Saṅgītaratnākara* (known to Sanskrit scholars as the "Poona Edition") was published by Anandashrama Press in two volumes (1896, 1897), number 35 in their Sanskrit Series, and was the definitive edition of the *Saṅgītaratnākara* until it was superseded by the Adyar Library Series, edited by S. Subrahmanya Sastri, published in four volumes between 1943 and 1953.

Displaying his thorough familiarity with the Poona Edition, Kaukab includes direct quotations—in their original language—from the *Saṅgītaratnākara* throughout his manuscript. Moreover, in many places Kaukab translates directly from Sanskrit to Urdu, as when, in his discussion of *grāma* (the ancient concept of "parent scales" discussed in the earliest works on Indian music), he quotes the *Saṅgītaratnākara*, and then immediately notes the Urdu translation (shown in Figure 14).

The Urdu reads: "Translation—Seven *sur*-s, three *grām*-s, twenty-one *mūrchanā*-s, twenty-two *śruti*-s; When they meet, the *rāg* will be complete" (Khan 1915: 40). Beyond his frequent invocation of Sanskrit slokas (verses) from the *Saṅgītaratnākara*, Kaukab also provides direct quotations in Sanskrit from *Nāradīyaśikṣā* (ibid.: 16), *Saṅgītadarpaṇa* (55), *Rāgavibodha* (86), and *Saṅgīta-*

pārijāta (132), while discussing (without direct quotations) passages from *Saṅ-gītakalādhar* (42) and *Saṅgīta-Bālbodh* (57). These texts inform Kaukab Khan's musicological arguments, but they also demonstrate his open-mindedness and his currency in the field, especially when he approvingly cites the *Saṅgīta-Bālbodh* as his model for the presentation of *alaṅkār*-s (scalar patterns), but does not mention the book's author, V. D. Paluskar, a towering figure in the Hin-duization of Hindustani music in the early twentieth century and thus an active adversary of Kaukab Khan and his vision of an Islamicate musical modernity. In this manner, Kaukab's informed use of Sanskrit treatises positions him cred-ibly to critique the overreliance on such texts by contemporary scholars. That is to say, Kaukab's intimate familiarity with the Sanskritic tradition illustrates that he is not a bigot who has dismissed Hindu musical scholarship out of hand.

Yet in contrast to Bhatkhande, who retained an ingrained respect for San-skrit as the language of authority in Indian music, both Kaukab Khan and Ka-ramatullah Khan specifically reject the overprivileging of the language. Kara-matullah Khan, for instance, explains, "However knowledgeable a man may be, by not mastering Sanskrit his own writings will be overshadowed by those of any ordinary pandit, whose writings will end up being written in stone for you" (1908: 148–49). Here Karamatullah Khan appears to anticipate his own meeting with Bhatkhande, in which Bhatkhande dismisses the authority of Karamatul-lah Khan's writings for their lack of Sanskrit references (Bakhle 2005: 110–11). Karamatullah Khan caustically suggests that despite the achievements of a given scholar, if he is not able to read and write Sanskrit, his contributions will be sec-ondary to the writings of even the most common and uneducated "pandit," by which he refers to Brahmans trained in Sanskrit language.

Kaukab Khan amplifies much the same point when he rails against the idea that Sanskrit language should possess the power to outweigh common prac-tice or common sense. In his discussion of contrasting explanations of *grāma*, Kaukab writes, "It is better to depend on one's reasoning and common sense rather than to accept anything old as written in stone" (1915: 45). Here Kaukab signals his informed engagement in the discussion of ancient and arcane con-cepts (*grāma*), and yet simultaneously rejects the approach to such a discussion that would arbitrarily privilege the statements of obsolete Sanskrit texts. His position is thus a nuanced one: he acknowledges that a thorough awareness of the concerns of the Sanskritic tradition is vital for any musician, thus agreeing strongly with Bhatkhande's vision of a theoretically informed musical practice, yet Kaukab also specifically attacks the perceived prestige of the Sanskrit language, thus performing a modernist skepticism and simultaneously leaving the possibility open that non-Sanskrit texts may also inform the history of Hindustani music.

While rejecting the uncritical veneration of Sanskrit texts, Kaukab also damns professional musicians who operate in the absence of the knowledge of theory. On this point Kaukab is again in strong agreement with Bhatkhande: they are both suspicious of "practical artists" who deviate from established norms through their ignorance of textual knowledge. Kaukab even criticizes musicians who may perform correctly but, "when asked about the names of their presentations, due to their lack of knowledge, give no response other than silence" (Khan 1915: 85). Reinforcing this point, Kaukab notes that there are twenty-two kinds of *gamak*-s (ornaments) as described by Somanatha in *Rāgavibodha*, and although "the experts of *ālāp* are able to almost perform all the twenty-two *gamak*-s, they merely call them all '*gamak*' and are unable to name them individually due to their lack of knowledge" (ibid.: 89). Yet while he cites the ancient treatise of Somanatha as a pivotal source for understanding the varieties of *gamak*, Kaukab does not agree with Somanatha's attempt to notate *ālāp*, which he says is inappropriate because the rhythmic, timbral, and melodic nuances of *ālāp* cannot be rendered in written notation (ibid.). In this regard, Kaukab once again stakes a nuanced claim, marshaling both his expertise as a performing artist and his knowledge of the textual tradition to assert that (a) musicians must participate in the theoretical tradition, and (b) the treatises themselves are not sufficient to capture the subtleties of the art.

Such nuance is lost, though, when in his tirade against "ustād-s," Kaukab overstates his case, suggesting that through their incompetence, professional musicians have squandered and destroyed the great inheritance of Tansen. Kaukab makes this point by asserting that in the beginning, the total gamut consisted of six rāga-s and thirty-six rāginī-s (thus evoking the so-called rāga-rāginī system that predominated from the seventeenth to the twentieth century), but these proliferated, producing thousands more.[17] When Tansen arrived on the scene, Kaukab further narrates, he selected from among these thousands 360 for *dhrupad* and *sādrā* (compositional forms associated with the Mughal court). However, Kaukab asserts, the musicians who followed Tansen lost most of these rāga-s and rāginī-s, such that now "even the biggest of ustād-s has no more than one hundred rāginī-s" (Khan 1915: 166). Even those hundred, Kaukab laments, are only claimed and not truly known by most musicians, because "the actual practice is done on very few rāga-s." Despite this great loss since Tansen's time,

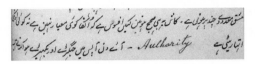

FIGURE 15 Manuscript excerpt from *Jauhar-e Mūsīqī*.

Kaukab would be satisfied if at least these "very few rāga-s" were practiced correctly, but he further contends that the musicians of his day have neither "standards nor authority" (ibid.). Strikingly, the word *authority* stands out from the Nastalīq text, written in English in a florid roman script (though with the first *t* uncrossed), as shown in Figure 15.

I believe this section—with its exaggerated harangue against professional musicians together with the invocation of the English word *authority*—provides a valuable clue to Kaukab's vision of the solution to the problems he (and the reformists) perceived in the status of music in his day. Despite his remonstrations, Kaukab Khan does not believe that the legacy of Tansen has been entirely annihilated: if such were the case, there would be little point in attempting to resuscitate the culture of Hindustani music in the twentieth century. Instead, such assertions serve a rhetorical strategy that highlights Kaukab's disdain for professional musicians who lack a dedicated investment in the relevant texts and treatises of music theory. However, Kaukab has also rejected an uncritical embrace of the textual tradition as the solution to deteriorating standards of performance. The solution will lie, Kaukab implies, with musicians who (like himself) are both masters of the oral art and scholars—"authors"—of the textual tradition.

Kaukab's use of the English word *authority* thus suggests a powerful conflation of the oral and the textual, signifying his own mastery of tradition as well as his embrace of a modern, scientific disposition. At other points in his manuscript, Kaukab further demonstrates his fluency in the colonial language and associates it with the scientific method. For instance, in his discussion of various theories of the production of vocal sound, Kaukab first discusses the theory of *cakr*-s ("shakras" to many today) laid down in the *Saṅgītaratnākara*, following this with a section titled "The Origins of Voice According to *Dāktari* [Western medicine]." In this section, Kaukab offers an extensive discussion of the anatomical processes involved in the production of the human voice, entailing the use of the following English words in roman script: *larynx, pharynx, trachea, diaphargm (diaphragm), thyroid, arytenaid (arytenoid), crycaid (cricoid), and glattis (glottis)* (Khan 1915: 21–22). Further displaying both his knowledge of English and his interest in the scientific method as it relates to music study, Kaukab includes a brief section titled "Animals Are Affected by Rāga," in which he reflects on a "surprising article written in New York's *Herald* about the science of music." The article concerned a scientific experiment by an American farmer who had a violinist play to his milk cows and compared the yield to those unexposed to music, concluding that music greatly increased the cows' output (ibid.: 126–27). Trained as an heir to the orthodox musical traditions of the Mughal court, fluent in a variety of languages, and invested in the values of textual knowledge and scientific skepticism, Kaukab Khan positions himself as a potential savior of Hindustani music, and thus as an ideal partner for leaders of the reform movement such as Bhatkhande. In this regard, Kaukab Khan volunteers himself in advance for the role of musical hero Bhatkhande envisions in his article from 1930: "It is to be expected that at no distant future we shall have people who combine in themselves both the art and the science of Music and then the progress we make will be both rapid and stable" (1930: 9).

As a potential partner with Bhatkhande, however, Kaukab Khan demonstrates that he draws on a distinct intellectual heritage that undermines the anti-Muslim bias of the reform movement. As a final attempt to thwart the onslaught of nationalist modernity and the threat it posed to the family traditions of Muslim hereditary musicians, Kaukab and Karamatullah Khan meet the arguments against them in the center of the battlefield, ready to proclaim their full engagement with musical modernity while remaining ensconced in an Indo-Persian tradition that bolsters the Islamicate contributions to Indian music history and thus provides powerful counterevidence to reformist claims of Muslim obstructionism.

Kaukab echoes Bhatkhande when he complains that "the whole condition has been reversed and turned into almost hell. That was a time of its peak, and now its ultimate decline. Where is Fāryābī, and where is Bu Ali Sīnā? Music is now standing alone, helpless in the terrifying fields of despair and disgrace, and because of all the divided groups of experts of this field of art, one does not know what its state will be in the future" (Khan 1915: 91). In a brilliant move, Kaukab here supports Bhatkhande's vision of a reformed, consolidated, and institutionalized future for Hindustani music, but draws sustenance from an Islamicate genealogy. Searching for past pillars of musical integrity, Kaukab does not cite Sharngadeva and Damodara. Instead, he invokes twelfth-century Persian poet Fāryābī—though he may have meant to name Fārābī, a tenth-century Persian philosopher and music theorist—and Bu Alī Sīnā (better known as Avicenna), a tenth- and eleventh-century Persian philosopher, physician, music theorist, and follower of Fārābī. In expressing his concern for the loss of Indian music's authenticity—thus demonstrating his allegiance to the vision propounded by Bhatkhande—Kaukab actively perpetuates a vital theme of the Indo-Persian tradition itself.

As Schofield argues, a focus on "performers' illiteracy and musical degeneracy" is a shared feature of both the Indo-Persian tradition and the colonial-era nationalist reform movement (2010: 496). As early as 1660, for instance, Mughal writer Qazi Hasan complained bitterly that "today's singers do not perform music as it is [set out] in the treatises" (ibid.). By railing against uneducated musicians and lamenting musical degeneracy while harkening back nostalgically to early ancestors of the Indo-Persian musical and literary legacy, Kaukab Khan illustrates the compatibility of his Islamicate worldview with the vision set out by Bhatkhande, thus implying that the exclusionary path of musical modernity paved by the British-inspired nationalist reformers is not the only way to arrive at a renewed and reinvigorated national musical tradition.

Moreover, this critique extends to colonialism itself. Throughout his manuscript, Kaukab Khan highlights his knowledge of the English language to demonstrate his education, his interest in Western science, and his awareness of the wider world in which his discussion takes place. Yet he also indicates his rejection of European claims to cultural and intellectual superiority. For instance, in his discussion of *śruti*, or the ancient Indian theory of intonation, Kaukab Khan reproduces a diagram from C. R. Day's book, noting that he will refrain from comment about the quality of Day's work and instead merely remark (perhaps with some sarcasm) that "though a European, you were interested in another country's science of music and you even wrote a book on it" (1915: 36). Like Bhatkhande, Kaukab apparently has little regard for Day's writing, yet patronizes the colonial scholar by congratulating him for making even an unsuccessful attempt to come to terms with India's musical systems.

In contextualizing the difficulty and specificity of the different *gamak*-s, Kaukab notes that only one kind of *gamak* is available on the harmonium, known as "tremolo" in English. Kaukab immediately declares, however, that European vocal technique, from which the notion of tremolo derives, is not pleasing to Indian ears: he asserts that its "trembling"—vibrato—is practiced at great length by European musicians, but does not reflect a grasp of the essence of musical pitch. By way of concrete example, Kaukab mentions "Melba [. . .] a popular singer in England these days, considered one of the best, whose voice does not rest on any *sur* [pitch]" (Khan 1915: 89). Kaukab is surely referring to the Australian opera singer Nellie Melba (1861–1931), and through this example deriding the tradition of European operatic technique in its inability to produce pure and steady pitches as desired by a knowledgeable Hindustani musician.

Kaukab's disapproval of Western singing style may be read as simple ethnocentrism, or, as I have suggested, as an attack on the claims of cultural superiority by India's colonizers. In the latter sense, Kaukab implies a critique of both the nationalist reform movement and the broader system of colonialism from which it grew. Taken together with his thoroughgoing defense of the place of Muslim musicians and Islamicate traditions in music's past and in its modern transformations, and with his embrace of both the Sanskritic and the Indo-Persian textual traditions, Kaukab's anticolonialism and simultaneous rejection of an incipient Hindu nationalism suggests a remarkably sophisticated plea for the value of long-standing cultural syncretism as the basis for a nonexclusionary modernity.

———

This chapter has pursued the voices and visions of the Lucknow gharānā through a focus on two significant texts: the published book and the unpublished manuscript, respectively, of the brothers Karamatullah and Kaukab Khan. Reading selections from those works has illuminated a number of important insights. First, we have seen that in the early twentieth century, the primary exponents of the Lucknow gharānā reveled in their participation in musical modernity, documenting their innovations, contributions, and interventions in shaping the new culture of Hindustani music as the feudal era drew to a close. Radical changes in the nature of Hindustani music, patronage, and performance practice were the necessary ingredients that propelled the Lucknow gharānā to preeminence. The waning of the kalāwant lines, the invention of new instruments, the collapse of the Lucknow court, the shift to Bengal, the establishment of educational institutions, the emergence of the recording industry, and the opportunities for global travel and performance allowed Niamatullah Khan and his sons to rise to the heights of renown in the late nineteenth and early twentieth centuries.

Further, the writings of the brothers Khan reveal their investment in the struggle to define and claim musical modernity both alongside and against its better-known reformers, especially V. N. Bhatkhande. In Kaukab Khan's writings, we see specific discussions that address the primary concerns of the reform movement: the neglect of the textual tradition by performing artists, the consequent detriment to musical integrity perpetuated by uneducated professional musicians, the pressing need to explain the discrepancies between present-day practice and established theory, the requirement of a new system that will address the discrepancies, and most centrally, the overriding concern that the great tradition of Hindustani music was losing its purity, thus requiring immediate resuscitation through these measures.

Yet as Muslims, the brothers were acutely aware that their legitimacy was undermined by the vision of Hindu-centricity propounded by the dominant voices of the reform movement. Karamatullah and Kaukab Khan's celebration of the Islamicate contributions to the development of Indian music thus serve the purposes of political expediency as well as historical accuracy. Marshaling a six-hundred-year tradition of Indo-Persian scholarship on Indian music, the brothers bring the epistemology of a distinctly Islamicate tradition directly into conversation with the twentieth-century reform movement, illustrating the great congruence of concerns while also powerfully rejecting the misperception that Muslim musicians are themselves the source of the problem. Instead, while agreeing that uneducated performers impede music's modernity, Karamatullah and Kaukab Khan underscore the unmistakable reality that Muslim musicians and theorists have a long tradition of addressing the very points the reformers press, and in fact have anticipated them by several centuries.

Most centrally, the texts by Karamatullah and Kaukab Khan reveal the insurgent consciousness of Muslim hereditary musicians intent on retaining control of their own musical traditions and determined to brand those traditions as products of Islamicate knowledge and practice. The visions of an Islamicate musical modernity propounded by the two brothers never came to fruition; moreover, the writings accessed in this chapter have been virtually forgotten. In breathing life back into the writings of Karamatullah and Kaukab Khan, we uncover a hidden history of Hindustani music and rediscover a vanished moment pregnant with possibilities for the musical identity of the incipient nation. And yet the thwarted vision offered in these forgotten texts—in which master musicians of the lineage of Lucknow might have defined the music of the nation—continues to inform the historical consciousness of the living Lucknow gharānā even today.

Epilogue

In 2010 Irfan Khan left his position as head of the department of music at the Delhi Public School, where I first met him in Numaligarh, Assam. He was convinced to do so by a generous offer from the founder of a new school of music in Kabul, Afghanistan: the Afghanistan National Institute of Music. Irfan had spent three years in Kabul as a teacher and performer in the 1980s and was eager to reunite with his now-grown students and to help train the next generation, the great majority having been traumatized by the successive catastrophes of Taliban rule and the subsequent United States–led war. Moreover, as the _khalīfa_ of the Lucknow gharānā, Irfan Khan felt a connection to Afghanistan as the homeland of his earliest known ancestors. He returned to Kabul and taught at the school for three years, but ultimately longed for Calcutta, where he had spent most of his youth. In 2012 he resettled in his Calcutta home and invested much of his accumulated pay in reestablishing his downstairs residence as a proper music room complete with elegant framed portraits of his gharānā ancestors, and a beautiful glass cabinet displaying half a dozen instruments that had belonged to his uncle and his father.

In January of 2011, during one of Irfan Khan's short leaves from Kabul, I was sitting with Ilyas Khan's old sitar in the refurbished downstairs music room, reviewing my recent lesson in rāga _Alhaiyā Bilāwal_, when my ustād's two college-aged daughters emerged from their room and paused to observe my practice. They were curious to know more about my interest in Indian music, but the manner of their questions exposed a stunning disconnection from the traditions of their father: they appeared to have virtually no knowledge of their own family's role in the history of Hindustani music. Traditionally speaking, it is not surprising that female offspring were uninitiated into the gharānā. And yet Irfan Khan was far from a traditionalist on this score: he made a valiant attempt

FIGURE 16 Irfan Khan, Berlin, 2015. Still from video by Markus Schlaffke.

to train both of his daughters in their childhood. For me, beyond the image of a fractured and discontinuous musical legacy, Irfan Khan's daughters presented a bracing vision of the evaporation of a long stream of embodied memory. The genealogical imagination crafted in and through numerous continuous generations of this musical family appeared to have arrived at its concluding chapter. The counternarratives and oppositional historical consciousness I had discovered through my research on the past and present members of the Lucknow gharānā now evoked a completed narrative arc with a beginning, a middle, and an end. Or was it possible that this genealogical and musical braid of practice and memory could live on?

Irfan Khan remains cautiously optimistic. Born in Lucknow in 1954, Irfan, shown in performance in Berlin in Figure 16, was the second son of Umar Khan. Soon after Irfan was born, Umar Khan relocated the family from Lucknow to Calcutta, where Irfan received his early training from his father. When Irfan Khan completed his high school education in the 1970s, his father sent him to Lucknow to begin learning from the sitarist Ilyas Khan, Umar Khan's younger brother. As mentioned earlier, Irfan Khan spent three years in Kabul in the mid-1980s under the auspices of the Indian Council for Cultural Relations (ICCR). Upon his return, he was married and subsequently accepted successive positions at music schools in Assam and Kabul. Since his return to Calcutta, he has restarted his concert career, traveling often to Europe and the United States, were he trains disciples in the diaspora and performs prestigious concerts on university campuses.

Growing up in Delhi, Gulfam Ahmad Khan (b. 1956) learned sarod initially from his father, Ishtiaq Ahmad Khan, who passed away in 1967 when Gulfam was still a young man. Gulfam then learned briefly from his elder brother, Mukhtiyar Ahmad Khan (1942–1997), who had received many more years of training from their father. In 1971 Gulfam relocated to Lucknow for training under Ilyas Khan. That same year, Gulfam moved back to Delhi, where he worked outside the music field for some eight years, struggling as a young man with neither father nor mother (she had passed away in 1970). In 1979, however, Gulfam rededicated himself to music practice, establishing himself as a player not only of the sarod, but of the Afghani rabāb. In the past decade, he has built a name for himself, especially in Afghanistan, where he was employed for several years as a staff artist and teacher by the Indian consulate in Kabul. Gulfam's son, Imran Khan (b. 1979), boasts a direct line of descent from Niamatullah Khan and demonstrates potential as a virtuoso instrumentalist. He is today the last such offspring of the Lucknow gharānā.

Son of the first wife of Umar Khan, Shahid Khan (b. ca. 1940) began his sarod training with his grandfather, Sakhawat Husain Khan. Shahid's mother passed away when he was only three years old, and his father remarried, taking as his second wife his first wife's sister. Somehow Shahid was not attached to his father, and felt much more comfortable in the home of Ilyas Khan, whose wife was also Shahid's late mother's sister. Shahid was able to study only until class (grade) 1, and otherwise spent his youth imbibing the traditions of his gharānā. When Sakhawat Husain Khan passed away in 1955, Shahid was sent by Ilyas Khan to learn from Ishtiaq Ahmad Khan in Delhi. Shahid remained in Delhi for two years and then returned to Lucknow, where he learned for many years from Ilyas Khan. As a young man Shahid defied his uncle, absconding to Bombay to find work as a musician, but he returned before too long and began his career as a staff artist at Lucknow's Doordarshan (public television station) in 1977. Thirty years later, in 2007, Shahid Khan retired from his service at Doordarshan and today leads a quiet life at home in Lucknow, where he enjoys frequent visits from his young grandchildren.

Born in 1966, Aqueel Khan lives and works in Gauhati, Assam, where his father, Akhtar Khan, served for many years as staff artist at the All India Radio station. Aqueel learned sitar from his father, and also from Ilyas Khan in

Lucknow. He insists that he is a rightful member of the gharānā—his mother was a daughter of Sakhawat Husain Khan—yet he is not entirely embraced by the heirs of the lineage today. Nevertheless Aqueel celebrates his role in perpetuating the oral traditions of the gharānā and remains hopeful for its survival.

On Wednesday, July 10, 2013, as I sat down at my computer to work on the manuscript that would become *Lineage of Loss*, I received a Facebook message from Irfan Khan, sorrowful that his train to Jabalpur had arrived too late; Idris Khan had passed away before Irfan could attend his deathbed. Suffering from kidney disease, in 2009 Idris had abandoned his ambitions as a professional musician, sold his ancestral home, quit Lucknow, and resettled some 500 kilometers away in the city of Jabalpur, Madhya Pradesh. There he lived with his longtime companion, endured daily dialysis, and ultimately succumbed short of his sixtieth birthday.

As discussed in the introduction to this book, I met Idris in Lucknow in 2007; he was the first member of the Lucknow gharānā I managed to contact when I began my field research in the city. He was generous, kind, accommodating, and insightful, yet clearly suffering physically and emotionally. The combination of the loss his family's renown, his own inability to make a living as a musician or music teacher, and his ongoing physical ailments produced a cloud of dejection and disappointment looming in the air around him. My experience with Idris shaped my research agenda, propelling my interest in the downfall of his gharānā: how could the son of a great ustād, the inheritor of a cherished oral tradition, the representative of an influential gharānā, have fallen so far into the depths of obscurity, poverty, and hopelessness? As I was eventually to learn, he was not alone. None of the living representatives of the Lucknow gharānā was a celebrated performing artist today, and many were so marginal that their names were unknown outside the small circle of their own relatives.

As I became a friend and colleague of the remaining lineage holders, I learned of their individual life circumstances and the specific obstacles—both internal and external—they faced in perpetuating the legacy of their gharānā through professional performance and instruction. Yet Idris opened the door for me to perceive the present condition of the Lucknow gharānā as more than the mere sum of individual failures, flaws, and frailties. He readily acknowledged that in his youth he was less interested in learning music than in carousing with his friends and riding his motorcycle, yet he insisted that his detractors have underestimated the extent of his training by his father. As a young man, Idris strongly desired to follow in his father's footsteps by becoming a professor at the Bhatkhande Music Institute University in Lucknow but could not achieve this goal despite his efforts. Whereas the institution had once offered exemptions to the requirement of a formal degree for hereditary musicians such as Idris Khan, this policy was subsequently reformed; without an official diploma, Idris lacked the qualifications for the job. To remedy this, he pursued an eight-year course (requiring his appearance for jury auditions for eight consecutive years), finally earning his Nipurn degree in 1998 from the Bhatkhande Vidya-peeth, the examining body responsible for administering exams and conferring degrees from the college across the country. In that same year, Idris obtained a position at the Almora branch of the Bhatkhande College, in the mountains 500 kilometers north of Lucknow. Yet he retained this position for only a few years; ultimately, when his contract was not renewed, Idris Khan returned to Lucknow to face unemployment for the rest of his life.

———

In this book I have attempted to inhabit the living historical consciousness of a genealogical entity forged through a continuous tradition of embodied, formal musical habitus and supported by both oral narratives and textual documents. My method has been to represent the history of the Lucknow gharānā as a coherent set of interlinked counternarratives. Like Shryock (1997) and Ho (2006), I ennoble the genealogical imagination as a powerful source of historical data, even when this sometimes grates against accepted methods of critical historiography. I have done so because I contend that the Lucknow gharānā deserves study as the subject of its own story. While the celebrated mansion of Hindustani music has been brightly illuminated by generations of talented scholars, the rise and fall of the Lucknow gharānā occupies within it a still-dark corner. Daniel Neuman has recently described this unlit recess as "completely unknown to the *Pandit* [or dominant, Hindu, textual] reality of Indian music history" (2014: 292–93).

As I have acknowledged, my habitation within the musical and genealogical consciousness of the Lucknow gharānā leaves me vulnerable to the charge of subjective historical interpretation. I believe, however, that my story of the Lucknow gharānā draws its strength—its effectiveness—from precisely this vulnerability. Against traditional historians who "take unusual pains to erase the elements in their work which reveal their grounding in a particular time and place, their preferences in a controversy," Michel Foucault advocates an "effective history" that boldly affirms "knowledge as perspective" (1977: 156). Effective history operates as an oppositional epistemology, denaturalizing all we have inherited as "immortal" and "immutable" (ibid.: 153); its aim is nothing less than to shatter the myths of "a completed development" and thus to undermine the inevitability of the present (ibid.).

My hope is that a history of Hindustani music from the perspective of the Lucknow gharānā may be both effective and practical (White 2014). I submit that a sustained encounter with the past through the eyes of a dying dynasty reveals the world anew, intimating uncharted streams of historical consciousness that flow beneath the surface, cut across settled histories, and propel oppositional interpretations of the present. In a search for ultimate origins and final consequences, such counternarratives constitute perhaps little more than footnotes. And yet the possibility remains that a foray into a subterranean world of music, memory, and meaning may transform not only our sense of the past but our outlook on the future.

NOTES

Introduction

1. Kippen writes of a population shift from Delhi to Lucknow when the capital was established there in 1775, stating that "the new capital promised to be an even greater centre of wealth and splendor" than Delhi had been (2005 [1988]: 2). Manuel writes of "the flowering of Indo-Muslim culture based in nineteenth-century Lucknow," noting that the city "had replaced war-ravaged Delhi as the center of fine arts patronage in North India" (1991: 350).

2. The eminent musician and musicologist S. N. Ratanjankar refers to the music performed by North India's late nineteenth-century masters as "the Royal Court art of Ragadari music" (1967: 7).

3. The surname Khan recurs throughout this book. Originally a title, the name is common among South Asian Muslims and thus does not necessarily indicate family relation.

4. See McNeil 2004 and Tamori 2008 for detailed genealogical charts.

5. Nearly all of the works named here could be listed in more than one of these contingent categories.

6. Adrian McNeil, in his book *Inventing the Sarod* (2004), presents a thorough history of the Paṭhān sarod lineages and their roles in shaping both the instrument and its repertoire.

7. When the college was founded in 1926, it was known as the All-India College of Hindustani Music. Some six months later, the name was changed to the Marris College of Hindustani Music (Singh 1952: 1). In 1936 an examining body was created named the Bhatkhande Indian Music University of Lucknow, of which the Marris College was the "constituent college" (Bakhle 2005: 205). The name of the college was later changed to the Bhatkhande College of Music, and later still to the Bhatkhande Music Institute, Deemed University. Today the official title of the college is the Bhatkhande Music Institute University. For simplicity's sake I will refer to it most often as "the college."

ONE "Oh Father, My Home Is Being Left Behind"

1. Except for those specializing in drumming, when one learns Indian music, the primary topic of concern is rāga. The concept of rāga enters the written discourse on Indian music in a treatise titled *Bṛhaddeśī* by Matanga written ca. 800 CE. From the seventeenth century until the early twentieth century, the most common system of rāga typology for Hindustani music categorized rāga-s into "families" in which major rāga-s were male, and lighter counterparts—rāginī-s—were female: it is from this system that Kaukab Khan described *Bhairaviṅ* as a "rāginī."

2. See Slawek (2000: 198–99) for further discussion of the *mohrā* in instrumental ālāp.

3. The history of Awadh as a polity caught between the old Mughal Empire and the new British Empire is well documented and analyzed by Fisher (1987) and Barnett (1980).

4. I have chosen to render the name as Niamatullah, where it could have been Ni'matullah, Ne'matullah, or Nematullah. Though Urdu texts do not usually include indications for short vowel sounds, formal Arabic writing often does. On the title page of his book, Niamatullah's own son offers an elaborate and Arabicized calligraphic rendering of the word *niamat*, his father's shortened name and also the final word in the title of his book. In this rendering Niamatullah's son offers four separate diacritical additions to *niamat*, including the small marking known as *zer* beneath the initial "n" consonant, thus indicating that it should carry its own short "i" vowel. The subsequent 'ain could certainly be represented with the single open quotation mark, but in Urdu, in this case, is pronounced as a short "a." Based on both the pronunciation practice of his own descendants and the most commonly employed spelling of his name in previous English texts, I have opted for "Niamatullah."

5. See Williams (2014: 213) for a more thorough attempt to sort out this chronology.

6. Sharma states that Enayat Ali Khan "was sent to England by the Raja for the Silver Jubilee Ceremony of Queen Victoria," where the "Queen and her courtiers were charmed by his performance" (1993: 197). Irfan Khan states that the occasion was Queen Victoria's "Golden Jubilee," that is, her celebration of fifty years on the throne, and that the year was 1887. Irfan Khan further states that Enayat Ali Khan was accompanied by the tablā player Ata Husain (personal communication, April 27, 2010).

7. Sakhawat Husain Khan's handwritten Urdu journal was translated by Farrokh Namazi.

8. Joshi gives a detailed (but partial) itinerary of the European tour in an appendix to her book (1989: 42–44).

1. See Delvoye (1997: 199) for a discussion of the documentation of Tansen's life and death.

2. Imam, writing in the mid-nineteenth century, states the proposition most starkly: "the rules of Been [bīn] are taught by the Ustads to their sons only and not even to their daughter's children" (1959 [ca. 1857]: 23). Daniel Neuman responds to Imam's statement of bīnkār-s training only their own sons by noting that, "among binkars, the inheritance of musical knowledge was strictly patrilineal" (1990 [1980]: 132).

3. As the first English-language scholar to address the issue directly, Solis writes, "It is manifestly evident that the modern sarod and Afghan rabab, almost identical in basic structure, are closely related" (1970: 23–26).

4. Translation by Farrokh Namazi.

5. See McNeil (2004) for the history of Paṭhān immigration to India and its musical ramifications.

6. In Delvoye's analysis, the relationship between Tansen and Haridas (entirely un-documented in the Indo-Persian literature) was established only in the Braj literature of the late Bhakti revival and thus represents an "appropriation" in the service of "Vaish-nava sectarian traditions" (1997: 210–11 n. 87).

7. Translation by Allyn Miner, brackets added.

8. Translations of Kaukab Khan's 1915 manuscript are by Farrokh Namazi.

9. Wajid Ali Shah's debauchery is discussed at length by Colonel William Sleeman, General James Outram, and governor-general of India Lord Dalhousie in the so-called "Oude Blue Book" (1856). Perkins argues that Sharar wrote against prevailing British characterizations of Lucknow's history, but he also documents the unmistakable influence of Victorian morality on Sharar's depictions of the effete and lascivious kings of Lucknow (Perkins 2011: 350–66), as when Sharar describes Wajid Ali Shah's character as "the most dubious in the records of history" (Sharar 2001 [1975]: 63, quoted in Perkins 2011: 365; see also Naim 2012). Similarly, Kaukab Khan appears to reject the legitimacy of British colonial rule while replicating the very charges against Wajid Ali Shah that served as the justification for the annexation of his kingdom by the East India Company.

10. "Dhurpad" reflects a common Urdu spelling and pronunciation of "dhrupad."

11. As pen names, Wajid Ali Shah used Akhtar, Akhtar Piyā, and Akhtar (Williams 2014: 145). Abdul Halim Sharar and Kaukab Khan (along with the editors and transla-tors E. S. Harcourt and Fakhir Hussain) are apparently alone in maintaining that Wajid Ali used Kadar Piyā as his pen name in his ṭhumrī-s (Sharar 2001 [1975]: 137, 269 n. 439).

12. See Manuel (1989a: 192–221) for a discussion of structural affinities among ṭhumrī rāga-s.

THREE Rival Tales and Tales of Rivalry

1. Seth apparently drew on the ethnographic work of Daniel Neuman, who discussed artist self-segregation at All India Radio canteens (Neuman 1990 [1980]: 179, passim; see also 2011: 135).

2. Karamatullah uses *khāndān* (family tradition), *silsila* (lineage or succession), and *aulād* (offspring) to refer to the notion of genealogical descent. He does not use any term to address the idea of stylistic or discipular descent evoked by gharānā. Likewise, Kaukab Khan uses *khāndān*, and *silsila* when speaking of the members of Basat Khan's (and thus Tansen's) genealogy.

3. I thank James Kippen for access to the original recording of this unpublished interview, conducted in Umar Khan's Calcutta residence, August 11, 1981.

4. Thanks to Allyn Miner for assistance with translation.

5. The late musicologist Ashok Ranade gives a variation on the interpretation of "Seniya," stating that "the descendants of the legendary Tansen led to the formation of three senia gharānā-s" (1997: 114). Ranade can be read as supporting Gulfam's claims of descent from the "son's line" when he notes that the descendants of the Dagari Bani "migrated to Jaipur," the descendants of the Khandari Bani moved to Varanasi, and the followers of the Gorari Bani, "descendants of Tansens' youngest son Bilas Khan [. . .] settled in Lucknow" (ibid.).

6. Allyn Miner writes that Rajab Ali Khan was the "most prominent binkar of [Maharaja Sawai] Ram Singh's Jaipur [. . . .] He was the Maharaja's ustad and the official head of the court musicians, and was so highly placed as to have been granted a village land holding" (1997 [1993]: 142). Maharaja Sawai Ram Singh ruled Jaipur from 1854 to 1880. According to Sharma, Rajab Ali Khan was also the teacher of Imdad Khan (Sharma 1993: 128).

7. I thank my friend and colleague Nasir Syed for this last interpretation.

8. While agreeing that such a confrontation occurred between Kaukab Khan and Wazir Khan in the presence of the nawāb of Rampur, Irfan Khan does not support the interpretation that Kaukab Khan would have spoken so rudely to the nawāb. Irfan specifically states that Kaukab Khan would never have used the "tu" form of "you" (in this context, the least polite form) in addressing the nawāb (personal communication, April 27, 2010).

9. I believe Gulfam means to refer to Nawāb Raza Ali Khan (1906–1966), who assumed the throne in 1930 as the final nawāb of Rampur, following his father, Nawāb Hamid Ali Khan. In another part of the interview, Gulfam explains that the nawāb himself had accompanied Ishtiaq Ahmad Khan by playing *kartāl*, a type of castanets: indeed, Nawāb Raza Ali Khan was well known as a player of this instrument (Narasimhan 2006: 20).

10. Irfan Khan notes that Nawāb Raza Ali Khan regularly visited the palace of the nawāb of Jalpaiguri in Calcutta where Umar Khan (Irfan Khan's father) served as a court

musician, and was so close with the family that he would call the begam (Umar Khan's disciple) his "sister." Irfan Khan himself witnessed Nawāb Raza Ali Khan play the kartāl in accompaniment of Umar Khan (personal communication, April 27, 2010).

11. One should give Amjad Ali Khan the benefit of the doubt that the misspelling of Umar Khan's name was a typographical error, and not one of memory. Indeed, in a backstage meeting with Amjad Ali Khan in Santa Barbara, California, on May 28, 2010, he immediately offered the names of Ilyas Khan and Umar Khan when I mentioned that my research concerned important musicians of Lucknow.

12. Irfan Khan adds that the name of the ḍomnī was Bismillah Jaan (personal communication, April 27, 2010).

13. I thank Zainab Cheema, a scholar of comparative literature, for her insight in this matter.

14. Irfan Khan agrees that Waliullah Khan refused to teach Vilayat Khan but does not accept the justification Gulfam has supplied. Instead, Irfan argues that Waliullah Khan refused because he believed that Vilayat Khan would not acknowledge the true source of the musical knowledge, and would instead cite his own lineage (personal communication, April 27, 2010).

15. As Brian Silver observes regarding the *adab* or manners of Hindustani musicians, "in the event that the soloist sees [a respected guest or fellow musician] sitting further back in the audience, it is not at all unusual for him to call that person up to the front of the audience" (1984: 320, brackets added).

16. Manuel was misled by a faulty but influential translation of Kaukab's letter to Sharar by E. S. Harcourt and Fakhir Hussain, who put the following phrase into the mouth of Kaukab Khan: "Ghazals and thumris were the vogue and no one paid any attention to heavy intricate ragas such as dhurpad and hori" (Sharar 2001 [1975]: 138). Sharar's original Urdu writings have recently been reprinted in a 2006 edition. Locating the passage in question, one finds that Kaukab's sentence does not contain the word rāga at all; the word Harcourt and Hussain have given as rāga is actually *cīzeṅ*, or "things." Thus, Kaukab's sentence should be more accurately rendered as "Ghazal and thumrī spread among the public while no one paid any attention to such intricate and heavy things as dhrupad and hori" (Sharar 2006: 184).

17. I thank my friend and colleague Dard Neuman for suggesting the phrase "politics of resentment" to address the dynamics discussed in this chapter.

FOUR The College and the Ustād

1. The historian William Gould has described the Congress Party as "the most prominent and successful movement of anti-colonial nationalism in the twentieth century" (2004: 1).

2. In an earlier article (1991), Qureshi highlights the anti-Muslim dimensions of the music reform movement, but moves away from this analysis in subsequent work.

3. Some scholars have argued that it is historically inaccurate to place the origins of communalism entirely within the period of British colonial rule. C. A. Bayly, for instance, offers an interpretation in which the preconditions for communalism—in his phrase, the "pre-existing lines of social fracture"—were established with the fall of the Mughal Empire in the early eighteenth century, well prior to the era of widespread British colonial intervention (1985: 203; see also Freitag 1989; O'Hanlon 1993; Sarkar 2000). Here Bayly's argument forms part of his larger project to document the agency of Indians throughout the colonial era, an approach that responds directly to an earlier historiographic tendency to ascribe omnipotence to British colonial rule. Against Bayly's work, a number of scholars reject a programmatic focus on cultural, economic, and political continuities that span the precolonial and the colonial eras, arguing that such an approach serves as an apology for British colonialism itself. Paul Brass, for instance, declares, "Whatever similarities, continuities, and persisting idioms may be found before the nineteenth century, it would seem idle to overemphasize them" (2003: 25–26). Partha Chatterjee singles out Bayly when he bemoans scholars who argue that colonial rule did not "represent a fundamental break in Indian history" (1993: 27). Dirks objects to the same point when he writes, "Curiously [. . .] Indian agency becomes a way of suggesting that colonial rule itself was an Indian project more than it was a European one" (2001: 307). Dirks summarizes his critique of Bayly's approach with the pithy phrase, "Blame the victim again!" (ibid.: 310).

4. The report was produced by a seven-member committee, including the former chief justice of the Delhi High Court, Rajinder Sachar, the chairperson whose name has come to stand for the report. After some twenty months of exhaustive research, the committee presented its findings in the form of a four-hundred-twenty-four-page report to the office of the prime minister of India in 2006 (see Sachar et al. 2006).

5. A "resolution of the conference" for the "establishment of the College of Music in the United Provinces [. . .] passed on the 11th January 1925" (Report 1925: 96).

6. For the story behind Bhatkhande's decision to join with Bali in establishing the college in Lucknow, see Singh (1952) and Bakhle (2005: 195–200).

7. Although these conferences were not overtly political, both Trasoff (1999: 143) and Bakhle (2005: 180) have noted that they shared important features with the Indian National Congress.

8. Bali's invocation of "the last 60 years" likely refers to the period following the war of 1857–58, when the British strengthened their colonial rule, now under the direct auspices of the royal crown. As already noted, Bali connects the "fall" of the Hindustani music tradition directly to British colonialism.

9. In 1924 Rai Umanath Bali's nephew (though three years his senior), Dr. Rai Rajesh-war Bali, was appointed minister of education for the United Provinces, and would go on to become the president of the managing committee of the college from 1929 to 1943. It was through his connection to the British governor of the United Provinces, Sir William Marris, that the college came to be redubbed the Marris College of Hindustani Music some six months after its grand opening (Singh 1952: 1).

10. Kumar Prasad Mukherji recalls a recital in his own home given by Ratanjankar. Mukherji writes that in response to the enthusiastic praise following his performance, Ratanjankar remarked, "I am a shagird of Aftab-e-Mausiqi Faiyaz Khan Saheb, the greatest ustad of my time, and a shishya of Bhatkhandeji, the greatest pundit of Hindustan. Agar kabhi thoda gaa leta hoon to kaun sa kamaal kiya maine (What is so amazing if I occasionally manage to sing well)?" (2006: 340).

11. All of the data presented in this section were gathered from documents titled "Academy of Hindustani Music Constitution," housed at the National Archives of India in New Delhi under the Department of Education, Branch A-2, 1948, Files 4–5.

12. I am grateful to Ghazala Rafiq for her kind assistance in checking and correcting my translation of this essay by Sakhawat Husain Khan.

13. The essay is dated 1932, but this is clearly an error for several reasons: from Sakha-wat Husain Khan's text, we understand that he wrote the piece after Bhatkhande had already passed away, yet the date of 1932 precedes Bhatkhande's death by four years. Sa-khawat Husain Khan also notes that the famed singer Faiyaz Khan had passed away by the time of writing; Faiyaz Khan died in 1950. I thus believe that date is misprinted as 1932 and should instead read 1952.

14. Interestingly, Bhatkhande's own primary disciple, S. N. Ratanjankar, advances a contrasting assessment of the utility of Bhatkhande's system of notation, arguing that it offers only "a basic skeleton" that requires "much to be read between the lines which has to be left to the experience and judgment of the student and the teacher" (1967: 52).

15. The college had become a cultural hub attracting students from all areas of British India, including Sri Lanka, Nepal, and Mauritius.

16. Bali describes Abid Husain in a handwritten note as "a tabla player of all India fame, awarded a gold medal, first prize in [the] 4th All India music conference" (1927: 32). According to Misra, Abid Husain was born in 1867 and died in 1936 (1985: 40–41). For Abid Husain's great significance within the Lucknow tablā gharānā, see Kippen 2005 [1988]: 76–77.

17. As Purohit caustically asserts, "Not a single musician has emerged out of these music factories, who is considered worth anything in Indian classical music circles. Nevertheless a self-perpetuating cycle has been set up. The schools produce graduate (sic) [who] later run the institutions which produced them" (1988: 880).

1. Naveena Naqvi (2010) discusses the writings of both brothers (largely emphasizing the work of Karamatullah Khan) in her unpublished MPhil thesis from Jawaharlal Nehru University in Delhi. As far as I know, hers is the only work besides my own to address Kaukab Khan's unpublished manuscript. I am grateful to Farrokh Namazi for her generous help with the translation and interpretation of both texts.

2. The Urdu-language journal in which these pieces were published, *Dil Gudāz*, was founded by Abdul Halim Sharar in 1887 (Sharar 2001 [1975]: 18).

3. My sincerest gratitude to Ryan Perkins for his generosity in locating and supplying me with the original text from Sharar's 1915 publication. Thanks also to Saher Rizvi for consultation in translation.

4. Bhatkhande writes that "until there is a consensus of opinion as to the right value of a Shruti [microtone] and until it becomes possible to determine the Shuddha [natural] scale of Natya Shastra and Ratnakara, the two works are bound to remain sealed books" (1930: 13).

5. In his 1916 speech, Bhatkhande includes a list of twelve prescribed treatises, including one in Persian, *Uṣūl al-Naghmāt-i Āṣafī* (Report 1917: 14). In the 1930 list, Bhatkhande has excised the final three sources from the earlier list (including *Uṣūl al-Naghmāt-i Āṣafī*) and added nine new titles. All eighteen on the 1930 list are Sanskrit treatises.

6. Rosse gives the date of publication of K. M. Goswami's book as 1879 (1995: 45).

7. Another Muslim patron intimately involved with Bhatkhande's efforts toward music reform was Nawāb Hamid Ali Khan, ruler of Rampur state (r. 1889–1930).

8. Tagore writes, "Within this royal lineage of invaders there have been born one or two knowledge-loving emperors who, understanding the exquisiteness of Hindu music, contributed their enthusiasm towards its advancement. But be it through chicanery or might, they started converting exponents of Hindu music to their own religion. We think this is the outstanding reason why cultivation of music is so rare among Hindus, and it is due to this that one sees more music-exponents among the Muslims [. . . .] What is a matter of even greater sorrow is that the Muslims are not easily inclined to teach music to Hindus. Even if they are favorably inclined, they are ignorant regarding how to teach in a simple way. Therefore, learning music from Muslims is not easily forthcoming" (Tagore 1872: 2–3, quoted in Basu 2011: 336 and translated by Basu, quoted in Scarimbolo 2014: 350, brackets added by Scarimbolo).

9. The document, complete with signatures of assent by Muslim musicians (in Nastalīq) and Hindu musicians (in Devanāgarī), is reprinted—as Rosse notes, "without title or comment"—in S. M. Tagore's *Hindu Music from Various Authors*, first published in 1875 (Rosse 1995: 139; Tagore 1994 [1875]: 389–97). As Richard Williams reveals, Niamatullah Khan is one of the signatories (2014: 233).

10. I know of only one other text by a Muslim Hindustani musician that argues explicitly against the defamation of Muslim musicians: Vilayat Husain Khan's *Saṅgītagyoṅ ke Saṅsmaraṇ* (1959). The author directly attacks the idea that ustād-s hoarded knowledge and refused to teach, or passed on substandard training to their students, citing as counterexamples Tanras Khan, Haddu Khan, and Behram Khan. Vilayat Husain Khan argues that if these three Muslim master musicians had not openly propagated their art, the knowledge of music would not have survived to the present (1959: 10).

11. In Wade's work on Mughal miniature paintings, she describes the nafīr as a wind instrument of the *naqqārakẖānā* (1998: 6), yet cautions that it "is still a mystery instrument not elucidated in the paintings" while speculating that it might be a conical horn (ibid.: 173).

12. A long-standing myth suggests that Aurangzeb's Islamic extremism led him to ban the performance of music in his court. Katherine Brown (Schofield) in her article "Did Aurangzeb Ban Music?" (2007) proves that although the emperor personally renounced music, musical patronage continued unabated in his court; a legacy of treatises from Aurangzeb's reign show that his was a fertile time for music and musical thought indeed.

13. Among Kaukab Khan's disciples, Sharma lists Becha Chandra, Dhirendra Nath Bose, Jitendra Charan Guha, Jnaanada Prasanna Mukherji, Hiralal Haldar, Kalidas Pal, Nanigopal Motilal, Satyendra Nath Mukherji, Shivkumar Thakur ("son of Raja Sir S.M. Tagore"), Harendra Krishna Sheel, and Sarat Chandra Singh (Sharma 1993: 198). Chatterjee additionally lists Premkumar Atarthi (1996: 269). Beyond the disciples already listed, Chatterjee notes that Karamatullah Khan trained Birendra Kishore Roy Chowdhury, Jogindranath Ray, Krishnachandra De, Kalicharan Ray, Ksitischandra Lahiri, Jagatprasanna Mukhopadhyay, Begam Jabbar Saheba of Jalpaiguri, and Sakhawat Husain Khan (ibid.). Irfan Khan adds that Kaukab Khan's disciple Jitendra Charan Guha was also known as Gobar Babu: he was a wrestler and a good sarod and banjo player. Irfan Khan further notes that Begam Jabbar Saheba of Jalpaiguri was not a disciple of Kaukab Khan, but rather of Kaukab Khan's son, Waliullah Khan, and subsequently of Umar Khan (personal communication, April 27, 2010).

14. Sharma lists Ghulam Muhammad Khan and his "son," Sajjad Muhammad Khan, as "court-musicians to Raja Sir Sourindra Mohan Thakur" (1993: 77). As Sharma writes, "Raja Sir Sourindra Mohan Thakur (a.k.a. S.M. Tagore, 1840–1914) was one of India's brilliant musicians [. . . .] He also received training from [. . .] Sajjad Muhammad Khan, a well-known Sitar player, the son of the Surbahar player Ghulam Muhammad Khan" (ibid.: 46–47). Chatterjee asserts that Sajjad Muhammad taught both S. M. Tagore and Kaukab Khan, and that Imdad Khan "benefitted [sic] by listening to him" (1996: 212). Irfan Khan, however, states strongly that Kaukab Khan did not learn from Sajjad Muhammad, but from Ali Muhammad Khan, elder son of Basat Khan, not to be confused

with Muhammad Ali Khan, Basat Khan's younger son (personal communication, April 27, 2010).

15. Although the visit to Europe by Karamatullah and Kaukab Khan is widely reported in the secondary literature and is noted in the writings of Karamatullah Khan, Sakhawat Husain Khan, and Umar Khan (three successive generations of the gharānā), I have not found any primary historical source that corroborates these claims. Motilal Nehru certainly took a large contingent of "performers, musicians, acrobats and artizans" (Nehru, quoted in Lunn 2014) to Paris for the exhibition in 1900; the visit is remembered chiefly for the bout Nehru organized there between India's great wrestler, Ghulam, and a Turkish champion, whom Ghulam defeated. Jann Pasler cites a text by French musicologist Julien Tiersot, who writes of Indian "folk musicians" he witnessed at the 1900 exhibition in Paris, but does not mention art music or any kind of stringed instruments in his descriptions (Pasler 2000: 89). This is not to call into question the veracity of the visit, but simply to note that it has not yet been verified in primary documentation.

16. *Tuḥfat al-Hind* (ca. 1675) is almost entirely derivative, including whole sections from *Rāga Darpan*, but it also presents the best summary of Indo-Persian theory to date. Most important, the author "reworked the Indo-Persian treatise on Hindustani music into a cohesive format, transforming the *Tuḥfat al-Hind* [. . .] into the quintessential model for the next generation of Indo-Persian theorists," apparently forming the model even for Imam's *Maʿdan al-Mūsīqī* (written most likely after the collapse of Lucknow in 1857) (Brown [Schofield] 2003: 76). The *Shams al-Aṣwāt* (1698) was written by a descendant of Tansen, cited by Sir William Jones (in Tagore 1994 [1875]: 136), and nearly copied in the *Uṣūl al-Naghmāt-i Āṣafī* (Brown [Schofield] 2003: 78). The *Shams al-Aṣwāt* was "intended to be a full translation of Damodara's text" (ibid.: 36). Damodara's treatise, the *Saṅgītadarpaṇa*, was itself a reworking of the *Saṅgītaratnākara*, and was highly influential in the Indo-Persian tradition. It was the "preeminent Sanskrit source for Indo-Persian treatises during Aurangzeb's reign" (ibid.).

17. Throughout this discussion, the terms *rāga* and *rāginī* are used interchangeably.

BIBLIOGRAPHY

Academy of Hindustani Music Constitution. 1948. Housed at National Archives of India in New Delhi, Department of Education, Branch A-2, 1948, Files 4–5.

Alavi, Seema. 2008 [2007]. *Islam and Healing: Loss and Recovery of an Indo-Muslim Medical Tradition, 1600–1900.* Basingstoke: Palgrave Macmillan.

Allen, Matthew Harp. 1997. "Rewriting the Script for South Indian Dance." *Drama Review* 41(3): 63–100.

Althusser, Louis. 2006 [1970]. "Ideology and Ideological State Apparatuses: Notes toward an Investigation." Translated by Ben Brewster. In *Lenin and Philosophy and Other Essays.* Delhi: Aakar Books.

Anderson, Benedict. 1991 [1983]. *Imagined Communities: Reflections on the Origin and Spread of Nationalism.* London: Verso.

Arnold, Alison E., and Jonathan Kramer. 2016. *What in the World Is Music?* New York: Routledge.

Attewell, Guy N. A. 2007. *Refiguring Unani Tibb: Plural Healing in Late Colonial India.* Hyderabad: Orient Longman.

Bagchee, Sandeep. 1998. *Nad: Understanding Raga Music.* Bombay: Eeshwar.

Baily, John. 1976. "Recent Changes in the Dutar of Herat." *Asian Music* 8(1): 29–64.

———. 1988. *Music of Afghanistan: Professional Musicians in the City of Herat.* Cambridge: Cambridge University Press.

Bakhle, Janaki. 2005. *Two Men and Music: Nationalism in the Making of an Indian Classical Tradition.* New York: Oxford University Press.

Bali, Rai Umanath. 1926a. Letter to the Secretary to Government Education Department, United Provinces, Allahabad, Dated January 21, 1926, Lucknow. Housed in Uttar Pradesh State Archives, Lucknow, Department of Education, List 21A, Box 127, File 807/1926.

———. 1926b. Letter to the Deputy Secretary to Government, Education Department,

United Provinces, Allahabad, Dated July 29, 1926, Lucknow. Housed in Uttar Pradesh State Archives, Lucknow, Department of Education, List 21A, Box 127, File 807/1926.

———. 1927. Handwritten Notes, Dated January 22, 1926, Lucknow. Housed in Uttar Pradesh State Archives, Lucknow, Department of Education, List 21A, Box 127, File 807/1926, 32–36.

———. 1928. Letter to the Secretary to Government, United Provinces, Education Department, Nainital. Housed in Uttar Pradesh State Archives, Lucknow, Department of Education, List 21A, Box 127, File 807/1926, 69.

———. 1931. Letter to the Secretary to Government, Education Department, United Provinces, Lucknow. Housed in Uttar Pradesh State Archives, Lucknow, Department of Education, List 21A, Box 127, File 807/1926, 102–4.

———. ca. 1931. The Marris College of Hindustani Music, Lucknow: Progress Report. Housed in Uttar Pradesh State Archives, Lucknow, Department of Education, List 21A, Box 127, File 807/1926, 105–11.

———. 1940. Bhatkhande University of Indian Music: Progress Report (from August 1926 to December 1939). Lucknow.

———. 1941. The Marris College of Hindustani Music, Lucknow: Annual Report, 1940–41. Housed in Uttar Pradesh State Archives, Lucknow, Department of Education, List 21A: Box 298, File 172/1941, 1–22.

Barlow, Jon. 2007. "The Sarod: Its Forms and Voices." In *Music and Modernity: North Indian Classical Music in an Age of Mechanical Reproduction*, edited by Amlan Das Gupta, 89–123. Calcutta: Thema.

Barnett, Richard. 1980. *North India between Empires: Awadh, the Mughals, and the British, 1720–1801*. Berkeley: University of California Press.

Basant, Rakesh. 2007. "Social, Economic, and Education Conditions of Indian Muslims." *Economic and Political Weekly* 42(10): 828–32.

———, and Abusaleh Shariff, eds. 2010. *Handbook of Muslims in India: Empirical and Policy Perspectives*. New Delhi: Oxford University Press.

Basu, Sharmadip. 2011. "Tuning Modernity: Musical Knowledge and Subjectivities in Colonial India, C.1780s–C.1900." PhD dissertation, Syracuse University.

Bayly, C. A. 1985. "The Pre-History of 'Communalism'? Religious Conflict in India, 1700–1860." *Modern Asian Studies* 19(2): 177–203.

Berman, Marshall. 1988 [1982]. *All That Is Solid Melts into Air: The Experience of Modernity*. New York: Penguin Books.

Bhatkhande, V. N. 1930. "A Comparative Study of Some of the Leading Music Systems of the 15th, 16th, 17th, and 18th Centuries." *Sangeeta: A Quarterly Journal of Hindustani Music* 1(1): 7–17.

———. 1974. *A Short Historical Survey of the Music of Upper India*. Baroda: Indian Musicological Society.

Bhatnagar, G. D. 1968. *Awadh under Wajid 'Ali Shah*. Varanasi: Bharatiya Vidya Prakashan.

Bhattacharya, Sabyasachi. 2010 [2007]. "Rethinking 1857." In *Rethinking 1857*, edited by Sabyasachi Bhattacharya. Hyderabad: Orient Blackswan.

Bor, Joep. 1986/1987. "The Voice of the Sarangi: An Illustrated History of Bowing in India." *National Centre for the Performing Arts Quarterly Journal* 15(3–4), 16(1): 1–183.

———, and Allyn Miner. 2010. "Hindustani Music: A Historical Overview of the Modern Period." In *Hindustani Music, Thirteenth to Twentieth Centuries*, edited by Joep Bor, Françoise "Nalini" Delvoye, Jane Harvey, and Emmie te Nijenhuis, 197–220. New Delhi: Manohar.

Bose, Sugata, and Ayesha Jalal. 1998. *Modern South Asia: History, Culture, Political Economy*. New Delhi: Oxford University Press.

Brahaspati, Sulochana. 2010. "Rampur as a Centre of Music." In *Hindustani Music, Thirteenth to Twentieth Centuries*, edited by Joep Bor, Françoise "Nalini" Delvoye, Jane Harvey, and Emmie te Nijenhuis, 267–83. New Delhi: Manohar.

Brass, Paul R. 2003. *The Production of Hindu-Muslim Violence in Contemporary India*. Seattle: University of Washington Press.

Brihaspati, Acharya Kailash Chandra Dev. 1976. *Dhrupad Aur Uskā Vikās [Dhrupad and Its Development]* [Hindi]. Patna, India: Bihar Rashtrabhasha Parishad.

Brown, Elaine. 2002. *The Condemnation of Little B: New Age Racism in America*. Boston: Beacon Press.

Brown (Schofield), Katherine Butler. 2000. "Reading Indian Music: The Interpretation of Seventeeth-Century European Travel-Writing in the (Re)Construction of Indian Music History." *British Journal of Ethnomusicology* 9(2): 1–34.

———. 2003. "Hindustani Music in the Time of Aurangzeb." PhD dissertation, School of Oriental and African Studies, University of London.

———. 2007. "Did Aurangzeb Ban Music? Questions for the Historiography of His Reign." *Modern Asian Studies* 41(1): 77–120.

———. 2010. "The Origins and Early Development of Khayal." In *Hindustani Music, Thirteenth to Twentieth Centuries*, edited by Joep Bor, Françoise "Nalini" Delvoye, Jane Harvey, and Emmie te Nijenhuis, 159–94. New Delhi: Manohar.

Capwell, Charles. 1991. "Marginality and Musicology in Nineteenth-Century Calcutta: The Case of Sourindro Mohun Tagore." In *Comparative Musicology and Anthropology of Music*, edited by Bruno Nettl and Philip V. Bohlman, 228–43. Chicago: University of Chicago Press.

———. 2010. "Representing 'Hindu' Music to the Colonial and Native Elite of Calcutta." In *Hindustani Music, Thirteenth to Twentieth Centuries*, edited by Joep Bor, Françoise "Nalini" Delvoye, Jane Harvey, and Emmie te Nijenhuis, 285–312. New Delhi: Manohar.

Chakrabarty, Dipesh. 2002. *Habitations of Modernity: Essays in the Wake of Subaltern Studies*. Chicago: University of Chicago Press.

———. 2008 [2000]. *Provincializing Europe: Postcolonial Thought and Historical Difference*. Princeton: Princeton University Press.

Chakravorty, Pallabi. 2006. "Dancing into Modernity: Multiple Narratives of India's Kathak Dance." *Dance Research Journal* 38(1/2): 115–36.

Chatterjee, Chhaya. 1996. *Śāstrīya Saṅgīta and Music Culture of Bengal through the Ages*. Vol. I and II. Delhi: Sharada.

Chatterjee, Partha. 1993 [1986]. *Nationalist Thought and the Colonial World: A Derivative Discourse*. London: Zed Books.

———. 1993. *The Nation and Its Fragments: Colonial and Postcolonial Histories*. Princeton: Princeton University Press.

———. 2004. "Empire after Globalization." *Economic and Political Weekly* 39(37): 4155–64.

Chaubey, Sushil Kumar. 1958. *Musicians I Have Met*. Lucknow: Prakashan Shakha, Information Deparment, Uttar Pradesh.

———. 1976. *Hindustānī Saṅgīt ke Ratn [Jewels of Hindustani Music]* [Hindi]. Lucknow: Uttar Pradesh Hindi Granth Akademi.

Chinchore, Prabhakar. 1988. "Pt. Bhatkhande's Thoughts on Thumri." *Journal of the Indian Musicological Society* 19: 22–25.

Clayton, Martin. 2000. *Time in Indian Music: Rhythm, Metre, and Form in North Indian Rāg Performance*. New York: Oxford University Press.

———. 2007. "Musical Renaissance and Its Margins in England and India, 1874–1914." In *Music and Orientalism in the British Empire, 1780s to 1940s: Portrayal of the East*, edited by Martin Clayton and Bennett Zon, 71–93. Burlington, VT: Ashgate.

Cohn, Bernard, S. 2002 [1996]. *Colonialism and Its Forms of Knowledge: The British in India*. New Delhi: Oxford University Press.

Dadheech, Puru, ed. 1976. *Swarṇ Jayantī Smārikā [Golden Jubilee Souvenir]* [Hindi]. Lucknow: Bhatkhande Hindustani Sangeet Mahavidyalaya.

Dalhousie, James Andrew Broun Ramsay. 1910. *Private Letters of the Marquess of Dalhousie*. Edited by John George Alexander Baird. London: William Blackwood and Sons.

Dalmia, Vasudha. 1997. *The Nationalization of Hindu Traditions: Bharatendu Harischandra and Nineteenth-Century Banaras*. Delhi: Oxford University Press.

Dalrymple, William. 2004 [1998]. *The Age of Kali: Indian Travels and Encounters*. New Delhi: Penguin Books.

Delvoye, Françoise "Nalini." 1997. "The Image of Akbar as a Patron of Music in Indo-Persian and Vernacular Sources." In *Akbar and His India*, edited by Irfan Habib, 188–214. Delhi: Oxford University Press.

———. 2001. "L'appropriation de Tānsen, premier musicien de la cour d'Akbar, par les traditions sectaires krishnaïtes." In *Constructions hagiographiques dans le monde indien: Entre mythe et histoire*, edited by Françoise Mallison, 221–55. Paris: Champion.

Dirks, Nicholas B. 2001. *Castes of Mind: Colonialism and the Making of Modern India*. Princeton: Princeton University Press.

Erdman, Joan. 1985. *Patrons and Performers in Rajasthan: The Subtle Tradition*. New Delhi: Chanakya.

Evans-Pritchard, E. E. 1940. *The Nuer: A Description of the Modes of Livelihood and Political Institutions of Nilotic People*. Oxford: Clarendon Press.

Farrell, Gerry. 1997. *Indian Music and the West*. Oxford: Clarendon Press.

———. 2002. "The Senia Style of Sitar Playing in Contemporary India." *British Journal of Ethnomusicology* 11(2): 29–60.

Fisher, Michael. 1987. *A Clash of Cultures: Awadh, the British, and the Mughals*. Riverdale: Riverdale Company.

Foucault, Michel. 1977. "Nietzsche, Genealogy, History." In *Language, Counter-Memory, Practice: Selected Essays and Interviews*, edited by Donald F. Bouchard, 139–64. Ithaca: Cornell University Press.

Freitag, Sandria. 1989. *Collective Action and Community: Public Arenas and the Emergence of Communalism in North India*. Berkeley: University of California Press.

Gaonkar, Dilip Parameshwar. 1999. "On Alternative Modernities." *Public Culture* 11(1): 1–18.

Gayer, Laurent, and Christophe Jaffrelot, eds. 2012. *Muslims in Indian Cities: Trajectories of Marginalization*. New Delhi: HarperCollins.

Glasser, Jonathan. 2015. "Andalusi Musical Origins at the Moroccan-Algerian Frontier: Beyond Charter Myth." *American Ethnologist* 42(4): 720–33.

Gommans, Jos J. L. 1995. *The Rise of the Indo-Afghan Empire C. 1710-1780*. Leiden: Brill.

Gould, William. 2002. "Congress Radicals and Hindu Militancy: Sampurnanand and Purushottam Das Tandon in the Politics of the United Provinces, 1930–1947." *Modern Asian Studies* 36(3): 619–55.

———. 2004. *Hindu Nationalism and the Language of Politics in Late Colonial India*. Cambridge: Cambridge University Press.

———. 2012. *Religion and Conflict in Modern South Asia*. Cambridge: Cambridge University Press.

Habib, Irfan. 2010 [2007]. "Understanding 1857." In *Rethinking 1857*, edited by Sabyasachi Bhattacharya, 58–66. Hyderabad: Orient Blackswan.

Hansen, Thomas Blom. 1999. *The Saffron Wave: Democracy and Hindu Nationalism in Modern India*. Princeton: Princeton University Press.

———. 2007. "The India That Does Not Shine." *ISIM Review* 19: 50–51.

Hasan, Zoya Khaliq. 1982. "Communalism and Communal Violence in India." *Social Scientist* 10(2): 25–39.

Ho, Engseng. 2006. *The Graves of Tarim: Genealogy and Mobility across the Indian Ocean.* Berkeley: University of California Press.

Hosain, Attia. 1992 [1961]. *Sunlight on a Broken Column.* New Delhi: Penguin Books.

Hussain, Fakhir. 2001. "Preface to the Omnibus Edition: The Construction and Destruction of Lucknow." In *Lucknow: The Last Phase of an Oriental Culture,* in *The Lucknow Omnibus,* n.p. New Delhi: Oxford University Press.

Imam, Hakim Muhammad Karam. 1959 [ca. 1857]. "Melody through the Centuries." Translated by Govind Vidyarthi. *Sangeet Natak Akademi Bulletin* 2(12): 13–26.

Jaffrelot, Christophe. 1996. *The Hindu Nationalist Movement in India.* New York: Columbia University Press.

———, ed. 2007. *Hindu Nationalism: A Reader.* Princeton: Princeton University Press.

Jairazbhoy, N. A. 1995 [1971]. *The Rāgs of North Indian Music.* Bombay: Popular Prakashan.

Jameson, Fredric. 1991. *Postmodernism, Or, the Cultural Logic of Late Capitalism.* Durham, NC: Duke University Press.

———. 2002. *A Singular Modernity: Essay on the Ontology of the Present.* New York: Verso.

Jeffery, Patricia, and Roger Jeffery. 1998. "Gender, Community, and the Local State in Bijnor, India." In *Appropriating Gender: Women's Activism and Politicized Religion in South Asia,* edited by Patricia Jeffery and Amrita Basu, 123–142. New York: Routledge.

Joshi, Damayanti. 1989. *Madame Menaka.* New Delhi: Sangeet Natak Akademi.

Katz, Max. 2012. "Institutional Communalism in North Indian Classical Music." *Ethnomusicology* 56(2): 279–98.

———. 2014. "Sites of Memory in Hindustani Music: Yusuf Ali Khan and the Sitar Shops of Lucknow." *Ethnomusicology Forum* 23(1): 67–93.

Khan, Alladiya. 2000. *My Life.* Translated by Amlan Das Gupta and Urmila Bhirdikar. Calcutta: Thema.

Khan, Amaan Ali, and Ayaan Ali Khan. 2009. *50 Maestros, 50 Recordings: The Best of Indian Classical Music.* Noida, UP: Collins.

Khan, Asadullah "Kaukab." 1915. *Jauhar-e Mūsīqī* [Urdu]. Unpublished manuscript, property of Irfan Khan.

Khan, Ilyas. 1986. "*Bhātkhaṇḍe ke Sakhi-Sakhā* [Bhatkhande's Sakhi-Sakha] [Hindi]." In *Hīrak Jayantī Smārikā* [*Diamond Jubilee Souvenir*], edited by Dyaprakash Sinha, Surendra Shankar Avasthi, and Puru Dadheech, 47–48. Lucknow: Bhatkhande Hindustani Sangeet Mahavidyalaya.

Khan, Karamatullah. 1908. *Isrār-e Karāmat Urf Naghmāt-e Niamat* [Urdu]. Allahabad: Janaki Press.

Khan, Sadiq Ali. 1875 [1869]. *Sarmāya-i 'Ishrat* [Urdu]. Delhi: Munshi Muhammad Ibrahim.

Khan, Sakhawat Husain. 1976 [1952]. "*Gāyan Kaimarā: Noṭeshan* [The Singing Camera: Notation] [Hindi]." In *Swarṇ Jayaṅtī Smārikā* [*Golden Jubilee Souvenir*], edited by Puru Dadheech, 34–35. Lucknow: Bhatkhande Hindustani Sangeet Mahavidyalaya.

———. n.d. Private memoirs [Urdu]. Unpublished manuscript, property of Irfan Khan.

Khan, Umar. 1976. "*Sarodiyoṅ ke Gharāne* [Gharanas of Sarod] [Hindi]." In *Swarṇ Jayaṅtī Smārikā* [*Golden Jubilee Souvenir*], edited by Puru Dadheech, 95. Lucknow: Bhatkhande Hindustani Sangeet Mahavidyalaya.

Khan, Vilayat Husain. 1959. *Saṅgītagyoṅ ke Saṅsmaraṇ* [*Remembrances of Musicians*] [Hindi]. New Delhi: Sangeet Natak Akademi.

Khanna, Lalita. 1973. "The Last Interview." In *Ustad Hafiz Ali Khan Memorial Music Festival*, n.p. Calcutta: Ananda Press.

Kippen, James. 2005 [1988]. *The Tabla of Lucknow: A Cultural Analysis of a Musical Tradition*. New Delhi: Manohar.

———. 2006. *Gurudev's Drumming Legacy: Music, Theory and Nationalism in the Mṛdaṅg Aur Tablā Vādanpaddhati of Gurudev Patwardhan*. Burlington, VT: Ashgate.

———. 2008. "Working with the Masters." In *Shadows in the Field: New Perspectives for Fieldwork in Ethnomusicology*, edited by Gregory Barz and Timothy J. Cooley, 125–40. Oxford: Oxford University Press.

———. 2014. "Eighteenth and Nineteenth Century Sources on Drumming in North India: Revealing Pleasure's Fortune in the Sarmāya-e 'Ishrat." Paper read at Transitions in Indian Music and Dance in the Colonial Indian Ocean, ca. 1750–1950, conference at the University of Pennsylvania, April 25–26, 2014.

Kobayashi, Eriko. 2003. "Hindustani Classical Music Reform Movement and the Writing of History, 1900s to 1940s." PhD dissertation, University of Texas–Austin.

Levy, Mark. 1982. *Intonation in North Indian Music: A Select Comparison of Theories with Contemporary Practice*. New Delhi: Biblia Impex.

Lipsitz, George. 1995. "'Swing Low, Sweet Cadillac': White Supremacy, Antiblack Racism, and the New Historicism." *American Literary History* 7(4): 700–25.

———. 2006. *The Possessive Investment in Whiteness: How White People Profit from Identity Politics*. Revised and expanded ed. Philadelphia: Temple University Press.

———. 2007. *Footsteps in the Dark: The Hidden Histories of Popular Music*. Minneapolis: University of Minneapolis Press.

Llewellyn-Jones, Rosie. 2014. *The Last King in India: Wajid 'Ali Shah, 1822–1887*. London: Hurst.

Longfellow, Henry Wadsworth. 2000. *Henry Wadsworth Longfellow: Poems and Other Writings*. New York: Library of America.

Lucas, Samuel. 1857. *Dacoitee in Excelsis: Or, the Spoliation of Oude by the East India Company*. London: J. R. Taylor.

Ludden, David. 2007 [1996]. "Ayodhya: A Window on the World." In *Making India Hindu: Religion, Community, and the Politics of Democracy in India*, edited by David Ludden, 1–23. Oxford: Oxford University Press.

Lunn, David J. 2014. "'Spectacular Performances over Seas': Travelling Artistes and the Indian Emigration Act of 1901." Paper read at Transitions in Indian Music and Dance in the Colonial Indian Ocean, ca. 1750–1950, conference at the University of Pennsylvania, April 25–26, 2014.

Maciszewski, Amelia. 2006. "Tawaʻif, Tourism, and Tales: The Problematics of Twenty-First-Century Musical Patronage for North India's Courtesans." In *The Courtesan's Arts: Cross-Cultural Perspectives*, edited by Martha Feldman and Bonnie Gordon, 332–51. Oxford: Oxford University Press.

———. 2007. "Nayika Ki Yadgar: North Indian Women Musicians and Their Words." In *Music and Modernity: North Indian Classical Music in an Age of Mechanical Reproduction*, edited by Amlan Das Gupta, 156–219. Calcutta: Thema.

Magriel, Nicolas, and Lalita Du Perron. 2013. *The Songs of Khayāl*. 2 vols. New Delhi: Manohar.

Maitra, Radhika Mohan. 1973. "Khansahib: My Khalifa." In *Ustad Hafiz Ali Khan Memorial Music Festival*, n.p. Calcutta: Ananda Press.

Malhotra, L. K. 1973. "My Father, My Guru: Ustad Amjad Ali Khan Talks to L. K. Malhotra." *Sangeet Natak* 29: 17–26.

Manuel, Peter. 1986. "The Evolution of Modern Thumri." *Ethnomusicology* 30(3): 470–90.

———. 1987. "Courtesans and Hindustani Music." *Asian Review* Spring: 12–17.

———. 1989a. *Thumrī in Historical and Stylistic Perspectives*. Delhi: Motilal Banarasidass.

———. 1989b. "A Historical Survey of the Urdu Gazal-Song in India." *Asian Music* 20(1): 93–113.

———. 1991. "The Popularization and Transformation of the Light-Classical Urdu Ghazal-Song." In *Gender, Genre and Power in South Asian Expressive Traditions*, edited by Arjun Appadurai, Frank J. Korom, and Margaret A. Mills, 347–61. Philadelphia: University of Pennsylvania Press.

———. 2000. "Thumri, Ghazal, and Modernity in Hindustani Music Culture." *Music and Culture (Korean Society for World Music)* 2: 133–56.

———. 2001. "Fifteen Cds of Hindustani Music: A Review Essay." *Ethnomusicology* 45(2): 370–75.

———. 2002. "Modernity and Musical Structure: Neo-Marxist Perspectives on Song Form and Its Successors." In *Music and Marx: Ideas, Practice, Politics*, edited by Regula Burkhardt Qureshi, 45–62. New York: Routledge.

———. 2007 [1996]. "Music, the Media, and Communal Relations in North India, Past and Present." In *Making India Hindu: Religion, Community, and the Politics of Democracy in India*, edited by David Ludden, 119–39. Oxford: Oxford University Press.

———. 2008. "North Indian Sufi Popular Music in the Age of Hindu and Muslim Fundamentalism." *Ethnomusicology* 52(3): 378–400.

McNeil, Adrian. 2004. *Inventing the Sarod: A Cultural History*. Calcutta: Seagull Books.

———. 2007a. "Making Modernity Audible: Sarodiyas and the Early Recording Industry." In *Music and Modernity: North Indian Classical Music in an Age of Mechanical Reproduction*, edited by Amlan Das Gupta, 60–88. Calcutta: Thema.

———. 2007b. "Mirasis: Some Thoughts on Hereditary Musicians in Hindustani Music." *Context* 32: 45–58.

Meer, Wim van der. 1980. *Hindustani Music in the Twentieth Century*. The Hague: Martinus Nijhoff.

Metcalf, Barbara D., and Thomas R. Metcalf. 2002. *A Concise History of India*. Cambridge: Cambridge University Press.

Miner, Allyn. 1997 [1993]. *Sitar and Sarod in the 18th and 19th Centuries*. Delhi: Motilal Banarsidass.

———. 2010. "Sources on the Early History of the Tambur, Rabab, Sitar, and Sarod." In *Hindustani Music, Thirteenth to Twentieth Centuries*, edited by Joep Bor, Françoise "Nalini" Delvoye, Jane Harvey, and Emmie te Nijenhuis, 373–90. New Delhi: Manohar.

———. 2014. "Wajid Ali Shah's Favorites: The Musical Non-Elites of Lucknow." Paper read at Transitions in Indian Music and Dance in the Colonial Indian Ocean, ca. 1750–1950, conference at the University of Pennsylvania, April 25–26, 2014.

Misra, Susheela. 1985. *Music Makers of the Bhatkhande College of Hindustani Music*. Calcutta: Sangeet Research Academy.

———. 1991. *Musical Heritage of Lucknow*. New Delhi: Harman.

Morcom, Anna. 2013. *Illicit Worlds of Indian Dance: Cultures of Exclusion*. New York: Oxford University Press.

Mujahid, Sharif Al. 1999. "Sir Syed Ahmad Khan and Muslim Nationalism in India." *Islamic Studies* 38(1): 87–101.

Mukherjee, Rudrangshu. 2001 [1984]. *Awadh in Revolt: 1857–1858*. Delhi: Permanent Black.

Mukherji, Dhurjati Prasad. 1934. "Classical Revival in Our Music and Principles of Composition." *Calcutta Review* 51(1): 63–71.

———. 1955. "The Great Masters I Have Heard." In *Radio Sangeet Sammelan: 10–15 November 1955*, 58–68. Delhi: Ministry of Information and Broadcasting, Government of India.

Mukherji, Kumar Prasad. 2006. *The Lost World of Hindustani Music*. New Delhi: Penguin Books.

Munim, Lakshman Das. 1924. *Saṅgīt -Samuccaya* [Hindi]. Edited by Shri Shivendranath Basu. Banaras, UP: Bharat Kala Parishad.

Mutatkar, Sumati. 2001. *Shrikrishna Narayan Ratanjankar "Sujan": A Many-Splendoured Genius*. New Delhi: Roli Books.

Naim, C. M. 2012. "Interrogating 'the East,' 'Culture,' 'and Loss,' in Abdul Halim Sharar's *Guzishta Lakhnaʻu*." In *Indo-Muslim Cultures in Transition*, edited by Alka Patel and Karen Leonard, 189–204. Leiden: Brill.

Naqvi, Naveena. 2010. "Aspects Concerning the 'Invention' of North Indian Classical Music in the Late Nineteenth and Early Twentieth Centuries." MPhil dissertation, Jawaharlal Nehru University, Delhi.

Narasimhan, Sakuntala. 2006. "Nawab Raza Ali Khan of Rampur: The Last of the Great Patrons." *Sangeet Natak* 40(4): 19–29.

Nayar, Sobhana. 1989. *Bhatkhande's Contribution to Music: A Historical Perspective*. Bombay: Popular Prakashan.

Neuman, Daniel. 1978. "Gharanas: The Rise of Musical 'Houses' in Delhi and Neighboring Cities." In *Eight Urban Musical Cultures: Tradition and Change*, edited by Bruno Nettl, 186–222. Urbana: University of Illinois Press.

———. 1990 [1980]. *The Life of Music in North India: The Organization of an Artistic Tradition*. Detroit: Wayne State University Press.

———. 2011. "String Theory: A Meditation on Lives in Ethnomusicology." In *Ethnomusicological Encounters with Music and Musicians: Essays in Honor of Robert Garfias*, edited by Timothy Rice, 129–52. Burlington, VT: Ashgate.

———. 2014. "A Tale of Two Sensibilities: Hindustani Music and Its Histories." In *Theory and Method in Historical Ethnomusicology*, edited by Jonathan McCollum and David G. Hebert, 279–308. Lanham: Lexington Books.

Neuman, Dard. 2000. Liner Notes. In *Shujaat Husain Khan: Legacy*. Ethnomusicology @ UCLA, Artists Series Vol. 1.

———. 2004. "A House of Music: The Hindustani Musician and the Crafting of Traditions." PhD dissertation, Columbia University.

———. 2012. "Pedagogy, Practice, and Embodied Creativity in Hindustani Music." *Ethnomusicology* 56(3): 426–49.

Nijenhuis, Emmie te, and Françoise "Nalini" Delvoye. 2010. "Sanskrit and Indo-Persian Literature on Music." In *Hindustani Music, Thirteenth to Twentieth Centuries*, edited by Joep Bor, Françoise "Nalini" Delvoye, Jane Harvey, and Emmie te Nijenhuis, 35–64. New Delhi: Manohar.

O'Hanlon, Rosalind. 1993. "Historical Approaches to Communalism: Perspectives from Western India." In *Society and Ideology: Essays in South Asian History Presented to Professor K. A. Ballhatchet*, edited by Peter Robb, 247–66. Delhi: Oxford University Press.

Oldenburg, Veena Talwar. 2001 [1984]. *The Making of Colonial Lucknow: 1856–1877,* in *The Lucknow Omnibus.* New Delhi: Oxford University Press.

"Oude Blue Book." 1856. *Oude, Papers Relating to.* Presented to both Houses of Parliament by Command of Her Majesty. London: Harrison and Sons.

Pandey, Gyanendra. 1996 [1990]. *The Construction of Communalism in Colonial North India.* New Delhi: Oxford University Press.

Pasler, Jann. 2000. "Race, Orientalism, and Distinction in the Wake of the 'Yellow Peril.'" In *Western Music and Its Others: Difference, Representation, and Appropriation in Music,* edited by Georgina Born and David Hesmondhalgh, 86–118. Berkeley: University of California Press.

Perkins, Christopher Ryan. 2011. "Partitioning History: The Creation of an Islami Pablik in Late Colonial India, C. 1880–1920." PhD dissertation, University of Pennsylvania.

Perron, Lalita Du. 2007. *Hindi Poetry in a Musical Genre: Ṭhumrī Lyrics.* New York: Routledge.

Peterson, Indira Viswanathan, and Davesh Soneji, eds. 2008. *Performing Pasts: Reinventing the Arts in Modern South India.* New Delhi: Oxford University Press.

Platts, John T. 2004 [1884]. *A Dictionary of Urdu, Classical Hindi, and English.* New Delhi: Munshiram Manoharlal.

Portelli, Alessandro. 1991. *The Death of Luigi Trastulli, and Other Stories: Form and Meaning in Oral History.* Suny Series in Oral and Public History. Albany: State University of New York Press.

Powers, Harold. 1970. "An Historical and Comparative Approach to the Classification of Ragas (with and Appendix on Ancient Indian Tunings)." *Institute of Ethnomusicology, UCLA: Selected Reports* 1(3): 1–78.

———. 1980. "Classical Music, Cultural Roots, and Colonial Rule: An Indic Musicologist Looks at the Muslim World." *Asian Music* 12(1): 5–39.

Pradhan, Aneesh. 2014. *Hindustani Music in Colonial Bombay.* Gurgaon: Three Essays Collective.

Prakash, Gyan. 1990. "Writing Post-Orientalist Histories of the Third World: Perspectives from Indian Historiography." *Comparative Studies in Society and History* 32(1): 383–408.

Purohit, Vinayak. 1988. *Arts of Transitional India: Twentieth Century.* 2 vols. Bombay: Popular Prakashan.

Qureshi, Regula. 1981. "Islamic Music in an Indian Environment: The Shi'a Majlis." *Ethnomusicology* 25(1): 41–71.

———. 1991. "Whose Music? Sources and Contexts in Indic Musicology." In *Comparative Musicology and Anthropology of Music: Essays on the History of Ethnomusicology,* edited by Bruno Nettl and Phillip V. Bohlman, 152–68. Chicago: University of Chicago Press.

————. 1999. "Other Musicologies: Exploring Issues and Confronting Practice in India." In *Rethinking Music*, edited by Nicholas Cook and Mark Everist, 311–35. Oxford: Oxford University Press.

————. 2000. "Confronting the Social: Mode of Production and the Sublime for (Indian) Art Music." *Ethnomusicology* 44(1): 15–38.

————. 2002. "Mode of Production and Musical Production: Is Hindustani Music Feudal?" In *Music and Marx: Ideas, Practice, Politics*, edited by Regula Burkhardt Qureshi, 81–105. New York: Routledge.

————. 2006. "Female Agency and Patrilineal Constraints: Situating Courtesans in Twentieth-Century India." In *The Courtesan's Arts: Cross-Cultural Perspectives*, edited by Martha Feldman and Bonnie Gordon, 312–31. New York: Oxford University Press.

————. 2007. *Master Musicians of India: Hereditary Sarangi Players Speak*. New York: Routledge.

————. 2009. "*Sīna Ba Sīna* or 'from Father to Son': Writing the Culture of Discipleship." In *Theorizing the Local: Music, Practice, and Experience in South Asia and Beyond*, edited by Richard K. Wolf, 165–84. New York: Oxford University Press.

————. 2010. "A Mine of Music History from Nineteenth-Century Lucknow." In *Hindustani Music, Thirteenth to Twentieth Centuries*, edited by Joep Bor, Françoise "Nalini" Delvoye, Jane Harvey, and Emmie te Nijenhuis, 221–37. New Delhi: Manohar.

Rahaim, Matthew. 2012. *Musicking Bodies: Gesture and Voice in Hindustani Music*. Middletown: Wesleyan University Press.

Ranade, Ashok. 1997. *Hindustani Music*. New Delhi: National Book Trust.

Ratanjankar, S. N. 1967. *Pandit Bhatkhande*. New Delhi: National Book Trust.

Report. 1917. *First All-India Music Conference*. Baroda, 1916: Baroda Printing Works.

Report. 1925. *4th All-India Music Conference*. Lucknow, 1925: Taluqdar Press.

Rosse, Michael D. 1995. "The Movement for the Revitalization of 'Hindu' Music in Northern India, 1860–1930: The Role of Associations and Institutions." PhD dissertation, University of Pennsylvania.

————. 2010. "Music Schools and Societies in Bombay C.1864–1937." In *Hindustani Music, Thirteenth to Twentieth Centuries*, edited by Joep Bor, Françoise "Nalini" Delvoye, Jane Harvey, and Emmie te Nijenhuis, 313–30. New Delhi: Manohar.

Rowell, Lewis. 1998 [1992]. *Music and Musical Thought in Early India*. New Delhi: Munishiram Manoharlal.

Roy Choudhuri, Birendra Kishore. 1957. "The Veena Paddhati of Hindustani Music." *Journal of the Music Academy, Madras* 29: 72–76.

Roy Chowdhury, Birendra Kishore. 1973. "My Ustad." In *Ustad Hafiz Ali Khan Memorial Music Festival*, n.p. Calcutta: Ananda Press.

Roy Chowdhury, Harendra Kishore. 1929. *The Musicians of India (Illustrated) Part I*. Mymensingh, India.

Roy Chowdhury, Vimalakant. 1975 [1965]. *Bhāratīya Saṅgīt Kosh* [*Dictionary of Indian Music*] [Hindi]. Delhi: Bharatiya Jnanpith.

Russell, William. 1957. *My Indian Mutiny Diary*. Edited by Michael Edwardes. London: Cassell.

Sachar, Rajinder, et al. 2006. *Social, Economic and Educational Status of the Muslim Community of India: A Report*. New Delhi: Prime Minister's High Level Committee, Cabinet Secretariat, Government of India.

Sakata, Hiromi Lorraine. 1983. *Music in the Mind: The Concepts of Music and Musician in Afghanistan*. Kent: Kent State University Press.

Sanyal, Ritwik, and Richard Widdess. 2004. *Dhrupad: Tradition and Performance in Indian Music*. Burlington, VT: Ashgate.

Sarkar, Sumit. 2000. "Orientalism Revisited: Saidian Frameworks in the Writing of Modern Indian History." In *Mapping Subaltern Studies and the Postcolonial*, edited by Vinayak Chaturvedi, 239–55. London: Verso.

———. 2007 [1996]. "Indian Nationalism and the Politics of Hindutva." In *Making India Hindu: Religion, Community, and the Politics of Democracy in India*, edited by David Ludden, 270–93. Delhi: Oxford University Press.

Sarmast, Ahmad. 2009. *A Survey of the History of Music in Afghanistan: Special Reference to Art Music from C. 1000 A.D.* Saarbrücken: VDM Verlag Dr. Müller.

Savarkar, V. D. 1947 [1909]. *The Indian War of Independence, 1857*. Bombay: Phoenix.

———. 2003 [1923]. *Hindutva*. New Delhi: Hindi Sahitya Sadan.

Scarimbolo, Justin. 2014. "Brahmans beyond Nationalism, Muslims beyond Dominance: A Hidden History of North Indian Classical Music's Hinduization." PhD dissertation, University of California–Santa Barbara.

Schofield, Katherine Butler. 2010. "Reviving the Golden Age Again: 'Classicization,' Hindustani Music, and the Mughals." *Ethnomusicology* 54(3): 484–517.

———. Forthcoming. "Chief Musicians to the Mughal Emperors: The Delhi *Kalāwant Birāderī*, 17th to 19th Centuries." *Journal of the Indian Musicological Society*.

Sen, Sharmistha. 1988. *String Instruments (Plucked Variety) of North India*. Vol. I. Delhi: Eastern Book Linkers.

———. 1992. *String Instruments (Plucked Variety) of North India*. Vol. II. Delhi: Eastern Book Linkers.

Seth, Vikram. 2005 [1993]. *A Suitable Boy*. New York: Harper.

Shankar, Ravi. 2007 [1968]. *My Music, My Life*. San Rafael: Mandala.

———. 1999 [1997]. *Raga Mala: The Autobiography of Ravi Shankar*. New York: Welcome Rain.

Shapiro, Thomas. 2004. *The Hidden Cost of Being African American: How Wealth Perpetuates Inequality*. Oxford: Oxford University Press.

Sharar, Abdul Halim. 1915. "Hindustān meṅ Mashriqī Tamaddun kā Ākhrī Namūna" [Urdu]. *Dil Gudāz* November: 257–64.

———. 2001 [1975] *Lucknow: The Last Phase of an Oriental Culture*. Translated by E. S. Harcourt and Fakhir Hussain. In *The Lucknow Omnibus*. New Delhi: Oxford University Press.

———. 2006. *Guzishta Lakhnaʻu* [Urdu]. Edited by Mohammad Ikram Chagahtai. Lahore: Sang-e Mil.

Sharma, Amal Das. 1993. *Musicians of India Past and Present: Gharanas of Hindustani Music and Genealogies*. Calcutta: Naya Prokash.

Shehadi, Fadlou. 1995. *Philosophies of Music in Medieval Islam*. Leiden: Brill.

Shryock, Andrew. 1997. *Nationalism and the Genealogical Imagination: Oral History and Textual Authority in Tribal Jordan*. Berkeley: University of California Press.

Silver, Brian. 1984. "The *Adab* of Musicians." In *Moral Conduct and Authority: The Place of Adab in South Asian Islam*, edited by Barbara Daly Metcalf, 315–29. Berkeley: University of California Press.

Silver, Brian, and R. Arnold Burghardt. 1976. "On Becoming an Ustad: Six Life Sketches in the Evolution of a Gharana." *Asian Music* 7(2): 27–58.

Singh, Raja Raghavendra Pratap. 1952. "India's Premier Music College." In *Rajat Jayaṅtī Granth* [*Silver Jubilee Book*], edited by Rai Umanath Bali, Chribhuvannath Singh "Saroj," and Shrikrishna Narayan Ratanjankar, 1–4 (English Section). Lucknow: Marris College of Hindustani Music.

Slawek, Stephen. 1991. "Ravi Shankar as Mediator between a Traditional Music and Modernity." In *Ethnomusicology and Modern Music History*, edited by Stephen Blum, Philip Bohlman, and Daniel Neuman, 161–80. Urbana: University of Illinios Press.

———. 2000. "Hindustani Instrumental Music." In *The Garland Encyclopedia of World Music. Volume 5: South Asia: The Indian Subcontinent*, edited by Alison Arnold, 188–208. New York: Garland.

———. 2000 [1987]. *Sitar Technique in Nibaddh Forms*. Delhi: Motilal Banarsidass.

———. 2007. "Review [Two Men and Music]." *Ethnomusicology* 51(3): 506–12.

Slobin, Mark. 1976. *Music in the Culture of Northern Afghanistan*. Tucson: University of Arizona Press.

Solis, Ted. 1970. "The Sarod: Its Gat-Toda Tradition with Examples by Amir Khan and Three of His Students." MA thesis, University of Hawaii.

Soneji, Davesh. 2012. *Unfinished Gestures: Devadāsīs, Memory, and Modernity in South India*. Chicago: University of Chicago Press.

Subrahmanyam, Sanjay. 1998. "Hearing Voices: Vignettes of Early Modernity in South Asia, 1400–1750." *Daedalus* 127(3): 75–104.

Subramanian, Lakshmi. 2006. *From the Tanjore Court to the Madras Music Academy: A Social History of Music in South India*. New Delhi: Oxford University Press.

———. 2008. *New Mansions for Music: Performance, Pedagogy, and Criticism*. New Delhi: Social Science Press.

Sugarman, Jane C. 1989. "The Nightingale and the Partridge: Singing and Gender among Prespa Albanians." *Ethnomusicology* 33(2): 191–215.

Tagore, Sourindro Mohun. 1872. "Introduction." *Sangit Samalochani* [*Music Review*] 1(1).

———. 1994 [1875]. *Hindu Music from Various Authors*. Delhi: Low Price.

Tamori, Masakazu. 2008. "The Transformation of Sarod Gharana: Transmitting Musical Property in Hindustani Music." *Senri Ethnological Studies* 71: 169–202.

Taylor, Diana. 2003. *The Archive and the Repertoire: Performing Cultural Memory in the Americas*. Durham, NC: Duke University Press.

Trasoff, David. 1999. "Sarod Performance Practice in the Twentieth Century: Tradition and Transformation in North Indian Classical Instrumental Music." PhD dissertation, University of California–Santa Barbara.

———. 2010. "The All-India Music Conferences of 1916–1925: Cultural Transformations and Colonial Ideology." In *Hindustani Music, Thirteenth to Twentieth Centuries*, edited by Joep Bor, Françoise "Nalini" Delvoye, Jane Harvey, and Emmie te Nijenhuis, 331–56. New Delhi: Manohar.

Trepagnier, Barbara. 2006. *Silent Racism: How Well-Meaning White People Perpetuate the Racial Divide*. Boulder, CO: Paradigm Publishers.

Trivedi, Madhu. 2010. "Music Patronage in the Indo-Persian Context: A Historical Overview." In *Hindustani Music, Thirteenth to Twentieth Centuries*, edited by Joep Bor, Françoise "Nalini" Delvoye, Jane Harvey, and Emmie te Nijenhuis, 65–90. New Delhi: Manohar.

Ture, Kwame, and Charles V. Hamilton. 1967. *Black Power: The Politics of Liberation*. New York: Vintage Books.

Van der Veer, Peter. 1994. *Religious Nationalism: Hindus and Muslims in India*. Berkeley: University of California Press.

Varadarajan, Siddharth, ed. 2002. *Gujarat: The Making of a Trajedy*. New Delhi: Penguin Books.

Wade, Bonnie. 1997 [1984]. *Khyāl: Creativity within North India's Classical Music Tradition*. New Delhi: Munshiram Manoharlal.

———. 1998. *Imaging Sound: An Ethnomusicological Study of Music, Art, and Culture in Mughal India*. Chicago: University of Chicago Press.

Walker, Margaret. 2014. *India's Kathak Dance in Historical Perspective*. Burlington, VT: Ashgate.

Weidman, Amanda. 2007 [2006]. *Singing the Classical, Voicing the Modern: The Postcolonial Politics of Music in South India*. Calcutta: Seagull Books.

White, Hayden. 1978. *Tropics of Discourse: Essays in Cultural Criticism*. Baltimore: Johns Hopkins University Press.

———. 2014. *The Practical Past*. Evanston, IL: Northwestern University Press.

Widdess, Richard. 1995. *The Rāgas of Early Indian Music: Modes, Melodies, and Musical Notations from the Gupta Period to C. 1250*. Oxford: Clarendon Press.

———. 2010. "The Emergence of Dhrupad." In *Hindustani Music, Thirteenth to Twentieth Centuries*, edited by Joep Bor, Françoise "Nalini" Delvoye, Jane Harvey, and Emmie te Nijenhuis, 117–40. New Delhi: Manohar.

———. 2013. *Dāphā: Sacred Singing in a South Asian City*. Burlington, VT: Ashgate.

Williams, Richard David. 2014. "Hindustani Music between Awadh and Bengal, C.1758–1905." PhD dissertation, King's College London.

Wortham, Simon Morgan. 2006. *Counter-Institutions: Jacques Derrida and the Question of the University*. New York: Fordham University Press.

INDEX

Note: Page numbers in *italics* indicate figures; page numbers with "n" indicate endnotes.

horī (music genre), 60, 98, 169n16
Hosain, Attia, 20
Husain, Abid, 126, 171n16
Husain, Ata, 166n6
Husain, Hamid, 126
Hussain, Bahadur, 71
Hussain, Musharraf, 41

'ilm-e-mūsīqī (musical science), 137
Imam, Hakim Muhammad Karam, 56, 79–80, 167n2, 174n16
India: Afghani rabāb players in, 45, 47; Bhatkhande College's connections with government of, 102; national identity of, 104–5; partition of, 2, 20, 100, 105; Paṭhān-s in, 49; patriarchal inheritance practices of, 48; role of Hindustani music in, 21–22
Indian National Congress, 101, 105, 170n7
Indian Rebellion (1857), 32–33
Indo-Persian musical theoretical tradition, 132–33, 138–40, 147–48, 155–56, 158, 174n16
institutional communalism, 106–7, 124–25, 128
institutional racism, 107
institutions. See Bhatkhande College
instruction methods, of hereditary musicians, 11
instrumentalist paradigm, 12–15
instrumental music: human voice, imitation of, 24, 56, 61–62, 64–66, 75, 94; instrumental gharānā-s, 70; instrumentalists for Menaka's dance troupe, 38–39. See also names of individual instruments
instrumentation, as sign of social transition, 54

instruments, invention of, 141–43. See also individual instruments
International Dance Olympiad (1936), 39

Jalal, Ayesha, 33
Jalpaiguri, nawāb of, 41
jalsā (musical gathering), 83–84
Jameson, Fredric, 15–16, 21
Jang Bahadur, Mahārājā, 34
jāwā (plectrum), 24
Jeffery, Patricia, 106
Jeffery, Roger, 106
Jones, William, 135, 174n16
Joshi, Damayanti, 38–39

Kabul, Afghanistan: Hindustani musicians at court of, 45
kalāwant, 51, 53–58, 69, 74–75, 81–82, 130, 157
Kālpī gharānā, 71–72
kathak (dance), 2, 38
Kaukab banjo, 142–43, 144
khalīfa, current, of Lucknow gharānā, 22
Khan, Abdul Karim, 136
Khan, Afaq Husain, 122
Khan, Afaq Hussain, 42
Khan, Ahmed Ali, 86, 88
Khan, Akhtar, 42, 161–62
Khan, Ali Akbar, 86, 87–88, 92
Khan, Allabande, 35
Khan, Alladiya, 9, 40, 76, 77, 79, 142–43
Khan, Allauddin, 4, 47, 78, 85–88, 91, 94–95, 98
Khan, Amaan Ali, 92, 97
Khan, Amir, 62
Khan, Amjad Ali, 89, 90, 92, 169n11
Khan, Aqueel, 161–62
Khan, Asadullah. See Khan, Kaukab
Khan, Asghar Ali, 88

143–45; on Niamatullah Khan, 4, 51; orthodoxy, support for, 75; overview of, 35–36; Paris, performances in, 146, 174n15; photograph of, *131*; professional musicians, critique of, 153–54; recordings by, 66, 143, *144*; relationships, 37, 86–87, 118; repertoire purity, claim to, 65–66; Sharar and, 130; teachers of, 173–74n14; on Wajid Ali Shah, 167n9; Wazir Khan, counternarrative of, 83–85; writings of, 3, 59–61, 130, 132, 137–38, 148–58. *See also* reform movement

Khan, Kifayet, 41

Khan, Muhammad Ali, 52

Khan, Mukhtiyar Ahmad, 42, 143, *144*, 161

Khan, Munawar, 41

Khan, Musharraf, 42

Khan, Najaf Ali, 50

Khan, Na'mat (Sadarang), 51, 81–82

Khan, Nanhe, 93

Khan, Nasir, 126

Khan, Naubat, 79–81

Khan, Niamatullah: Basat Khan and, 45, 47–48, 50–52, 53; career of, 34–35; as creator of modern sarod, 93, 142; Goswami's notation system and, 172n9; Karamatullah Khan on, 138; name of, 166n4; photograph of, *35*; renown, 4, 98, 157; rise of lineage of, 74–75; role in Lucknow gharānā traditions, 65; writings of, 131–32

Khan, Noorullah, 145

Khan, Pyar, 45, 51, 56–57, 71

Khan, Rafiqullah, 41

Khan, Rajab Ali, 40, 83, 168n6

Khan, Ras Baras, 150, 174n16

Khan, Raza Ali, 168–69n10, 168n9

Khan, Sadiq Ali, 56–57, 70

Khan, Sahabdad, 94, 96

Khan, Sajjad Husain, 96

Khan, Sajjad Muhammad, 173n14

Khan, Sakhawat Husain: on Afghani rabāb, 49; Basat Khan manuscript and, 51; at Bhatkhande College, 101–2, 116–19, 126; on Bhatkhande's musical notation, 119–22; career, 37–40; communal perceptions of, 113; as duo with Sakharam Ramchandra, 100–101; on family's instrumental style, 61–62, 64; gharānā, use of term, 71–72; marriages of, 37; orthodoxy, support for, 75; overview of, 17; photograph of, *63*; recordings by, 66; reformist vision of, 116–19, 120; relationships, 41, 87, 95, 97, 161; renown, 4, 98, 99; training of, 36–37

Khan, Shafayat, 36

Khan, Shafiqullah, 41

Khan, Shahid, 42, 161

Khan, Shujaat, 94

Khan, Tassaduq Hussain, 136

Khan, Thakur Nawab Ali, 108, 112, 135, 136

Khan, Umar: on Afghani rabāb, 45; Basat Khan manuscript and, 51; at Bhatkhande College, 40, 122–23; career, 40–41; disciples, 173n13; on family's class origins, 73; gharānā, use of term, 72–73; mentioned, 92; orthodoxy, support for, 75; on own public reception, 64; photographs of, *25*, *63*; relationships, 87–88, 160–61; 168–69n10; repertoire, purity of, 65; Sakhawat Husain Khan on, 117, 118

Khan, Vilayat, 62, 78, 94–95, 97, 169n14

Khan, Vilayat Husain, 76, 77, 79, 82, 98, 136, 173n10

Khan, Waliullah, 41, 66, 94–95, 145,
169n14, 173n13
Khan, Wazir, 78–80, 82–88, 90
Khan, Yaqub Husain, 121
Khan, Yusuf Ali, 42, 71–72
Khusrau, Amir, 52–53, 132–33, 138–39
khyāl (vocal genre), 2, 55
Kindi, Ya'qub ibn Ishaq al-, 137, 140
Kinnear, Michael, 143
Kippen, James, 5–6, 13, 64, 72, 122–23,
136, 165n1
Kobayashi, Eriko, 136
koṭhā (courtesan salon), 8

Lal, Ganeshi and Chukha, 89
light music forms. See ṭhumrī
lineages. See gharānā-s
Lipsitz, George, 15, 107
Longfellow, Henry Wadsworth, 141
Lucknow: collapse of, 43; communal
riots in, 111; as cultural and musical
center, 1–2, 34, 50–52, 114–16;
disparagements of, 112; importance
to Lucknow gharānā, 130–31;
instrumental legacy, 3; population
shift to, 165n1. See also "Bābul Morā
Naihara Chūṭo Jāya"
Lucknow gharānā: ancestors of, 49–50;
Bhatkhande College and, 100–128;
conclusions on, 163–64; decline of,
23, 47, 127, 128, 162; early history of,
19–43; future of, 159–63; Lucknow's
importance to, 130–31; overview,
1–18; paradox of, 65, 75–76; reform
movement and, 129–58; rise and fall
of, 34–43; rivalries of, 68–99; ṭhumrī,
controversies over, 44–67; ṭhumrī
and, 57–58, 61–66
Lucknow-Shahjahanpur gharānā, 73

Ma'dan al-Mūsīqī, 79, 167n2, 174n16
Maihar gharānā, 85–88
Maitra, Radhika Mohan, 62, 88–89
Manuel, Peter, 55, 58, 62, 98, 103–4,
165n1, 169n16
marriage, 19–21, 33, 36–37, 43, 48
Marris, William, 112, 171n9
Marris College of Hindustani Music. See
Bhatkhande College
Matiyaburj, India: Wajid Ali Shah in, 34
Mazumdar, Ambika Charan, 38
McNeil, Adrian, 5, 49–50, 66, 69, 73, 143,
165n6
medicine, Unani medical tradition,
139–40
Melba, Nellie, 156–57
memory, 12, 76
Menaka, Madame, 38–40, 118
Metcalf, Barbara, 32
Metcalf, Thomas, 32
military, Afghani rabāb's association
with, 49
Miner, Allyn, 5–6, 35, 55–58, 73, 81, 141–
42, 145, 167n7, 168n6
mīrāsī (accompanist class), 9, 10, 68–69,
74
Misra, Susheela, 126
modernity, 7–9, 11, 20–21, 23, 33, 43,
57–58, 67, 155–58
mohrā (cadential phrase), 28
Morcom, Anna, 8
Mughal Empire, 30, 45, 51, 55, 139
Mukherji, Dhurjati Prasad, 91–92, 113
Mukherji, Kumar Prasad, 171n10
mukhṛā (cadential phrase), of "Bābul
Morā," 27–29, 28, 66
Munim, Lakshman Das, 71
Munshi, K. M., 125
music: Bali on British Raj's impact on,

Peterson, Indira Viswanathan, 7–8
physicality, in music, 11–12
pitch (musical, *sur*), theories of origins
   of, 149
Piya, Kadar. *See* Wajid Ali Shah
Piya, Lallan, 58
Portelli, Alessandro, 14–15
Powers, Harold, 7
Prasad, Rajendra, 100–101, 124
professional musicians, criticisms of,
   148–49, 153–54, *154*
Purab bāj (Eastern style), 56, 57, 64
Purohit, Vinayak, 6, 171n17
Pythagoras, 137, 140–41

Qaiserbagh Baradari, 19
qaum, meaning of, 146–47
qawwāl-bacce (Sufi lineage), 55
Qureshi, Regula, 7–8, 103, 107–8, 113, 121,
   170n2

rabāb (early sarod), 34, 47–50, 55, 73. *See
   also* Afghani (Kabuli) rabāb; sarod
rabābiyā-s (*rabāb* players), 36, 75, 79,
   80–81
racism, institutional, 107
rāga-s: monsoon rāga-s, 117; *rāga*-
   based art music, in Lucknow, 2;
   rāga *Bhairavīṅ*, 24–29, 27, 28, 45;
   rāga *Jhinjhoṭī*, 47; rāga *Kāfi, gat* in,
   57; rāga *Khamāj*, 97; *rāga* practice,
   historical bifurcation of, 54; rāga
   Shuddha Kalyān, 44, 83–85; typology
   of, 166n1
Rāgavibodha, 153
Rahaim, Matthew, 11–12
Rahamin, Atiya Begum Fyzee, 108
Rahman, Abdul, 126

Ramchandra, Sakharam, 100–101
Rampur, 83–85, 90
Ramsay, James Andrew Broun, Marquess
   of Dalhousie, 30–32, 167n9
Ranade, Ashok, 168n5
Rashtriya Swayamsevak Sangh (RSS),
   104–5
Ratanjankar, Shrikrishna Narayan, 113–
   14, 124, 165n2, 171n10, 171n14
Ray, Narayan, 36
Razākhānī bāj, 56–57
Razākhānī gat, 65
reform movement, 129–58; Bhatkhande,
   Lucknow gharānā's engagement
   with ideas of, 147–57; Indo-Persian
   musical theoretical tradition, 138–
   40; institutions and education,
   143–45; instrumental invention,
   141–43; Karamatullah and Kaukab
   Khan, confluence of texts, 132–38;
   al-Kindi and Pythagorean science,
   employment of, 140–41; national
   pride and, 146–47
reputations. *See* counternarratives
rivalries of Lucknow gharānā, 68–99;
   Etawah gharānā counternarratives,
   94–97; gharānā-s, debate over,
   70–76; gharānā stories, 76–77;
   Gwalior-Bangash gharānā
   counternarratives, 88–94; Maihar
   gharānā counternarratives, 85–88;
   two-streams theory, 78–82; Wazir
   Khan counternarratives, 82–85
Rosse, Michael, 136, 172n9
Roy, Leila, 38
Roy Chowdhury, Birendra Kishore, 54,
   79, 88, 90, 173n13
Roy Chowdhury, Harendra Kishore, 93

MUSIC / CULTURE

A series from Wesleyan University Press

Edited by Deborah Wong, Sherrie Tucker, and Jeremy Wallach

Originating editors: George Lipsitz, Susan McClary, and Robert Walser

Frances Aparicio
Listening to Salsa: Gender, Latin Popular Music, and Puerto Rican Cultures

Paul Austerlitz
Jazz Consciousness: Music, Race, and Humanity

Harris M. Berger
Metal, Rock, and Jazz: Perception and the Phenomenology of Musical Experience

Harris M. Berger
Stance: Ideas about Emotion, Style, and Meaning for the Study of Expressive Culture

Harris M. Berger and Giovanna P. Del Negro
Identity and Everyday Life: Essays in the Study of Folklore, Music, and Popular Culture

Franya J. Berkman
Monument Eternal: The Music of Alice Coltrane

Dick Blau, Angeliki Vellou Keil, and Charles Keil
Bright Balkan Morning: Romani Lives and the Power of Music in Greek Macedonia

Susan Boynton and Roe-Min Kok, editors
Musical Childhoods and the Cultures of Youth

James Buhler, Caryl Flinn and David Neumeyer, editors
Music and Cinema

Thomas Burkhalter, Kay Dickinson, and Benjamin J. Harbert, editors
The Arab Avant-Garde: Music, Politics, Modernity

Patrick Burkart
Music and Cyberliberties

Julia Byl
Antiphonal Histories: Resonant Pasts in the Toba Batak Musical Present

Daniel Cavicchi
Listening and Longing: Music Lovers in the Age of Barnum

Susan D. Crafts, Daniel Cavicchi, Charles Keil, and the Music in Daily Life Project
My Music: Explorations of Music in Daily Life

Jim Cullen
Born in the USA: Bruce Springsteen and the American Tradition

Anne Danielsen
Presence and Pleasure: The Funk Grooves of James Brown and Parliament

Peter Doyle
Echo and Reverb: Fabricating Space in Popular Music Recording, 1900–1960

Ron Emoff
Recollecting from the Past: Musical Practice and Spirit Possession on the East Coast of Madagascar

Yayoi Uno Everett and Frederick Lau, editors
Locating East Asia in Western Art Music

Susan Fast and Kip Pegley, editors
Music, Politics, and Violence

Heidi Feldman
Black Rhythms of Peru: Reviving African Musical Heritage in the Black Pacific

Kai Fikentscher
"You Better Work!" Underground Dance Music in New York City

Ruth Finnegan
The Hidden Musicians: Music-Making in an English Town

Daniel Fischlin and Ajay Heble, editors
The Other Side of Nowhere: Jazz, Improvisation, and Communities in Dialogue

Wendy Fonarow
Empire of Dirt: The Aesthetics and Rituals of British "Indie" Music

Murray Forman
The 'Hood Comes First: Race, Space, and Place in Rap and Hip-Hop

Lisa Gilman
My Music, My War: The Listening Habits of U.S. Troops in Iraq and Afghanistan

Paul D. Greene and Thomas Porcello, editors
Wired for Sound: Engineering and Technologies in Sonic Cultures

Tomie Hahn
Sensational Knowledge: Embodying Culture Through Japanese Dance

Edward Herbst
Voices in Bali: Energies and Perceptions in Vocal Music and Dance Theater

Deborah Kapchan
Traveling Spirit Masters: Moroccan Gnawa Trance and Music in the Global Marketplace

Deborah Kapchan, editor
Theorizing Sound Writing

Max Katz
Lineage of Loss: Counternarratives of North Indian Music

Raymond Knapp
Symphonic Metamorphoses:
Subjectivity and Alienation in
Mahler's Re-Cycled Songs

Laura Lohman
Umm Kulthūm: Artistic Agency and the
Shaping of an Arab Legend, 1967–2007

Preston Love
A Thousand Honey Creeks Later:
My Life in Music from Basie to
Motown—and Beyond

René T. A. Lysloff and
Leslie C. Gay Jr., editors
Music and Technoculture

Allan Marett
Songs, Dreamings, and Ghosts:
The Wangga of North Australia

Ian Maxwell
Phat Beats, Dope Rhymes: Hip Hop
Down Under Comin' Upper

Kristin A. McGee
Some Liked It Hot: Jazz Women in
Film and Television, 1928–1959

Rebecca S. Miller
Carriacou String Band Serenade:
Performing Identity in the
Eastern Caribbean

Tony Mitchell, editor
Global Noise: Rap and Hip-Hop
Outside the USA

Keith Negus
Popular Music in Theory:
An Introduction

Johnny Otis
Upside Your Head!: Rhythm and
Blues on Central Avenue

Kip Pegley
Coming to You Wherever You Are:
MuchMusic, MTV, and Youth Identities

Jonathan Pieslak
Radicalism and Music: An Introduction
to the Music Cultures of al-Qa'ida, Racist
Skinheads, Christian-Affiliated Radicals,
and Eco-Animal Rights Militants

Matthew Rahaim
Musicking Bodies: Gesture and
Voice in Hindustani Music

John Richardson
Singing Archaeology:
Philip Glass's Akhnaten

Tricia Rose
Black Noise: Rap Music and Black
Culture in Contemporary America

David Rothenberg and
Marta Ulvaeus, editors
The Book of Music and Nature: An
Anthology of Sounds, Words, Thoughts

Nichole Rustin-Paschal
The Kind of Man I Am: Jazz Masculinity
and the World of Charles Mingus Jr.

Marta Elena Savigliano
Angora Matta: Fatal Acts of
North-South Translation

Joseph G. Schloss
Making Beats: The Art of
Sample-Based Hip-Hop

Barry Shank
*Dissonant Identities: The Rock 'n' Roll
Scene in Austin, Texas*

Jonathan Holt Shannon
*Among the Jasmine Trees: Music and
Modernity in Contemporary Syria*

Daniel B. Sharp
*Between Nostalgia and Apocalypse:
Popular Music and the Staging of Brazil*

Helena Simonett
*Banda: Mexican Musical Life
across Borders*

Mark Slobin
*Subcultural Sounds:
Micromusics of the West*

Mark Slobin, editor
*Global Soundtracks:
Worlds of Film Music*

Christopher Small
The Christopher Small Reader

Christopher Small
*Music of the Common Tongue:
Survival and Celebration in
African American Music*

Christopher Small
Music, Society, Education

Christopher Small
*Musicking: The Meanings of
Performing and Listening*

Regina M. Sweeney
*Singing Our Way to Victory:
French Cultural Politics and Music
During the Great War*

Colin Symes
*Setting the Record Straight: A Material
History of Classical Recording*

Steven Taylor
*False Prophet: Fieldnotes from
the Punk Underground*

Paul Théberge
*Any Sound You Can Imagine:
Making Music/Consuming Technology*

Sarah Thornton
*Club Cultures: Music, Media
and Sub-cultural Capital*

Michael E. Veal
*Dub: Songscape and Shattered
Songs in Jamaican Reggae*

Michael E. Veal and
E. Tammy Kim, editors
*Punk Ethnography: Artists and Scholars
Listen to Sublime Frequencies*

Robert Walser
*Running with the Devil: Power, Gender,
and Madness in Heavy Metal Music*

Dennis Waring
*Manufacturing the Muse:
Estey Organs and Consumer
Culture in Victorian America*

Lise A. Waxer
*The City of Musical Memory:
Salsa, Record Grooves, and Popular
Culture in Cali, Colombia*

Mina Yang
*Planet Beethoven: Classical Music
at the Turn of the Millennium*

ABOUT THE AUTHOR

Max Katz is associate professor of music at the College of William and Mary.